Praise for *Creating Passion Brands*

"This book addresses the biggest challenge marketers and brands face today. It shows how without passion and a clear brand belief, brands are at risk. And unlike so many business books it is written in an engaging style and is very practical!"

Gary Bembridge, Vice President Global Marketing Development, Johnson & Johnson

"You'll read this important book and think: 'I know all this.' And then you'll think: 'So what stops me from doing it?' Creating Passion Brands charts and celebrates the commercial value of good old-fashioned conviction."

Jeremy Bullmore, WPP

"A call to arms to marketers to utilise the culture of the organization to drive the brand. Informed by the authors' many years of practice, it also draws on recent academic theory and builds a model to guide implementation."

Richard Elliott, Professor of Marketing, Warwick Business School

"The importance of differentiating on emotional grounds is increasing. This book is full of insights on how to meet this challenge."

Raoul Pinnell, Chairman, Shell Brands International AG

"This book marries the insight of the practitioner with the substance of the academic. Intelligently written and elegantly argued it challenges some of the important industry preconceptions and gives vivid examples of a whole new way of looking at brands, with a passion."

Leslie Butterfield, Managing Partner, The Ingram Partnership

"A lucid examination of brand DNA. The reader is successfully navigated through the mystique of marketing, which itself can often be vague and somewhat incomprehensible."

Tim Clark, President, Emirates Airline

"*Creating Passion Brands* is the perfect text for today's planner. Part visionary polemic and part practical manual, the way you think about brands and the way you practise brand development will be forever altered by reading it."

Malcolm White, The Account Planning Group

"Knowledge on branding usually falls between two stools: academic impenetrability or jargon-filled over-simplicity. With *Creating Passion Brands* Edwards and Day have managed to find the sweet spot. This is a book of tremendous practical application that also includes high-level, intellectual debate. It's a book that I would recommend to brand managers, MBA students and academics alike."

Mark Ritson, Professor of Marketing, London Business School

"I read it in a single sitting, yelling 'Bravo!' every few pages. A wise and inspirational book."

David Abbott, Founding Partner, Abbott Mead Vickers BBDO

"At last the branding holy grail! This book shows us that by combining rigour and creativity we can make the intangible, tangible. A must read."

Louise Jones, Executive Strategy Director, PHD

"A rare treat: a beautifully-written business book with a genuinely fresh point of view."

William Eccleshare, Chairman/CEO, BBDO Europe

"Very rarely do you get a business book that moves the game on whilst simultaneously giving open practical steps for all to discover their very own passionpoint."

Jon Wilkins, Founder, Naked Communications

creating PASSION BRANDS

how to build emotional brand connection with customers

Helen Edwards and Derek Day

KOGAN PAGE

London and Philadelphia

First published in Great Britain and the United States in 2005 by Kogan Page Limited
Reprinted 2006
Paperback edition 2007
Reprinted 2008

120 Pentonville Road
London N1 9JN
United Kingdom
www.kogan-page.co.uk

525 South 4th Street, #241
Philadelphia PA 19147
USA

© Helen Edwards and Derek Day, 2005

The right of Helen Edwards and Derek Day to be identified as the authors of this work has been asserted by them in accordance with the Copyright, Designs and Patents Act 1988.

ISBN-10   0 7494 4762 1
ISBN-13   978 0 7494 4762 5

British Library Cataloguing-in-Publication Data

A CIP record for this book is available from the British Library.

Library of Congress Cataloging-in-Publication Data

Edwards, Helen, 1965–
  Creating passion brands : how to build emotional brand connection
  with customers / Helen Edwards and Derek Day — 1st ed.
    p. cm.
  Includes bibliographical references and index.
  ISBN 0-7494-4370-7
  1. Brand name products. I. Day, Derek, 1949– II. Title.
HD69.B7E38 2005
658.8'343—dc22   2005009398

Typeset by Saxon Graphics Ltd, Derby
Printed and bound in India by Replika Press Pvt Ltd

Contents

Acknowledgements

We would like to thank the business leaders, marketing professionals and marketing academics who have spared the time to give us personal interviews to help shape (or to challenge) the themes and ideas of this book:

- David Arkwright, Global Brand Director, Unilever HPC;
- Martin Beaumont, Chief Executive, The Co-operative Group;
- Leslie Butterfield, Managing Partner, The Ingram Partnership;
- Tim Clark, President, Emirates Airline;
- David Cowan, Independent Consultant, London;
- Cliff Dennett, Consultant, Lego;
- Jonathan Durden, President, PHD;
- James Dyson, Founder, Dyson;
- William Eccleshare, Chairman/CEO, BBDO Europe;
- Professor Richard Elliott, Professor of Marketing and Consumer Research, Warwick Business School;
- Lorenzo Fluxá, Founder, Camper;
- James Foxall, Motoring Journalist;
- Helen Fraser, Managing Director, Penguin Books;
- Roddy Glen, Qualitative Researcher;
- Nigel Hollis, Global Strategic Planning Director, Millward Brown;
- Professor Theodore Levitt, Emeritus Professor of Marketing, Harvard Business School;
- Raymond Nasr, Director of Executive Communications, Google;

- Nigel Pocklington, Commercial Director, FT.com;
- Richard Reed, Founding Partner, Innocent;
- Professor Mark Ritson, Professor of Marketing, London Business School;
- Richard Rivers, Senior Vice-President, Home and Personal Care Division, Unilever;
- James Rothnie, Director of Corporate Affairs, easyGroup;
- Sue Sim, Operations Director, The Sanctuary Spa;
- Tony Tompkins, CEO, The Sanctuary Connections;
- Gordon Torr, Innovation Coach, London;
- John Wilkins, Founder, Naked Communications;
- Simon Williams, Director of Corporate Affairs, The Co-operative Bank;
- Rebecca Wynberg, Head of Sadek Wynberg Millward Brown.

Thanks also, for various contributions, to: Nick Brearley, Alexena Collins, Tim Davis, Alan Edwards, William Fawcett, Paul Fisher, Dominic Frain, Tim Gilchrist, Dinah Gray, Louise Jones, Peggy Kreller, Suresh Mistry, Debbie Sandford, Laura Scanga, Debra Van Gene, Peter Walshe and Malcolm White.

Preface:
We're getting what we ask for, but is it what we want?

Imagine you are at a major conference waiting for the keynote speech. Everyone has just settled into their seats and there is a palpable air of expectation in the hall. This is the person you have all come to see and hear. This is the talk that is going to challenge preconceptions, raise sights, inspire confidence, take you to the next level.

The chairperson introduces the speaker; the low-level audience murmur recedes to a respectful hush. But the speaker doesn't launch straight into the talk, preferring instead to check out a few things with the audience first.

'Look,' says the speaker, 'there are a number of ways we can do this – and I want to make sure it works for you.' This is followed by a few questions to sound out your communal preferences. 'Is the advertised theme OK – is it what you really want to hear about?' 'What about examples – do they help or get in the way?' 'Do you want me to quote sources as I go, or shall I just circulate them at the end?' The show of hands, tentative at first as people overcome their natural embarrassment, becomes brisker with each question, working to signal the audience view.

More questions, more hands. 'What about graphics? I have this kind – or this kind.' 'Is it better if I walk about the stage or stay put?' 'Humour: how do you feel about that? A little? A lot? None? You tell me.'

And now, with each show of hands, there is a growing sense of impatience around you. When will the talk actually begin?

It finally does. But the speaker, from time to time, still checks back with the audience. 'Pace OK?' 'Am I teaching grannies to suck eggs here?' 'Prefer a different typeface on those charts?'

There's some good stuff from the stage, no doubt about that, but also a disconcerting tendency, just as some contentious point is to be expressed, to hedge it about a bit, robbing it of its potential thrill.

'Look,' assures the speaker, 'mine is just one way to view this; if you feel strongly that my view here is wrong, then, hey, that might indicate a need to go back and explore other possibilities. We're all learning, and I can learn from you.'

And so it continues: speaking, checking, adjusting, speaking, through to the conclusion of the talk and the appreciative applause. And it is appreciative: a lot of thought and care have gone into the talk, and the audience knows it.

But, at a deeper level, what is the effect of this speaker and this speech? Probably, if you're honest, a sense of disappointment, of heights left unscaled, of challenges deferred. Sometimes, it seemed as if everything was up for negotiation, even the speaker's most cherished beliefs. Where was the passion? It was agreeable, comprehensive and clearly tailored to audience needs but – perhaps because of that – lacked surprise. You were wooed but not wowed. You didn't talk about it when you got home.

This is the feeling that modern consumer-led brands confer on modern consumers. Think of most of the brands you come into contact with every day. Think of almost entire brand categories like mid-size cars, haircare, cook-in sauces, business hotels. They are consumer-led brands because they make extensive use of research, usually focus groups, to sound out consumer opinions on just about every aspect of the brand. Like the speaker on the stage, they ask a lot of questions and they act on the findings. Within the constraints of commercial reality, they deliver.

In so doing they sort of get everything right and yet, at the same time, seem to leave something missing. Frothing with personality, yet lacking in soul, these brands fail to surprise, fail to thrill, fail to excite conversation. They are, if we're honest, for all their consumer-friendly charms, just a little disappointing. They give us what we ask for – but is it what we want?

Introduction

This book is written for CEOs, marketing professionals and MBA students. Since all of these busy people value summaries of detailed or subtle arguments, we offer, by way of introduction, just that: a 10-point summary of the book's main contentions, themes and ideas:

1. Current brand management practice, with its slavish devotion to consumer whims and directives, is leading brands on a road to nowhere.
2. Many apparently healthy brands are in trouble. With the help of Millward Brown's BrandZ™ database of 23,000 brands worldwide we show that consumer-led brands display five tell-tale symptoms of malaise that point to future loss of share.
3. Marketers are right to believe that greater emotional connection with consumers is the route to better brand health, but they are wrong if they believe that this can be achieved through superficial means like communications or 'brand personality'. If only.
4. Emotional connection starts with brand belief – a concept that is not just reserved for brands in naturally heroic categories, nor just for challenger brands, nor just for niche brands, nor just for one-off brands like Harley and Apple. We demonstrate, with examples, the tremendous power of belief for everyday, mainstream brands too.
5. A brand (or more precisely the company behind it) needs to be good at something that is good for people. This is an old-fashioned notion, but one with increasing relevance in a newly cynical world.

6. Brands that combine 4 and 5 above, and do it with imagination, integrity and guts, are Passionbrands, and there are reasons why they will be disproportionately successful in the unforgiving global economy.

7. Passionbrands can be created from the basis of existing brands. The methodology we describe, with its combination of analysis and creativity, is proven but is not for the faint-hearted.

8. There is too much smoke and mirrors, and not enough discipline, in the discipline of marketing. Passion and belief do not preclude plain language and rigour. Quite the opposite.

9. Practitioners can learn from academics – despite the latter's lack of practical experience, and arcane terminology. We decode the gobbledegook and show how the latest thinking from academia can transform your brand.

10. If branding were a sport, it would be the decathlon. Those yearning for a simple, one-stop solution to the mysteries of brand stewardship would be advised to seek another book.

PART 1

Why

1 From understanding to obsession

Consumer understanding is so much part of marketing today that it is hard to imagine a time when it wasn't. Yet midway through the 20th century the consumer, and especially the US consumer, was someone to be sold to, the dutiful recipient of the bounty that big business had become ever more practised at providing. Detroit made huge cars because it could, and because it was inclined to, not because of any evidence that huge was what people really wanted.

It was the Harvard academic Theodore Levitt who first persuaded US business that it was guilty of subordinating the needs of consumers to its own. His landmark paper, 'Marketing Myopia', written in 1960, opened eyes to the growing gulf between what people wanted and what business wanted them to want. Others had voiced similar opinions before, Peter Drucker among them, but it was the clarity and audacity of Levitt's challenge that hit home. His main proposal sought not merely to tinker with the US business machine but to throw it into reverse: marketing should start with the consumer and work back from there. Product should come last, not first. Unafraid to take on big targets, Levitt chose the petroleum industry to exemplify this radical view:

> The industry is implicitly defined as beginning with the search for oil and ending with its distribution from the refinery. But the truth is, it seems to me, that the industry begins with the needs of the consumer for its products. From that primal position its definition moves steadily back-stream to areas of less importance, until it finally comes to rest at the 'search for oil.'

By placing the consumer at the forefront of the business process Levitt laid the foundations of modern marketing. In a paper that was massively influential in its time can be found thinking that cuts through every bit as keenly today. Nobody, for example, should embark upon a career in marketing without first reading Levitt's classic distinction between marketing and selling:

> Selling focuses on the needs of the seller, marketing on the needs of the buyer. Selling is preoccupied with the seller's need to convert his product into cash, marketing with the idea of satisfying the needs of the customer by means of the product and the whole cluster of things associated with creating, delivering, and finally consuming it.

Levitt has written several times about the surprising influence of 'Marketing Myopia', the first as early as 1975. With the candour that characterizes the business academic (who after all has no stock options to nurture) he took care to list both positive and negative outcomes. In the credit column he cites, among other things, the increased tendency for companies to define their core competence in terms that reflect what people derive from it, rather than what the company puts in: from oil to energy companies, for example. But from today's perspective it is something written on the debit side that draws the eye: 'Some companies have developed what I call "marketing mania" – they've become obsessively responsive to every fleeting whim of the consumer.'

In other words, if you think of the marketing function as a pendulum that can swing from producer-centric to consumer-centric, Levitt saw that there was a danger in it swinging too far. Three decades on and it has swung further still in the direction that Levitt first launched it. The implications of that pendulum swing will form one of the central themes of this book.

The consumer in the brand's inner sanctum

For today's sophisticated brand companies, consumer-centric marketing is something not just to be practised but to be worn as a badge of honour. 'Getting closer to consumers' – to quote the kind of phrase routinely deployed for journalists and in annual reports – is seen as the ultimate source of competitive advantage, something worth striving for and worthy of pride when achieved. Typical of the genre is the claim made by the British industrial conglomerate ICI, on its new website: 'It is by getting closer to the consumer that we are able to create imaginative solutions to the challenges of a modern lifestyle.'

Niall FitzGerald, chairman of Unilever, in a talk entitled 'Understanding people to build brands' (2003), puts the point with more feeling: 'We must strive for consumer intimacy. Our great strength is the knowledge of what the consumer wants.'

The British Chartered Institute of Marketing (2003) picks up the theme in *Eight Ways to Revive Your Brand for Better Business Performance*. Right up there at no 1 is 'Find new ways to listen to your customers.'

Few in Europe champion the approach with greater zeal or justification than Sir Terry Leahy, CEO of the UK's leading grocery retailer Tesco. In a *Sunday Times Business* interview (16 November 2003) exploring his role in turning Tesco into a 'customer-led business', Leahy said, 'We were determined to follow the customer – so the business would go wherever the customer took us, and we would never try to shoehorn the customer into what we wanted to offer. We stopped following the competition and followed the customer.'

Meanwhile, across the Atlantic, the clothing retailer Nordstrom has gone one further. Its corporate organogram places The Customer at the very top of the chart, ahead of the CEO and all those occupying humbler stations in the hierarchy. If you think of where the customer stood at the time Levitt was picking up the 1960 McKinsey Award for the year's seminal paper, this is some promotion.

Nor is it merely symbolic, like the position accorded to some fêted yet powerless head of state. Modern brand marketing companies increasingly look to the consumer for leadership across the board. These companies not only generate concepts like 'consumer insight mining' or 'implicit consumer-psychographic-space mapping', but they put their money where their tongue-twisted mouths are. Consumer research is a $16-billion business worldwide and its tentacles probe deeply into the 'cluster of things' associated with any given brand. Consumers are now consulted routinely on a whole range of issues of which their own needs, in the normal sense of that word, constitute an ever-diminishing proportion. Line extensions, pack design, livery, colourways, advertising, brand values, brand personality, service strategy, ethos, even the much vaunted 'brand essence' – all these are viewed as reasonable subject matter to be set in front of the consumer's emperor-like thumb.

Let us look, just for a moment, at an example at one extreme of that list. An international beer brand with over 130 years' heritage decides to involve consumers in determining its brand essence. The methodology will be focus groups. Consumers will look at stimulus in the form of concept boards, each one a montage of related images titled by a single word. On one, for example, are images of lakes, snow-capped mountains and similarly tranquil images, all governed by the word 'Calm'. On another the images are more assertive: party-goers, groups rather than singles, active poses and high-octane smiles. The caption for this board reads 'Social'. Other boards depict the themes of 'Confidence', 'Natural', 'Independent' – and so on. The task of the professional qualitative researcher will be to tease out from consumers where they would most like to see this brand represent itself at its deepest, most essential, level. (In the end, it came down to a hybrid of two.)

Now brand essence is no trifling thing; it is not just something to help get a piece of communications right. It is not simply 'image' or 'personality' or 'attitude' – although it should guide all of those things. The marketing guru David Aaker (Aaker and Joachimsthaler, 2000) defines brand essence as 'A single thought that captures the soul of the brand'. An additional point is that brand essence is an active force, not inert ballast; it should find expression in everything the brand does and is; it should infuse new product development, distribution strategy, pricing, targeting, sampling, joint ventures, advertising, everything. It is, after all, the essence.

It is curious, then, that a brand with a 130-year heritage should need to ask others what its own essence should be. If it doesn't have its own sense of that, what does it have? Curious, too, that the research in this case was commissioned for Europe alone, although the brand has global reach. For while it is normal enough for brand communications to vary by market somewhat, to reflect local cultural mores, brand essence should be consistent everywhere; you can't really split your soul. Most curious of all, perhaps, is that the marketing fraternity doesn't seem to find this process curious; brand essence research has become common over the past decade, mirroring the tendency, if you will, of individuals within wealthy societies to turn to counsellors for help in discovering 'who they are'.

If you think about it, brand essence research is an exotic example of outsourcing, of the kind that the entrepreneur Stelios Haji-Iaonnou has made famous: outsourcing to the consumer. This is the phrase

Stelios likes to use to describe his easyCar rental policy of asking customers to bring the car back clean, and charging them extra if they don't. It's one of the ways his company can offer the lowest deals in town. Ikea outsources the assembly of its furniture to the consumer, often with frustrating results, but it works because the arrangement helps to provide high quality at low cost. Outsourcing rental-car cleaning? Smart idea. Outsourcing furniture assembly? Good business. *But outsourcing your soul?*

And if brand essence research is at the rarefied end of things, you don't have to come in too far along the spectrum to see consumers making extraordinarily fundamental decisions on behalf of the brands they buy. Hence the kinds of phrases you will hear in modern marketing departments and their agencies:

- 'We know from consumers that this brand can't come out of the chill cabinet.'
- 'Heavy users want to see the brand move into the haircare category.'
- 'According to research, the 15- to 18-year-old coffee target thinks our taste credentials are secondary in importance.'
- 'Consumers tell us our commercials have to feature "mum".'
- 'Our conquest target tells us that the marque is respected but needs to become more likeable.'

Of course, consumers wouldn't issue these directives unless asked, but asked they are – and you have to wonder about the appropriateness of some of the questions. There is a quantum difference between Tesco learning from research how vexatious people find checkout queues and then taking action to shorten them, and a brand inviting consumers into its inner sanctum to help define its core values. The former shows a brand genuinely striving to get closer to consumers, the latter the precise reverse: it is about bringing consumers smack up close to the brand, and reflects less a desire for understanding than a kind of corporate aimlessness. The leading British brand strategist Leslie Butterfield is a forceful exponent of consumer research but his enthusiasm does not extend to its casual substitution for professional judgement. As he puts it, 'There are people earning six-figure salaries who are going to consumers to get answers to issues that should be decided with the analytical skills and fundamental marketing judgement they are being paid for.'

Examples abound. The no 3 pasta sauce brand goes to consumers to ask if it should be about 'Italian-ness'. Isn't this something that is either central to the brand or not? A financial institution uses consumer research to determine whether its offer should be built on flexibility or trust. Shouldn't this be decided at the level of company culture? Or consider the no 1 objective cited by a long-established European airline for a piece of qualitative consumer research briefed through the advertising agency: 'To develop a relevant, profitable and sustainable business model.' Well, the airline's customer base is bound to include some pretty smart business brains so, hey, why not?

The UK-based international qualitative researcher Rebecca Wynberg comments that she is frequently asked to 'go to research to answer questions that should be housed internally'. And her normal reaction is to challenge the marketer to come at the issue from the brand out. A recent, polite refusal to conduct some brand architecture research, for example, was rooted in her belief that 'consumers don't buy ranges' and that this was a highly inappropriate, company-led issue to be putting in front of end users. Other researchers, though, might have no such compunctions, and so another $1-billion chunk of corporate assets would find itself pored over in the consumer's lay hands.

How has marketing got to this stage? How has it arrived at such a state of abject dependence on the consumer? Is it because each step along the way has been carefully considered and evaluated and proved to have worked? Is it because the fashionable dictum that 'brands only exist in the minds of consumers' has lulled us into the acceptance of an altogether more specious conclusion: that consumers, therefore, are the only credible force that can shape a brand, mould its offer and determine its values? Or have things just kind of tripped along from one stage to the next, an increment here, an increment there, without us really noticing? One way or another, the consumer has become more and more influential in decisions that were once strictly the province of the professionals closest to the brand. The question is, why?

Factors in the rise of consumer influence

Many factors have combined to ensure the increased acceptance of the consumer-centric approach to marketing, not least of which is the eminent good sense of its more basic premises: of course it is important to understand people before attempting to engage them in a commercial transaction; of course consumer needs should come before those of the organization. Most powerful movements in business start this way. Good sense leads to good results, which leads others to follow. The technology and internet advance was set in train by the promise of real efficiencies, and fuelled by early successes, but then accelerators kicked in and we reached extremes that were not envisaged at the outset. The rise of consumer influence within the discipline of marketing, too, has had its accelerators, its own internal forces, which have helped propel its progress unchecked. We now turn our attention to the more significant of these.

The separation of marketing from making

Early in her best-selling book *No Logo* (2000), Naomi Klein evokes the notion of the 'weightless brand'. Citing household names like Nike, Microsoft and Tommy Hilfiger, she notes the growing desire of companies to divest themselves of the apparatus required for making things, in order to focus solely on branding:

> These pioneers made the bold claim that producing goods was only an incidental part of their operations and that, thanks to recent victories in trade liberalisation and labour law reform, they were able to have their products made for them by contractors, many of them overseas. What these companies produced were not things, they said, but images of their brands.

Free from the gravitational pull of the making part of the organization, with all its constraints and sturdy logic, it is easy to envisage marketers floating off into an ever-closer embrace with the consumer. Brands would be defined solely by consumer desire, unchained by corporate capability. This is the theory, at least, and it would be testable were it not for the fact that most marketing professionals are still waiting for the weightless brand: in spite of its supposed desirability it is not, for most, reality. The direct provision of things, or of services, is still the province of most brand marketing companies.

And yet a degree of separation has been contrived through simple geography. Marketing, despite the pleas of those who claim that it should be neither a discrete discipline nor a separate department, has become both. And it is a department increasingly housed away from the factories and R&D labs and service centres and anything else that smacks of the 'business end' of the organization.

A certain sense of weightlessness, then, is experienced by the typical marketing team. The marketing director and the production director aren't exactly likely to bump into each other at the water cooler and exchange a bit of business news, since their respective workplaces will often be hundreds of miles apart. The loss of dialogue that distance inevitably creates is to the detriment of all. Marketing ceases to stay close enough to disciplines like product formulation, service strategy and innovation in order to influence them, and be influenced by them, as it should. Instead it tends to focus on what it can influence, which is communications. Once inside this ghetto, the intimate bond with the consumer becomes stronger, the influence of the rest of the business weaker.

The need to justify actions

In recessionary times – and there have been a few during the brief history of modern marketing – chief financial officers look to find savings where they can and it doesn't take long for their gaze to fall on marketing. Millions of dollars going out, and what, exactly, in return, coming in? Any marketing director with more than a few miles on the clock, therefore, will have had some practice in defending budgets, staff levels, perhaps the very existence of the department at all. Not that the need to justify expenditure disappears entirely during better times; it simply becomes a question of defending the more ambitious projects, and of competing with peers in the same company for finite marketing funds.

The difficulty, in either good times or bad, is that marketing is a fuzzy discipline and its role is diffuse in the short-term performance of any given brand. Capital expenditure on a new production-line machine can be expected to produce a finely calculated saving across a known period of time; marketing investment famously eludes such precision.

Unable to demonstrate a linear correlation between marketing expenditure and return – retrospectively, let alone prospectively – marketing teams fall back on the use of proxies, indicators that help to show how the brand is faring. Tracking studies, awareness data, usage and attitude data are all well-accepted forms of research designed to monitor the progress of the brand and value for marketing dollar spent. Although none of these indicators is as direct as raw sales figures, or brand share, their quantitative status serves to give them a certain respectable solidity.

Increasingly, however, less robust, purely qualitative, findings are gracing the PowerPoint charts of the presentations marketing teams make to impress budget holders. The aim is to secure the budget; the research will be used as ammunition. Typically, the top-line findings from focus groups will be captured complete with pithy verbatims, each enclosed in a jauntily coloured speech bubble to show it is the consumer speaking. The message is clear: look, our proposed new line extension – or ad campaign or service innovation or whatever – has the direct endorsement of the consumer.

The tactical use of qualitative research is understandable but it is not without its dangers, principal among which is that the process tends to become self-reinforcing. Budget holders, CFOs, the board come to expect precise consumer endorsement of any project that requires significant expenditure or implies some kind of variation from the norm. This brings its own consequences: consumer research becomes more about endorsement than illumination, consumers play referees in the struggle between the competing aims of different groups and projects, and innovation is blunted by the need to stay within the consumer's comfort zone – or risk losing the project to something less challenging.

Short tenure of marketing managers

Twenty years ago the typical tenure of a marketing manager on the same brand was six to eight years in both the United States and Europe. Today, according to estimates provided by leading recruitment consultants on either side of the Atlantic, those figures have plummeted to between 18 months and two years. On 10 May 2004, *AdAge* noted that 'Only 14% of chief marketing officers had been in their jobs for more than three years.' Marketing has become a revolving door, as the best talent gets headhunted for the next challenge, creating a whirlwind of job-switching activity further down the line.

It is not hard to see one consequence of this instability: the diminution of internal focus. Marketing leaders fail to put down roots in any one brand culture, decline to become steeped in the beliefs and ethos of any single company and, perhaps, underestimate the depth and power of what resides inside the brand in favour of opinions and ideas from outside. It is with consumers, researchers and advisers that modern marketing professionals form lasting bonds as they move from one challenge to the next. There is no discontinuity of practice to match the discontinuity of brand. Today's marketing teams are outer-directed partly because that is what they know best; their relationship with consumers runs deeper than their relationship with any given brand.

The rise of the advertising planner

The discipline of account planning emerged more or less simultaneously from the London agencies BMP and JWT in 1968 and spread gradually throughout the industry worldwide. David Cowan, who joined BMP at the time, and who went on to run the agency's planning function for 16 years, observes that the original remit of the planner was 'the analysis of quantitative market data and its fusion with qualitative consumer research in order to find ways to make people want the brand'.

Quickly, though, the planner simply became known as 'the voice of the consumer'. Early on, it was a voice that much needed to be heard, to counterbalance the other voices in the marketing mix: clients who overestimated the interest of their new wonder ingredient to consumers, account people who reported and frequently amplified what the client said, and creative teams whose driving obsession was the pursuit of awards. In this context planning acted as both a restraining hand on self-indulgence and a source of inspiration for ideas that could, for the first time, create a real bond of empathy with people.

Today, planners are the stars in the advertising industry firmament, their rise in status reflected in their rise in salaries (Kendall Tarrant, 2003): up 46 per cent over five years, compared with 12 per cent for their peers in account management. Like creatives they are permitted their eccentricities and a casual sartorial style; unlike creatives they enjoy not just respect but an extraordinary level of trust from marketing teams. Planners are the people who bring 'consumer insights' into the debate, a commodity that seems to have an almost gem-like value in the eyes of marketing people. But planner power is best exemplified in their unique ability to close down a heated discussion about where the brand or the advertising should be going, simply by quoting from research: the consumer has spoken; so be it. From voice of consumer to voice of God in just over three decades.

But if planning is a factor in the increased propensity for marketing teams to look to the consumer for answers, it is, on balance, a benign one. The discipline of advertising, at least, is a lot more focused, entertaining and effective than before planning came along. However, as we shall see, the rise of planning has more serious implications when taken in conjunction with the next issue: the proliferation of advisers.

The proliferation of advisers to marketing departments

The modern marketing department deals with a matrix of advisers of bewildering complexity. It used to be simpler; the media function was part of the advertising agency, direct marketing was done in-house and digital didn't exist. Now, media alone will involve dealing with up to three separate companies, one each for strategy, buying and auditing. The typical marketing team will also visit separate advisers for brand strategy, pack design, corporate image design, PR, direct marketing, digital communications, internal communications, sponsorship, events management and more specialist functions – like trade-marketing, for example – according to market segment.

A quite recent feature of many of these adviser niches is their adoption of the planning discipline. A marketing team working on a brand extension, for example, might receive planning presentations from the advertising agency, brand consultancy, pack design company, PR company, media strategist and direct marketing company. In each case the debrief will of course be tilted towards the discipline in question, but many of the essentials, the consumer insights, consumer attitudes to the brand, and so on, will be the same. (In the rare cases where it isn't, there is usually an answer: more research.)

What is repeated tends to become amplified in the mind even though its importance remains consistent each time. If one person says you look tired, you shrug it off. If six people in a row say the same thing, it might occasion a visit to the doctor. Imagine, for example, the advertising agency planner concluding from research that a certain brand is 'respected but not loved' (a common enough finding in the world of brands). The brand manager hearing this would probably be neither too surprised nor fazed; it would probably fit with empirical knowledge about the brand, and would be taken in stride, seen in proportion, judged in the context of other factors in the marketing mix. Action, if action were deemed appropriate, would be limited to sensible measures. The finding, in other words, would be one input among many that influence brand strategy.

But now imagine hearing the same input again and again in presentation after presentation from the various advisers on the circuit.

'Respected but not loved' would come to dominate through sheer repetition. The insight would be no truer the eighth time than it was the first, but its apparent importance, with the best will in the world, would become exaggerated. Perhaps of all the factors in the growing obsession with consumer opinion, this is the most insidious, the one that's crept up on everyone unawares. The proliferation of advisers to marketing departments, combined with the spread of planning, has turned the voice of the consumer into a chorus.

The line that's been crossed

To summarize: for reasons that have much to do with marketing fundamentals, but more to do with the peculiarities and dynamics of the marketing industry, today's brands counsel consumer opinion on an ever-widening range of brand issues. If this in turn were leading to an ever-deepening understanding of people, if it were helping us more fully appreciate their needs, if it were giving us fresh insight into the role of brands within the context of their everyday personal, social and cultural lives it would, of course, be a good thing. The reality, however, is somewhat different.

Before moving on, it would be well to dispel any notion that this book takes an anti-research stance. It does not, as will become increasingly apparent. What it does question is the kind of objective to which research is typically shackled. Much of what is undertaken in the name of 'getting closer to consumers' – a phrase that seems to be open to suspiciously wide interpretation – amounts to little more than a narrow discussion about the brand. If you take a dispassionate look at the role of consumer research within the discipline of modern marketing you will observe that, time and again, a line has been crossed. It is the line that separates 'consumers on consumers' from 'consumers on the brand'.

It could be argued, of course, that this division is an artificial one, that things are more fluid in practice, that well-crafted research naturally embraces both the subject of consumers on themselves and their relationship with the brand. But sometimes it is necessary to draw a line solely to make graphic the fact that a bias exists, that activity is far greater on one side than the other. The common practice of getting a few consumers together to talk about some aspect of the brand is not the same thing as a thorough, holistic exercise aimed at a more general understanding, in spite of the fact that they both happen to be subsumed under the label of 'consumer research'. So let's stick with our line for now, and look at the difference between the typical objectives and methodologies on either side.

Consumers on consumers

At its holistic best this approach would be called 'people on people' since it aims at a rounded understanding of the way people lead their lives and go about their day, of which consumption is but a part. It looks at what people do, not just what they say, explores issues like social and personal identity, and develops a picture of the individual within the context of contemporary culture. Where consumption is examined the lens will be widened to give a view that is broader than the confines of any one brand or category.

This is the classical, post-Levitt approach, and it strives to foster an intuitive feel for people, the kind of close-woven understanding that leads to empathy and even affection. At a brand level the objective is not to seek direction from consumers but to find better ways to serve them through the juxtaposition of enhanced understanding and the company's own distinct culture and capability. Implied in this approach, then, is the need for the company to have a *strong sense of itself*, not just the customers it serves.

The methodology will tend to be multi-layered to reflect the nature of the enlightenment sought. Depending on the time and money available, the mix should approach the academic ideal of 'triangulation', first described by the interpretive theorists Denzin and Lincoln (1998), which not only combines qualitative and quantitative research, but interleaves several different techniques in each, in order to expose and corroborate important underlying themes.

The full-on holistic approach can hardly be recommended for the unconfident, the impoverished, the impatient or the culturally challenged but it is, we contend, the most promising route to richer, more creative, longer-lasting relationships between people and brands.

Consumers on the brand

The majority of consumer research today falls on this side of the line. The aim is to cut to the chase, to focus on the brand in question – or perhaps the brand and its nearest rival. Typically the research will set out to get immediate answers to quite narrow and specific brand questions: What do you think of this proposed advertising? Should the brand move into this new category? Is this packaging right? Which celebrities do you think are right for this brand? Which of these values should we stand for? If this brand were a person, who would it be? To loyalists: what makes you warm to this brand? To rejecters: what puts you off buying this brand? To opinion leaders: how do we make this brand cool?

The objective, though it might be unspoken, is not merely understanding but direction. The brand team wants direct input on how to make the brand and its values more attractive to consumers; where better to get it than from the consumer's own mouth?

This quest for directness drives the choice of methodology. Despite the wealth of qualitative options to hand – ethnography, friendship pairs, co-operative enquiry, accompanied shopping trips, video diaries, discourse analysis – it is focus groups that now command some 85 per cent of marketing's total qualitative research budget. It's not hard to see why. Focus groups are convenient, fast and relatively inexpensive. But not least among their attractions is the one that defines them: focus. There is an intensity of content to focus groups that captivates the marketing teams who observe them from behind those two-way mirrors. Consumers – in what must be one of the more artificial kinds of conversation on the planet – discuss the brand at a level of detail that simply doesn't happen in any other context. In just a couple of hours you have a whole cache of 'learnings' to seize and to turn into action.

It is significant that the professional qualitative researchers who conduct these groups are beginning to express concern about both the narrowness of objectives going in and the trend towards immediate feedback coming out. The veteran UK qualitative researcher Roddy Glen observes that clients are increasingly determined to 'get straight to the brand', and goes on to deplore 'the adoption of the American tendency to dispense with a carefully considered debrief'. According to David Cowan, 75 per cent of US groups are never debriefed; there is no careful sifting and weighing and extrapolation; marketing teams simply draw their own conclusions on the hoof. Marketers are mainlining consumer opinion now, and compared with the slow, considered stuff of the holistic approach it's heady and exhilarating and fast. But what kind of brands is it leading to?

Giving them what they ask for

Common practice is not the same thing as universal practice and there will always be marketing teams who resist the dubious extremes of the consumer-centric approach, who cherish consumer understanding without falling prey to consumer obsession, and who use focus groups as just one tool among many, for illumination not direction.

That said, the pressures on marketing teams are not getting any lighter, and best practice cannot be sustained without the proper time, money and encouragement from above. In a commercial world where brands and brand teams are stretched across wider geography and a more complex social and media landscape, resources have become only too finite. In this context, ever mindful of the penalties of slow brand growth, and confronted with the homogenized views of the people with the money in their pockets, it is a rare marketing team that has not simply, and gladly, implemented the 'findings' from a few brand-specific consumer groups.

And what is the consequence? It is the proliferation of consumer-led brands. These brands hold an undoubted attraction for consumers, which is hardly surprising given their influence in shaping them. But there is a danger, and it is this. What consumers have at heart is their own short-term interest, not the brand's long-term health. Hence, in category after category, market after market, the superficial attraction of consumer-led brands masks an inner malaise. This malaise, like some of the most insidious human pathologies, may cause no immediate pain. But its presence is consistent with five tell-tale symptoms. Look closely at your brand. If it suffers from any two or more of them, you have cause for concern.

2 The five symptoms of malaise of consumer-led brands

We live in a world of consumer-led brands. We are surrounded by them – in the supermarket, at the service station, in our shopping malls, in our homes, on our TVs. There is an easy familiarity to them, a kind of ready-made acceptability, even when these brands are brand new. The colours are attractive, the packs feel right in our hands, the fragrances beckon, the flavours are yummy and unchallenging, the personalities are as disarming as a smile. We walk into an unfamiliar brand of hotel, one we have never experienced before, and immediately feel a sense of déjà vu. We sit in a new car and it almost feels like a friend. We watch a TV commercial and see our own lives, only better, hum along to a 30-second blast of one of our all-time favourite tracks, enjoy the little twist we know will be there at the end, and file that clever slogan away with all the others that sound, well, just a little bit like it, just so, just the kind of thing we expected.

In the world of consumer-led brands there aren't too many shocks or surprises. How should there be? Consumer-led brands have gone beyond the mere understanding of our needs to co-opt our collective consciousness into the very design and substance and atmosphere of the brand itself. With our help, these brands have expunged all traces of their own corporately derived awkwardness, moderated their idiosyncrasies and smoothed out their quaint bumps and imperfections, so that they engage us like one of those photos of a human face that is, in fact, a composite of all the faces we find most attractive. Consumer-led brands want us to want them, and they take the most direct route possible. These brands say to consumers: we can be anything you want us to be. Just tell us what it is, what features you want, what personality you like, what values you favour. Tell us, tell us, tell us.

Emblematic of this quest to get straight to the heart of consumer desire is the exponential growth of the consumer research industry. In 1993 just over $7 billion was spent on consumer research worldwide. By 2001 it had grown to $16 billion, a 6 per cent increase on the previous year. Three-quarters of that money was spent in Europe and the United States, and just 13 per cent in Asia, despite its mighty population. But with Asian markets exploding and capitalism assurgent, that proportion will rise fast and help to swell the total pot to an estimated $25 billion by 2008. Thanks to the modern brand, consumer research is one of the world's most buoyant industries.

There is an irony, then, that this same industry should harbour some of the clues that all is not well. Consumer research is not simply a stream of information that flows one way, from the consumer via the research company to the brand owner. Information also collects in vast pools and reservoirs, created and tended by the research industry itself, and in these depths can be observed the underlying currents and eddies that cannot be perceived at the surface, at the level of the single brand. The world's biggest reservoir of consumer information is owned by the marketing services group WPP and managed by Millward Brown, one of the world's largest consumer research companies. Called BrandZ™ (pronounce that 'Brand-Zee'), it constitutes a database of over 23,000 brands, updated constantly through fieldwork with over 700,000 people in 30 countries. It is to this database that we were allowed privileged access in order to explore and corroborate some of the themes of this book. Since two of its proprietary metrics – Voltage and Bonding – are relevant to several of the symptoms of malaise in this chapter, we give a brief overview of them here.

The predictive power of BrandZ™

BrandZ™ measures the relative strengths of brands within their category. It generates, for any given brand, a BrandDynamics™ Pyramid like the one in Figure 2.1. At the bottom of the pyramid is Presence, an indication of the number of consumers whose contact with the brand extends no further than knowledge of its existence. At the top of the pyramid is Bonding, an indication of the number of consumers who

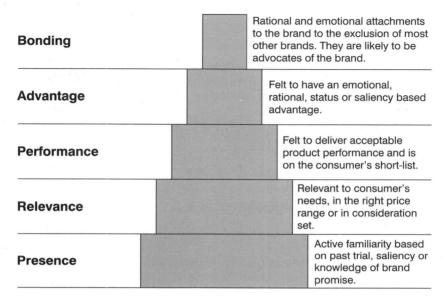

Figure 2.1 BrandDynamics™ Pyramid

have a relationship with the brand that runs deep enough to inspire loyalty.

The vigour with which a brand manages to convert consumers up the pyramid is captured in a one-digit number called Brand Voltage™. A small brand could have high Voltage, and a big brand low Voltage. It's the rate of conversion all the way up to the top that matters. If brand A starts with a Presence figure of 25 and brand B with 75, but they both end up with a Bonding figure of 9, it is brand A that has the higher Voltage.

Voltage is interesting to us for two reasons. The first is that it exhibits a proven, positive correlation with future brand share. Thousands of data inputs across hundreds of brands have corroborated this relationship. The higher the Voltage score, the greater the chance that the brand will grow its share in the coming year. The lower the Voltage score, the greater the chance that the brand will shrink. (See Figure 2.2.)

Given this predictive power, the constituent factors that determine Voltage must interest us too. What are the brand qualities that drive consumers up the pyramid into that box at the top? Well, consumers can be bought with very low prices. But this is hardly the most attractive route to future share growth. There are four more qualities that count, and they would figure on any marketer's wish-list: Leadership

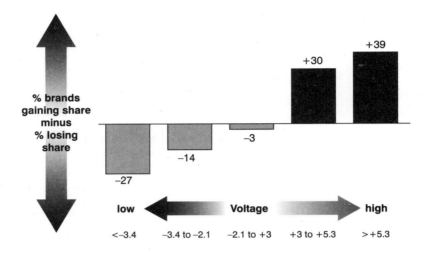

Figure 2.2 A proven link between Brand Voltage™ and future market share

(challenging the status quo); Difference (standing for something unique); Affinity (being rationally strong and emotionally warm); and Fame (dominating by sheer salience). But on all of these, as we shall show, consumer-led brands are vulnerable. It is this chain of reasoning, this proven link to future share, that justifies the word 'symptoms' rather than simply 'characteristics' for what we are about to describe.

Symptom no 1: an increased similarity between brands

Brands that canvass and act on consumer opinion must at some point confront a sobering reality: in any one category, at any one time, consumers will articulate the same desires, needs, preferences and whims. Therefore the more literally – and, from the consumer's point of view, satisfactorily – the brand translates these desires into reality, the greater the danger that it will fall into line with other brands in the same sector or the same niche of the same sector. This is the one potential flaw in the Terry Leahy school of argument; if Tesco does indeed simply follow the consumer – and there are reasons for supposing that things are not quite that basic – then the competitive advantage lasts only as long as his rivals choose not to do so. The consumer's voice is there for anyone who'll listen, and it will tell Asda the same thing as it tells him. Consumers are not interested in preserving the differences between brands; they are interested in getting what they want.

At a category level, therefore, what we see is brands collectively satisfying consumer desires and exhibiting values and associations that please them. The petroleum industry that Levitt originally singled out for opprobrium, for example, today drills for consumer insights as enthusiastically as it drills for oil, spending an estimated $200 million per year on consumer research. Viewed as a category it says all the right things about the environment, boasts a strong corporate social responsibility commitment and provides the basics people want: efficiently run, clean and convenient service stations.

At the level of any single brand, however, success derived from following consumers is bought at the price of convergence, unless the brand has the courage to filter consumer opinion through its own, necessarily strong, culture and create solutions that are far more imaginative and challenging than those offered by its competitors. In the petroleum category, as in so many others, no such hero brand has emerged. All are saying and doing much the same kind of thing, values are interchangeable, prices are virtually identical and competitive differences are few. These brands coalesce around what Kevin Keller (Keller *et al.*, 2002) calls the sector 'points of parity' – the must-haves, features and associations that serve to provide consumers with a frame of reference for the category. But what brands also desperately need, if they are to score on the BrandZ™ dimension of Leadership, is points of difference. In consumer-led brands, these are becoming ever more rare.

The tendency for brands to converge is seen with more gladiatorial drama when just two brands dominate a category, a not infrequent occurrence. The $1.4-billion German soups and convenience foods market provides an example. Just two brands – Knorr and Maggi – account for 65 per cent of the market. In terms of everything that makes a brand a brand – product performance, range, distribution, usership base, values and associations – these brands are very evenly matched. Similarities abound; differences are few and slight. Both make a range that extends from soups and bouillon cubes to salad dressings and meal-makers. Both favour vibrant house colours for packs and communications: Maggi is red and yellow, to put the colours in order of dominance; Knorr is green and yellow. On the packs you'll see similarly sized, similarly appetizing shots of the cooked finished dish to which the

Figure 2.3 Spot the difference: Knorr and Maggi packs in late 2003. The growing design convergence persuaded Knorr into a complete packaging redesign in 2004

product contributes. (See Figure 2.3.) The overlap in product offer is matched by the overlap in user base, which hovers around the 90 per cent mark. In other words, 90 per cent of the homes that have one brand will also have the other. This seeming ambivalence toward precise choice of brand was illustrated anecdotally in 2004 by a researcher exploring brand preference outside a German supermarket. She approached a couple and asked them what had driven their choice of the Maggi stock cubes visible in their shopping baskets. 'Oh,' came the reply, 'did we buy Maggi? I thought we'd bought Knorr. Oh, well.'

The lay observer might look at these brands and simply draw the conclusion that they continually copy one another, that their convergence is due to mutual obsession; what one does today, the other does tomorrow, so that they end up entwined with each other like two strands of the DNA molecule's iconic double helix. There is some truth in this, but only some; big, competitive brands do of course keep a constant eye on each other, and cannot allow breakthroughs to go unchallenged. But these brands, and others like them, would tend to be drawn together even if blind to one another's activities, for they both dance to the same tune, and it is that of the consumer. Both Knorr and Maggi carefully monitor consumer trends in eating and general lifestyle, both carefully test new product concepts and the formulations that follow them, and both canvass consumer opinion on the fine details of pack design, right down to nuances like how deeply the meat-balls should be submerged in the tomato sauce in the picture of the finished dish. From the consumers, in turn, the brands are getting similar answers, and it is leading to similar solutions on the shelf.

Convergence in communications

Recognizing the inevitability of convergence at the substantive product level, consumer-led brands look to communications to signal a differ-ence. After all, while product ingredients like wild mushrooms and saffron, say, are available to any brand with the expertise to use them, the company's own culture and heritage are unique to itself. Communications, by tapping into this unique set of internal values, can offer consumers an attractive way to differentiate between other-wise similar brand offers. So the argument goes.

In reality, to the resigned dismay of advertising creative teams all over the globe, marketers also turn to consumers for input on commu-nications planning and, in any one sector, consumers are pretty consis-tent on what they like. Any advertising copywriter or art director with more than a few years' experience will be able to recite by heart the list of interchangeable adjectives that accompany the brief for a brand in any given sector; in fmcg, for example, it will invariably include notions like: natural, vital, appealing, bright, vibrant, open and socia-ble. The advertising ideas that emerge from these briefs are then passed through the filter of consumer approval so that they, too, tend to converge with the others in the same, or related, sectors.

Why is convergence an issue, one might ask, for a pair of brands that between them have two-thirds of a billion-dollar market? In that context, does specific brand loyalty really matter? Isn't it better to maintain an uneasy truce with your main competitor and stand together against others in the sector who are seeking to take share? In fact the threat comes from outside the immediate sector. It is the power of the retailer that threatens big established brands and it is the very tendency of these brands to converge around nice, tightly grouped points of parity that makes it so easy for own-label to copy them. In Germany, own-label, at about 25 per cent, is relatively small but it is growing fast. In the UK, it accounts for over 40 per cent of fmcg sales, and it is in precisely those sectors where differentiation between the leaders is weak that it enjoys greatest success. As the INSEAD academics Judith and Marcel Corstjens remark in their book *Store Wars* (1995), the characterful 'eponymous brands' like Marmite or Twix, with their strong emotional brand loyalty, are the ones the retailers find it hard to emulate.

Few sectors are immune from the power of retailer brands where consumers display emotional ambivalence towards the leaders. Look at the banking sector in the UK, for example. The big, traditional bank brands converge with almost perfect cohesion around the sector points of parity, offering virtually identical products and services, at virtually identical rates, and seeking to reassure consumers in communications about the same kinds of issues like security and financial complexity. These banks got where they are by listening to consumers but those very consumers now shrug and say, 'Banks are all the same.' Emotional affinity to any one is markedly low. This has provided the opportunity for retailer brands like Sainsbury's and Tesco to leverage the consumer trust they enjoy, and offer an attractive alternative to the traditional banks simply by copying the points of parity to which they all so conveniently cleave. These same retailer brands are making inroads into the petrol, telecoms and insurance markets, too, and you have to wonder what's next.

For any given brand to survive and thrive in this context it needs to foster true, emotional brand loyalty with consumers. To achieve that it will need to find, at the very minimum, less literal, more inspiring, ways to turn their desires into brand reality. The alternative – convergence around sector points of parity – is growing more dangerous by the day.

Symptom no 2: an inconsistent brand image and offer

Following the consumer might seem like sound advice in principle but it can lead to a merry old dance in practice. Consumers don't live their lives in a straight line. They are human so they are fickle. As Rebecca Wynberg puts it, 'Consumers can tell you what they did yesterday; they can't tell you what they are going to do tomorrow.' Actually, it's worse than that; they can tell you passionately and categorically what they intend to do tomorrow, but there is no guarantee that they will actually do it, and a sporting chance that they will do the precise reverse.

For marketers the constantly moving target makes for a life of finely balanced decisions. To ignore consumer trends completely is to become eventually a blind brand, out of touch with real people in the real world. On the other hand, to react to every capricious wish and whim is like negotiating a choppy sea in a small boat: the brand is tossed about with abandon and it's an uncomfortable and dangerous ride.

The distinction to keep in mind, of course, is that between tactics and strategy, with change at the former level acceptable only insofar as it contributes to stability at the latter. As Kevin Keller writes in *Strategic Brand Management* (1998), 'Being consistent in managing brand equity may require numerous tactical shifts and changes in order to maintain the strategic thrust and direction of the brand.' What can make consumer-led brands so flaky, however, is their propensity to allow the attitudinal and behavioural volatility of consumers to exert undue influence directly at the strategic level.

A poignant example is the suncare brand Uvistat (Feldwick, 1991a), which until 1990 enjoyed a small but profitable niche in the $230-million European suncare sector. Uvistat's heritage and expertise – built up over 46 years – was at the protection end of the business. It was a brand for people with sensitive skin or for those who were uncomfortable with too much sun. Having spent years as a prescription-only brand, it had recently become available as a self-select brand in pharmacies and looked forward to a somewhat broader consumer franchise.

It's hard to imagine now, but as the 1980s gave way to the 1990s the suncare market was characterized by tanning values and dominated by tanning brands. Most people didn't care about protection, they cared about a sexy tan, and brands like Bergasol and Hawaiian Tropic built huge shares by promising a deeper, darker colour faster. Ambre Solaire's slogan was 'Deep tanning technology'. Nivea claimed 'The loveliest tan under the sun'. Ninety per cent of volume was in SPF factors lower than 6, the point where Uvistat's range got going. In those pre-health-scare days, mainstream consumer attitudes to brands like Uvistat were along the lines of 'Don't spoil my holiday fun.' At first Uvistat dealt with this resistance at a sensibly tactical level, by developing a communications programme that was sensitive to people's attitudes while alerting them to the dangers of too much sun.

Brand growth was good enough for the campaign to win an industry effectiveness award but not good enough for the brand's owners, Boehringer Ingelheim, who felt the protection niche to be too constrained. Against all professional advice they reacted to prevailing consumer attitudes at the strategic level and opted for a mainstream positioning as a tanning brand, moving into lower SPFs and talking the language of tanning in their new advertising campaign. Consumer attitudes, though, proved to be fickle as the skin cancer publicity took hold and people started to place their desire for a tan on a lower priority than their desire not to die. Almost overnight the market lurched away from tanning towards protection. When Uvistat tried to scramble back to its old positioning, much of its credibility, and all of the built-in impetus it should have enjoyed, had gone. Today it has a 2.2 per cent share.

You could argue that Uvistat just got unlucky, that timing and circumstances intervened in what would otherwise have been a reasonable attempt to play in a bigger market. We would argue that to abandon a brand's heritage and long-term strategy is to become a hostage to fortune, and that the voice of consumers can be like that of the sirens of Greek mythology: seductive but deadly.

Not all examples are quite that cut and dried, of course. More typical is the tendency for previously clearly defined brands simply to blur their strategic edges in the pursuit of fickle consumer obsessions. The 2004 spa phenomenon in the bath and body brands sector is instructive. Testing new product ideas with consumers at concept stage had convinced many brand owners that the world of the spa was the place to be. Consumers, for their part, were ready for the spa mood thanks to a combination of editorial coverage, celebrity usage of exclusive world spas and the trend towards an ever-busier lifestyle, prompting the desire for the kind of relaxation that spa values bring. The result was a rush of spa line-extensions and sub-brand launches from players like Palmolive, Nivea, Dove, Ponds, FCUK and numerous retail brands including M&S and Boots. For some of these brands, responding to this new consumer desire at a tactical level made sense since spa values could be seen to fit well with long-term brand strategy. But more questionable was the fit between the values of the spa and the family values of the Palmolive brand, for example, or the extrovert, street-fashion positioning of FCUK. For these brands, an inconsistent brand image looks to be the price paid for a place in an attractive, though crowded, consumer-led sector. But since consistency is one of the defining characteristics of powerful brands, this is not an inconsequential price to pay.

Our first two symptoms of malaise are each serious enough in isolation. More serious still, as the spa example shows, is the tendency for brands to display them in combination. The result is that the very fundamentals of good branding become reversed. Brands are meant to be consistent within themselves and different from their competitors. Consumer-led brands gradually become inconsistent within themselves and similar to their competitors. It is not something consumers give too much thought to, apart from the odd critical aside, but for marketers it is a worrying sign of the erosion of saliency and brand fame.

Symptom no 3: a lack of real innovation and surprise

Consumer-led brands, by definition, have blunted their power to surprise. Their tendency to ask before they offer, reflecting both a genuine desire to please and an understandable fear of making mistakes, disqualifies them from knocking our socks off. By communing so earnestly with consumers about what they want from the brand or the sector they tether creativity to the limits of the average person's imagination. Many brands do dare to think differently, on paper at least, but if they do not dare to act before they ask they will frequently find their inventiveness rebuffed in consumer groups; in these gatherings of instant opinion, where the herd instinct is never far away, innovations that challenge rarely make it beyond the stage of initial shock.

The University of Chicago's Professor William I Zangwill, author of *Lightning Strategies for Innovation* (1998), lists some of the products that would not exist if early consumer reactions had been taken to heart. They include styling mousse ('goopy and gunky' was the verdict in initial market tests), the telephone answering machine (using a mechanical device to answer the phone was felt to be disrespectful and rude) and the computer mouse. The British design guru Wally Olins, in his book *On Brand* (2003), tells the story of the inauspicious beginnings of the now highly successful Bailey's Irish Cream liqueur. Tom Jago, a new product development expert behind the brand, reveals that when it was researched in focus groups it received a 'unanimous negative response. They hated the stuff and didn't believe it was Irish or even real. We suppressed the results.'

It is no different in the business-to-business arena. The Harvard academics Bower and Christensen, in their work on disruptive technologies (1995), list the factors that deter leading companies from investing sufficiently in the technologies that the customers of the future will demand. Chief among them is the fact that they talk to the customers of today. Citing the failure of companies like IBM, Xerox and Bucyrus-Erie to maximize the disruptive innovation originating under their own roofs, the Harvard pair warn against focusing on the attributes that mainstream customers historically value. Rather, it is new customers that point the way forward. 'At first, then, disruptive technologies tend to be used and valued in new markets or applications; in fact they generally make possible the emergence of new markets.' Eventually, the new technologies do gain acceptance among the mainstream customers that first rejected them – but by this stage the companies that first developed them have frequently lost their initiative to others. It is, as Bower and Christensen phrase it, one of the 'dramatic dangers of staying too close to customers'.

But let's approach this issue from the other side, and look for a moment at companies that do have a record of successful brand innovation. How do they achieve it? Do they test it? What is their view on the consumer's involvement at the fragile early stages of a new idea?

Emirates, the international airline of Dubai, is an example of rapid-fire innovation. Among its many 'firsts' were on-board phones, personal video systems in economy, choc ices with the movie, and an external camera so passengers could watch themselves take off and land. Its most recent innovation is the fully enclosed 'pod' for its first-class passengers. Inside this 'cabin within a cabin', with its electronic sliding doors, room-service console and private minibar, passengers feel like they are in a flying hotel suite. Perks of travel in the pod can include a massage from the seat and a choice of 500 channels of entertainment from a hand-held, icon-driven screen.

None of these innovations was tested with consumers before implementation. The pod concept went straight into development from a sketch on the back of an envelope. As the airline's chief executive, Tim

Clark, explains, 'We know what customers want, and we use the experience of our own people to assess new ideas. If we tested innovations every time with a posse of consumers, we would lose the initiative. We prefer to back our judgement.'

In this he is in good company. Sony's Akio Morita, in his book *Made in Japan* (1987), evokes the notion of an 'Oriental sixth sense' to describe the Japanese approach to innovation. Morita himself was the inspiration behind the Walkman and its most impassioned supporter in face of early scepticism, yet he candidly puts it all down to 'a hunch'. It was a hunch he was prepared to back to the limit, as he made clear to his doubting colleagues: 'If we don't sell 100,000 pieces by the end of the year, I will resign my chairmanship of this company.'

Sixth sense, instinct, hunch, courage – to judge from the example of the Walkman, these are the qualities that make for profitable innovation. But we have strayed into the realm of argument by anecdote, and must be wary of accepting too uncritically the winner's-eye view of the world. There is always a danger in drawing an inference from a starting point of success: it doesn't take into account the alternative outcomes that were only too possible at the outset. For every hunch that leads to the Walkman there are hundreds that lead to oblivion, and the losers tend to keep their anecdotes to themselves. Innovation implies risk. Brand marketing companies know this so they try to minimize it by checking with consumers as they go. It's not an unreasonable thing to do in order to win a little extra certainty, as long as they can live with the downside.

And there is a downside. In the end, consumer-led brands are a bit like the life-partner who asks you what you want for your birthday, with the intention of getting it for you. This most sensible and adult of arrangements immediately makes two things certain: 1) you will not end up with something you do not want; and 2) you will not, on unwrapping your gift, experience the bitter-sweet thrill of surprise. It is a trade-off in which something has been gained by all parties but something perhaps more valuable has been lost. Surprise, even challenging surprise, is a powerful factor in our sense of feeling alive, a glimpse back to the vivid emotional clarity of childhood and, if we are lucky, a contributor to a capacity for zest that we never lose. Marketers should remember the answer Bob Hope is reported to have given, in his final days, when asked where he wished to be buried: 'Surprise me.'

Symptom no 4: an increasing gulf between brand offer and brand capability

Consumers know a great deal about themselves; they do not know a great deal about your company, even if they think they do. They do not understand the limits of its capability, the strength of its financial resources, the elasticity of its management structure or the depth of its roots. In sum, they do not really understand what your company can do now, could credibly do in the future or, just as crucially, what its culture inclines it to do.

But they are consulted on these issues nonetheless. The classic example is the involvement of consumers in decisions about brand extension. This is where brand owners learn that consumers 'want' the brand to move into a proposed new territory or, conversely, that it 'cannot' move there. Either verdict can lead companies to pursue a misguided strategy, but the former is the more dangerous if the company ends up venturing into a territory that lies outside its sphere of expertise.

Richard Rivers, VP Personal Care for Unilever, is refreshingly candid about the painful learning curve the team travelled when trying to extend its men's fragrance brand, Lynx, in 2000. In a talk given at London Business School in October 2002 he admits, 'We fell on our face.' Seeking new ways to penetrate the teenage market in which the Lynx brand was so successful, the marketing team had put a range of exciting new concepts in front of brand loyalists: Lynx razors, Lynx shampoos and Lynx hairdressing salons. The methodology was qualitative and the results were unequivocal: consumers were hugely enthusiastic about the prospect of seeing their brand move into these seemingly adjacent territories.

But they were adjacent only in consumer terms, not when examined from the point of view of corporate capability. The leap from aftershave to razors might not seem so far conceptually, but the technologies involved are utterly different. Gillette has invested billions in razor R&D over 30 years; how could a fragrance brand from a broadly based fmcg company compete? It couldn't, despite the efforts of one of the world's most creative advertising agencies to switch the shaving agenda from technology to style. The launch commercials through BBH London were strong enough to encourage trial, but repeat purchase was low. Then Gillette came in with the Mach 3, on which they'd spent $750 million in development, and Lynx had no way to compete. 'We didn't have the metal-bashing skills' is Rivers's laconic assessment.

The razors were withdrawn, Lynx shampoos lasted a year, and the Lynx salons – promoted as a kind of 'bloke heaven' cross between a barber's shop and an amusement arcade – were closed after a 14-month trial during which Unilever's inexperience in the service sector had been exposed. Lynx is still a remarkably successful brand, reporting faster growth than any other Unilever brand in 2003. But as Rivers concludes, 'We know more now about the limits of its extendibility than we did, and now approach the pronouncements of adolescents with considerably more caution.'

Even for brands rooted in an attitude rather than a specific capability, consumers can be a poor guide to the limits of brand stretch. Most consumers, and many pundits come to that, seem happy to accept the presence of the Virgin brand in totally diverse business areas, just so long as it sticks to its policy of challenging the status quo. But Mark Ritson, Professor of Marketing at London Business School, takes a contrarian view of the brand's fabled elasticity: 'They've identified good markets and, although their brand is extendable, can they actually then go to market and deliver it in a profitable way? The answer most of the time is "no".'

Ritson cites the example of Virgin Cola to make the point that issues of capability don't end with the product. 'In theory you could take on Coke with an equally good-tasting cola and actually make some money. It's an attractive market to be in. But could Virgin actually go in there, break distribution chains, get the advertising right? No, they couldn't. They haven't got the time, resources or the know-how.'

Consumers and corporate culture

Sitting with consumers, discussing the brand as though it were a blank piece of paper, it is easy to forget that behind it is a living organization with that amalgam of values, proclivities, tradition and accident we call culture. In the outside world, this culture might be poorly perceived and little prized, but inside the organization it's a different story. As companies become larger and more dispersed, culture is a vitally important force in keeping people together and motivated. In this context, few things are more divisive than the pronouncements of marketing teams that the qualities the company cares most deeply about are not valued by consumers.

This can occur when new advertising campaigns are unveiled. For example, in May 2003 the UK advertising trade magazine *Campaign* quoted a press release from the coffee brand Kenco highlighting its new TV campaign for Kenco Rappor. The ads dramatized a category generic – the caffeine hit – rather than the traditional Kenco virtue of taste. As the release explained, 'According to research, the 18–25 year-old target thinks our taste credentials are secondary in importance.' Perhaps so, but you have to wonder how that message played to the company's coffee-growing, buying, blending and R&D professionals as they were going the extra mile to improve the brand's flavour appeal. Of course, communications must take into account the attitudes, desires and 'so-what' shrugs of its primary target, but does that mean it has to ignore completely the passion and commitment coming the other way?

Perhaps we can answer that with an example from the world of car advertising. In the mid-1990s the Honda account for Europe was handled by the London advertising agency BDDH, of which both authors were then senior directors. (No, this isn't going to be one of those weren't-we-clever stories: just the reverse, in fact.) Honda's passion, as the agency knew well from its in-depth cultural briefings in Japan, was engineering. Honed in Formula One competition, enshrined in the company mantra, engineering excellence was Honda's *shimei* – a Japanese concept that can loosely be translated as 'mission' but that means, more literally and more heroically, 'the reason for our existence'.

But the agency's planners had bad news. Consumers, they assured, were not interested in engineering. It was not motivating. They knew this because they had tested various concept-board propositions based on engineering in groups. What loyalists liked most about Honda was driving feel. This is where the planners decided the advertising focus should be. After much wrangling inside the agency, and between agency and client, this rather nebulous concept was given to the creative teams to dramatize as best they could. The results were forgettable.

None of this implies that the knowledge gained by the planners was worthless. It's good to know what you are up against, and chastening to hear the consumer's sigh of indifference. But what consumers were indifferent to, literally, was the planner's concept boards on the engineering theme. This is not the same thing as indifference to the subject presented with all the verve and ingenuity that ensue when creative talent intersects with as powerful a force as *shimei*. Agency creative teams are galvanized when they come across genuine conviction inside an organization; it raises their sights and gets the blood coursing through their veins. Planners and marketers might do better to note what consumers have to say on the subject that is closest to a company's heart – *and ignore it.*

In 2003 a more courageous agency and Honda marketing team did exactly that. Wieden + Kennedy's 'cog' commercial blew everyone away from the moment it was aired. It was about nuts and bolts and springs and valves and sheets of shiny metal self-assembling in a mechanical bit-by-bit fashion to complete a car. It was a paean to engineering – the very subject that consumers, apparently, didn't care about. Well, they did now, when it was dramatized like this. The spot won not just every creative award in sight but also the 2003 APG gold award for the most effective commercial for an established brand. That plaudit was for measured performance against the end consumer; but think what it must have done for the spirits of the 130,000-strong audience who worked on the inside. They count too. Sometimes they count more.

Symptom no 5: something hollow at the heart of the brand

In 1997, global research with consumers persuaded British Airways that it was a bit too, well, British. The airline obligingly took steps to become less so by painting its tails the colours of the world. The project, code-named Utopia, is probably the most graphic example on record of a brand voluntarily hollowing out the meaning at its core and declaring, 'We can be anything you want us to be.' But British Airways wasn't just any old brand at the time. Influential people cared about its heart and soul more than it did itself; letters were written, complaints lodged; Baroness Thatcher, famous for 'handbagging' those who crossed her, took out a handkerchief to cover the tailfin of a model BA plane at a press function. British Airways was made to understand that it couldn't accommodate the comparatively shallow desires of its new global consumers without sacrificing something of what made it special to others, including loyalists, customers closer to home and, crucially, its own staff.

Not every brand is as lucky. Many modern brands are left to drift on the tide of consumer opinion until they lose sight of the shores of meaning from which they have become detached. Are they waving or drowning?

In 1960 Levitt said that marketing should start with the consumer. When we interviewed him in 2004 even he acknowledged the danger of brands abandoning their 'foundational belief'. If you look at the examples in our first four symptoms of malaise, a common theme emerges: the brand, by identifying with the consumer, loses sight of itself, of what it stands for, of what it's good at and what it believes in. In so doing it ends up sacrificing authenticity, specialness, distinction, cohesion and pride. It joins the ranks of other characterless consumer-led brands vying for the attention of an increasingly uninterested public. In that sense, then, perhaps symptom number 5 is not really a symptom at all, but a cause. Brands can't thrive forever with hollowness at the core. They need to be good at something that is good for people, need to regain an appetite for leading rather than following, need to have a view on how to make the human condition just a little better and work towards making it happen.

You can call this 'purpose'; you can call it 'conviction'; you can call it *shimei*; we prefer to call it 'belief'. But whatever you call it, if you want your brand to survive in an increasingly hostile marketing environment it needs to be there.

Note

Market research expenditure figures were derived from ESOMAR (2003).

3 Why brands need belief

Nothing so eloquently sums up the diffuse, fluid nature of the concept 'brand' as the diversity of the attempts at defining it. WPP's marketing guru Jeremy Bullmore (2003) referred to this imprecision in a lecture given to the British Brands Group. 'Brands', he said, 'are fiendishly complicated, elusive, slippery, half-real/half-virtual things. When CEOs try to think about brands, their brains hurt.' Bullmore shied away from offering a definition himself, in that lecture at least, perhaps to spare himself a little brain-strain. But we cannot; after all, one can hardly determine what a brand needs before determining what it is. To do so would be like prescribing medicine without knowing the patient. So what is a brand? Let's consult some of the leading specialists on the subject.

First, the marketing bodies on both sides of the Atlantic:

Brand: Name, term, symbol or design or a combination of them intended to identify the goods and services of one seller or groups of sellers and to differentiate them from those of the competition.

American Marketing Association

Brand: the set of physical attributes of a product or service together with the beliefs and expectations surrounding it – a unique combination which the name or logo of the product or service should evoke in the mind of the audience.

British Chartered Institute of Marketing

Right away, an interesting distinction emerges: the British definition, unlike its US counterpart, starts to accommodate the emotional texture that goes beyond the mere 'goods or services'. It is a theme picked up by many others and one that we will include in our own definition. There are good grounds for doing so; as the US anthropologist Grant McCracken writes in *Culture and Consumption* (1988), 'Consumer goods have a significance that goes beyond their utilitarian character and commercial value. This significance consists largely in their ability to carry and communicate cultural meaning.' Virtually all marketing academics agree on this symbolic content, as the following definitions exemplify:

> A brand constitutes a primary locus of meaning whereby the typical consumer goods company forges lasting exchange relationships with its customer base.
>
> *Professor Argun Chaudhuri, Fairfield University;*
> *Professor Morris Holbrook, Columbia University*

> A brand is the sum total of all perceived functional and emotional aspects of a product or service.
>
> *Alan Bergstrom, Danielle Blumenthal, Institute for Brand Leadership*

Those closer to the practitioner end of the spectrum not surprisingly introduce concepts like consumers and profit into the mix:

> Brand: product or service which has symbolic significance beyond its functional value for which its consumers are prepared to pay a premium.
>
> *Roddy Glen, Qualitative Researcher*

> A brand is a product, protected by a trademark, which through careful management and skilful promotion has come in the minds of consumers to embrace a particular and appealing set of values, both tangible and intangible.
>
> *Paul Stobart, Interbrand*

> A brand is the consumer's idea of a product.
>
> *David Ogilvy*

And so finally, thanks to the most famous advertising man of all time, we are reminded of the virtue of brevity. The problem with the definitions that try to cover all the bases is that their ungainly sprawl numbs our minds to the essentials. It might be better if certain things were accepted as given and could therefore be left out of the definition itself. For example, we might assume that the word 'product' embraces intangibles like services, charities, whole countries and so on; and we could equally assume that the brand will be distinguished in some way by a logo or a sign. Accepting these as given would clear the way for a definition that combines brevity with potency. It is with this criterion in mind that we offer our own definition for a brand, which we will use for the remainder of this book:

A brand is a product plus values and associations.

If you are prepared to accept this definition, or at least to work with it for now, then certain arguments flow automatically. First, we can quickly see that of the three defining elements (product + values + associations) two tend towards fluidity and one towards permanence. We would expect a product to change over time: from Kodak dry plate film in 1888, for example, to Kodak digital cameras in 2005; in fact, failure to evolve at the product level would probably mean death, as the Kodak company recently was forced painfully to acknowledge. Similarly, we would expect associations to change; in this category are included things like music, colours, advertising style, outlets where the brand is sold, celebrities who use the brand, and so on. It would be bizarre, for example, if the top-of-mind associations for the Irish beer brand Guinness were still toucans and brawny construction workers carrying steel girders. Brands need to stay current, and updating brand associations is a way of signalling this.

But values are another matter. We expect something deeper here. We expect values to remain intact, come what may, and to hold even when the going gets tough. More than that, we expect values to be cohesive, to relate to one another as a conceptual group. We would feel uncomfortable, for example, confronted with a brand that attempted to combine the values of decency and consistency with promiscuity and provocation.

You can think about a brand in the way you think about a person. Over a long period we might know someone as, say, a student, a doctor, a parent and a pensioner. That's the product bit, if you like. We accept and expect this kind of change, and would doubtless find it odd if the person had stayed a student forever. We expect the associations that surround people to change, too: the kind of music they like, places they go, clothes they wear. The 50-year-old who still wears a Mohican haircut and safety pins through PVC trousers is apt to strike us as amusing, pathetic even. Change at the level of associations is more accepted than stasis. But the person who's a democrat one minute, autocrat the next, who veers from radicalism to racism, who embraces a ragbag set of values that neither relate nor endure, is a subject of suspicion.

In people and in brands, values should be consistent and cohesive; this is the foundation of trust. But it doesn't happen by accident. Values will be subject to randomness, fashion, whim and drift like anything else unless anchored. And what anchors them is belief. What a person believes in, at the deepest level, will determine that person's values and ensure both consistency and cohesion. A brand needs nothing less than belief to ensure the same.

Brand belief: what it is and what it isn't

At an absolutely literal level, of course, it is an impossibility. The brand can't literally believe anything; but the organization and the people behind it can, on its behalf. From the consumer's point of view, though, belief can be seen to reside either at the level of the organization or at the level of the brand (and these, of course, can sometimes be the same thing). This is a distinction we'll explore in Chapter 6. Either way, the belief must hold even when the personnel change; it is bigger, in other words, than the individuals who happen to be managing things at any one time.

Brand belief is the brand's take on the world. It is a view on what would make the world a little better and how the brand can work towards making it happen. And here we have introduced an important caveat: there should be some kind of link between brand belief and brand capability. Brand belief is irrelevant if the brand can do nothing to contribute to its fulfilment. A brand that believes in Third World equality but makes confectionery sold only in Canada, for example, would be an absurdity. Belief, in a brand, must relate to purpose. In this sense, brand belief is not so far from the Japanese notion of *shimei* that we looked at in Chapter 2: 'the reason for our existence'.

To take a simple example, Lego believes that 'Through creating the world you understand it better.' This underpins not merely the company's values of creativity, imagination, trust, fun and love of knowledge, but also its business activity: creative play for young people – not just toys but 'development aids'.

The link between brand belief and capability is not as limiting as it might first appear. In the Lego example there is a linear connection. But it is fascinating to see how a similarly inspiring belief has galvanized a brand from a completely different, more humdrum, category, where the connection is less straightforward. Unilever's stain-removal detergent brands around the world share a belief in what they call 'modern parenting'. This is a recognition that children best learn about the world through direct experience. What is the brand's role in this? It offers the freedom to get mucky because the product, with its advanced formulations, can take care of the stains. And getting mucky, of course, is a natural part of exploring the world and learning how it works. No stains: no learning. Kids can't experiment with painting a picture, or making a cake, or climbing trees, or simply engaging in the rough and tumble of life without their clothes looking a good deal less clean and white at the end of the day than they were at the beginning. In the developing world especially, where pride in cleanliness combines with the reality of hand-washing and fewer garments to rotate, this can imply a hard burden for mothers. Who could blame them for trying to restrict their children's activities? In these markets, expressed through brands like Omo in Brazil and India, Breeze in Thailand and Rinso in Indonesia, the message is 'Go ahead, let them get dirty. Let them learn about the world. We'll help make it easy and economical for you to get the clothes clean and white again.'

This is brand belief that relates to capability without being cramped by it. 'Modern parenting' is an inspiring way to think about an everyday subject like laundry, and helps guide the brand team through many kinds of decisions. It anchors the brand's values: 'integrity, optimism, care'. It inspires new product development: faster, better ways to make stains disappear, focusing on the ones children tend to attract most often. And it suggests natural, seamless ways to involve the brand deeper in the community, through local programmes that help children realize their full potential. In Brazil, for example, the brand sponsors the construction and maintenance of sports facilities and play zones in the *favelas*.

Brand belief can embrace many different ideas and qualities, not all of them earnest or grandiose, and we'll cover a range of examples as we progress through the remainder of this book. For now though, having taken a first look at what brand belief is, we'll turn to the things it isn't.

Brand belief isn't just 'mission' or 'vision'

The problem with the whole vision–mission thing is that the language has become blurred and people are using terms interchangeably that were never that sharply etched to start with.

If you care to delve deep enough into the literature you'll find academically accepted definitions for vision and mission, but you'll probably be the only one bothering to make the effort. The academic consensus, summarized by Parikh and Neubauer (1993), is that vision is more inward-looking and embraces 'an image of the desired future of an organisation'. Mission, on the other hand, relates more to the organization's external purpose and 'why it exists'.

In this sense, it is mission that is closer to belief, but you wouldn't know it from the flaccid, formula-speak mission statements of companies around the world. Most seem to be some kind of permutation of the usual business buzzwords: excellence, highest standards, superior quality, partnership, performance, people, choice, achievement, potential, value, leadership, commitment, admired, world class and customers.

Brand belief should be just that: a genuine belief. It demands language that will do it justice. But perhaps the biggest difference between belief and mission is that belief doesn't end with the statement, to be forgotten in the day-to-day cut and thrust of business life. That, unsurprisingly, is the fate of many mission and vision statements around the world – only brought out, as one senior manager put it in a recent survey, 'like the best china, on special occasions'.

Brand belief isn't just 'attitude'

Attitude is something temporary, something you wear when it suits. Belief is more permanent and profound. In brands, therefore, attitude tends to come into play most often at the level of communications; advertising people are particularly given to talking about the need to inject a bit of attitude into a brand, usually when there's not much else going for it. Attitude is what bland brands try to assume; belief is what characterful brands have at their core. The power of a real brand belief, clearly understood by everyone on the team, is that it suggests its own way of approaching communications and, for that matter, everything else.

Brand belief isn't just CSR

'Corporate social responsibility' (CSR) is the modern term for a long-established business practice. The tendency of commerce and philanthropy to quietly coexist dates to the origins of some of our biggest companies. In 1897 Lord Hesketh, the founder of Lever, created Port Sunlight near Liverpool in England to provide decent homes for people working in Lever factories. In Pennsylvania, in 1888, Hershey created a 'real home town' around its factory, complete with tree-lined streets, comfortable homes, an inexpensive transport system and good schools. Earlier still, Carlsberg was founded along philanthropic principles by the Danish brewer JC Jacobsen. In 1876 this was formalized with the establishment of the Carlsberg Foundation with its remit 'to promote and financially support Danish scientific research within the areas of natural sciences, mathematics, philosophy, the humanities and social sciences'.

These arrangements were seen as a natural consequence of the founding beliefs of the companies, an integral part of what they stood for. The difference today is that CSR tends to be something separate from the main business activity, a programme run by a specialist department, promoted in PR releases and worn as a badge of respectability. This can go awry. The UK charity Christian Aid has taken to task several leading companies for hiding what the charity considers dubious activities behind CSR programmes. Shell, British American Tobacco and Coca-Cola are all accused in a 2004 report of using 'an image of social responsibility to oppose regulation and convince governments in rich countries that business can put its own house in order' (Pendleton *et al*, 2004).

In the end, the tacked-on CSR programme is tantamount to an admission that the brand does no real good in its day job, rather like the investment banker who helps out with deprived kids at the weekend in an effort to 'put something back'. But for a brand with real belief, nothing is tacked on; the belief itself infuses what the brand does commercially and this becomes inseparable from all other activity. If you start with a belief in how to make the world just a little better, then everything you do will play its part in a seamless, cohesive and inclusive effort. In that sense, corporate social responsibility becomes everyone's responsibility.

Two contemporary brands that started with belief

A belief in making things better has been a powerful force in the establishment of some of the world's most enduring brands. As well as Lever, Hershey and Carlsberg, brands like Cadbury, Philips, Krupp, Lloyds, John Lewis and Kellogg's were all built on a strong foundational belief, often that of a single person. Many of these brands date from the 19th century and were inspired by the unique commercial morality of the Quakers. But it is not our intention to root the concept of brand belief in the past; although the paternalism associated with the founding of these brands would be out of step with today's values, belief still counts as much as it always has. To highlight the power of brand belief in a modern context, we'll look at its role in the success of two recently founded brands: the British smoothies brand Innocent and the US internet phenomenon Google.

Innocent: a belief in purity

'What is an Innocent Smoothie?' asks a heading on one of the brand's famously disarming pack labels. The answer is 'A blend of crushed fruit, pure and fresh juices and absolutely nothing else at all'. Absolutely nothing else unless you count the conviction, persistence, wit and iconoclasm of its founders, Richard Reed, Adam Balon and Jon Wright, who in six years have built Innocent from scratch into a £16-million brand growing at 80 per cent year on year. The brand has attracted customers and admirers in equal measure, winning, as Richard Reed puts it, 'an embarrassing amount of business awards'. These include Entrepreneur of the Year, Growing Business of the Year, National Business of the Year and Marketing Strategy of the Year. So what's behind this success? What is the founding belief that has counted for so much in the early fame of this brand?

We talked to Richard Reed at Fruit Towers, the company's playfully named single-storey warehouse headquarters in a west London industrial park. The three founders, he explained, had been university friends and had long talked about creating a business based on 'a simple idea, something that was genuinely good, that would make life a little bit better, a littler bit easier'. Their first idea turned out to be not so simple in practice: an 'electric bath' that would fill to a pre-selected depth at a pre-selected temperature. It failed the overnight test when it dawned upon the friends that electricity and water were not a good mix.

The idea of pure juice drinks was based on a recognition that, in the busy modern world, 'it is a really nice, easy way of doing yourself some good'. But there was a caveat: the drinks would have to be completely natural. No concentrates, preservatives or flavourings. This is the distinguishing feature of Innocent, a brand belief enshrined in the very company name. To do yourself a bit of good, this team believes, your chosen fruit drink must be 'fresh and unadulterated and pure'. This, as often happens with a strongly held conviction, has implied some commercial sacrifice. First, it slowed down the launch of the new brand, as the team were told again and again by potential suppliers that their desired purity was impossible in a commercial context. Second, it has resulted in higher costs than those of competitors who all use cheaper concentrates. 'We'll take less margin for one simple reason,' vows Reed. 'We are only about making fresh, healthy drinks that taste better than any other and are better for you than any other. And you can't have that principle without sacrificing something.'

The Innocent example makes two crucial points that are usually overlooked by authors writing on the subject of brand belief:

1. Belief isn't just something for brands in naturally heroic categories like cars, technology and business systems. While it's always interesting to read the stories of Harley, Apple and BMW, most marketing professionals spend their lives in more workaday categories, where the notion of belief can seem inappropriately haughty. Innocent shows otherwise. In the end, it is just a drink, just something you buy on a whim when you're in that mood, and yet its belief in purity combined with its eco-humanist values has caught the imagination of a loyal following. And if you find its positioning still a little too niche to seem relevant to the mainstream world most brands inhabit, then you might want to consider that in

1906 Kellogg's was founded with a similar ideal to make 'high-quality, palatable, nutritious products to help people stay healthier'. Belief can carry a brand, and an entire category, a long way, and can bring its own kind of heroism to subjects that have hitherto seemed just a trivial part of life.

2. Belief, though profoundly felt, can be lightly worn. There is no doubting the genuineness of the Innocent team's desire to 'do something good'. It has long been a part of their personal identities and is reflected, at a company level, in support for reforestation projects and NGOs in the poorer fruit-growing countries with which the company trades; we learnt from Reed that half the company's profits were donated this way in 2004. But there is nothing remotely earnest or po-faced in the way the brand communicates its ideals either internally or to the outside world. From its 'hairy grass van', which has to be seen to be believed, to its company rule book containing headings like 'Thou shalt not commit adultery', there is a charm and openness in everything the brand does. When, for example, was the last time you read pack copy like this? 'It's quite tricky staying healthy these days. Pizzas and cold beer are often more enticing than mung bean surprise

Figure 3.1 Delivery with a difference: Innocent's 'hairy grass van'

and cabbage water, and jogger's nipple has always put us off the idea of wearing skimpy vests and pounding the pavements.' The copy went on to extol the virtues of Innocent's orange, banana and pineapple smoothie, one of 18 product variants as this book went to press.

It is still early days for Innocent, which competes in a crowded sector where customers and retailers alike wield instant power. But through the imaginative presentation of a strong core belief, Innocent has achieved a salience way beyond the normal expectations of its minuscule paid-for communications budget, and a cohesion that bigger brands, for all their brand-onion and brand-bull's-eye diagrams, can only dream of. Perhaps, with a dose of good fortune, Innocent can be the Kellogg's of the 21st century.

Google: 'We want to organize the world's information'

There is something almost childishly simple about Google. The candy-coloured logo; the open clarity of its interface; the eye-blink speed with which it searches 8 billion web pages to produce its sanely ordered results. This is Google from the user's-eye view. But behind this deceptive simplicity is a belief of breathtaking scale, implying the mastery of almost unimaginable complexity. Google exists, as co-founder Sergey Brin states, 'to organize the world's information, making it universally accessible and useful'. Since the world's information increases at the rate of 800 megabytes per person, per year – the equivalent of 30 feet of books for every person on the planet – this is no mean undertaking.

Google was founded by Brin and Larry Page in 1998, the fruit of a research project on which they'd collaborated at Stanford University since 1995. From the outset they believed in creating 'a very simple and easy-to-use website that offers the best search engine in the world'. The quest to get ever closer to this ideal is what drives the company and inspires the dedication with which it goes about its business. It is an ethos crisply described by *Fast Company* in a special feature on Google (Hammond, 2003): 'Make it easy. Make it fast. Make it work. And attack everything that gets in the way of perfection.'

And so we glimpse the essential Google paradox. The laid-back, open-plan, sofas-and-lava-lamps community with its ruthless focus, its aggressive genius for eliminating the impediments to perfection.

'Relaxed zealots' is the phrase we tried on Raymond Nasr, Google's Director of Executive Communications, in a 2004 telephone interview. 'That sums us up,' he agreed, adding, 'I'd say we're passionate but modest: there is a deep passion around search tempered by humility because of the magnitude of the task.' The passion, if not the modesty, is celebrated in Google's own Corporate Information website. In a section headed 'Fast is better than slow', it claims, 'By fanatically obsessing on shaving every bit and byte from our pages and increasing the efficiency of our serving environment, Google has broken its own speed records time and again.'

Central to this achievement is the motivation of 'Googlers' – what any other company might call 'employees' or 'staff'. Numbering around 2,000, and including over 150 PhDs, these are some of the cleverest people on the planet, and every one of them could take their talents somewhere else if they chose to. Super-bright people aren't 'fanatical' just because the company provides a pay cheque each month. Science PhDs don't 'obsess' just because senior management demands it. For Googlers, the motivation to break records, improve and invent has to come from something other than purely commercial considerations, something loftier than adding a few more dollars to the share price. That 'something' is the all-pervasive belief at Google that what the company does really, really matters. Brin and Page have talked about the social importance of search in virtually every interview they've given. Nasr likes to illustrate the point with the example of a suicidal teenager turning to the internet for help; in these circumstances, getting quickly to the right site could mean the difference between life and death.

Google is an example of a 21st-century enterprise founded on the kind of morality that inspired the successful Quaker companies of the 19th century, the essence of which is that business prosperity is both achieved and justified by *being good at something that is good for people*. Google is proud of its commercial success but prouder still of its perceived social contribution. 'Deep down in our DNA is the desire to be something useful,' Nasr told us. 'The implications of achieving it will have a deep impact on humanity.'

Beyond the founder effect

Clearly, companies like Innocent and Google benefit from the vision and continued day-to-day commitment of passionate founders. One question that often arises is whether brand belief can *only* really work when tied in this way to the personal ideology of individuals. What about companies like P&G and Nestlé, on the other hand, whose founders are long since departed and whose empires are widely dispersed; can brand belief really flourish and have a positive influence here? Our answer is an emphatic 'yes', and the second half of this book, with the exposition of a commercially and academically validated step-by-step method, is dedicated to showing how.

For now, though, this chapter is about 'why'. We've already looked at the importance of belief in anchoring brand values; we've shown through Innocent how it can promote saliency and cohesion, and through Google how it can inspire passionate internal dedication; we'll now look at its power to forge stronger customer loyalty through its relevance to personal identity.

The role of brands in personal identity

'We are what we buy' is a phrase that's gaining currency in smart marketing circles. It is an oversimplification, of course, and can be attacked as such by those who recoil at the suggestion that the human sense of self can be reduced to the question of whether you happen to favour Nike or Adidas. In the end, we are what we are – and we have many ways of affirming this to ourselves and communicating it to others. Some of these are subtle; some are obvious. But that one of these ways is through brand choice is not in doubt.

Much is known about the role of consumption in personal identity, virtually all of it due to the theory and research generated by social and marketing academics from the mid-1960s onwards. This is precisely the kind of research that practitioners never commission, since the subject matter is too broad to justify investment by those whose focus tends to be at the level of a single brand. Yet it could have a surprisingly profound effect on the way brands are marketed.

The fate of the academic literature, in respect of its use by practitioners, has followed the typical path: ignored for decades and then seized upon by a few looking for new ways to think about brands. Today it tends to pop up in epigrammatic form on PowerPoint charts to illustrate the shift in the social role of brands from that of signalling status to that of signalling affinity. The theory deserves a little more engagement than that and we shall seek to do it justice here.

The search for self in the modern world

Key to the flow of reasoning is the concept of 'self'. Socrates' admonition to 'know thyself' dates back to three centuries BC, yet for almost the entire intervening period the freedom to 'be thyself' – Maslow's nirvana of self-actualization – has been a privilege denied to all but a few (Maslow, 2002). Even in Western societies, even until as recently as the 1960s, what a person really was at heart would be buried beneath the welter of circumstance. As Giddens illustrates in *Modernity and Self-identity* (1991), the self was bounded by birth, location, occupation and social class. The rigid social stratification of medieval times that divided the populace into noblemen, knights, yeomen, freemen, labourers, cottagers and paupers had disappeared in name but continued in spirit. Well into the 20th century, to be a farmhand or craftsman or shop-girl or teacher or clerk – or simply to be a person in your 40s or 50s – implied the acceptance of distinct codes of behaviour, dress and speech, deviation from which would be considered eccentric, at charitable best. For most of history, to know yourself was, in large part, simply to know your place.

This changed during the period social academics call the 'post-modern era'. Bauman (2000) and Featherstone (1992), among others, showed how the dismantling of the barriers of social class since the 1970s created a new freedom: the freedom of individuals to express who they really were, and to vary that expression over time, rather than accept the stable social roles society had hitherto mandated.

Like all new freedoms this one posed dilemmas and came at a price. The price was the increasing fragmentation of society and the loss of certainty and comfort that the more structured world had ensured. The dilemmas were of a nature that had scarcely before troubled the individual within society. Giddens reduced it to three reflexive questions: 'What to do? How to act? Who to be?' The way that individuals went about answering these questions came to be known as 'the project of self' and has been the subject of intense scrutiny ever since. It is summarized by Thompson (1990) as the process by which a person actively constructs an identity out of 'the available symbolic resources in order to weave a coherent account of who she or he is'.

The 'available symbolic resources' include brands. They include, of course, famously symbolic brands like Harley, Apple and Saab, with their redolent power to assert and project the inner spirits of their owners. But they also include, at least potentially, and much more surprisingly, everyday brands in everyday categories, the kinds of brands that get tucked away inside cupboards in bathrooms and kitchens and garages. The point is that there is more to the link between brands and personal identity than badge values, and it is perhaps the tendency of marketing professionals to conflate the two that inhibits the potential of mainstream marketing. It's not just a question of 'What does this brand say about me to others?' Just as important is 'What does this brand say about me – *to me?*' As Fournier (1998) and Elliott (Elliott *et al.*, 1995, Elliott and Wattanasuwan, 1998) have shown, brand choice, in areas as private as cooking and cleaning, is as much to do with fit as it is with function; the brand has to feel right as 'a part of me'.

More recent research conducted by one of the authors in conjunction with London Business School and Warwick Business School endorses the important role of everyday brands in self-affirmation. The chosen methodology is one of the most illuminating in the pantheon of qualitative brand research: a deprivation study. For those unfamiliar with this kind of research, the technique is simply described: find people who are fiercely loyal to a brand and then, with their (albeit reluctant) consent, take it away from them! As the box shows, the insights into what motivates brand loyalty can be surprising, richly textured and deeply personal.

Brand deprivation research: an academic study

This 2004 study was funded by London Business School and conducted by Professor Mark Ritson of London Business School, Professor Richard Elliott of Warwick Business School, and Helen Edwards of Leicester University.

The research was designed to provide empirical data for the reasons behind strong brand loyalty. Fifteen respondents were selected on the basis of demographics and the strength of their loyalties to a representative range of brands. These brands were then withdrawn from their lives for a period of six weeks and replaced with generic alternatives in unbranded containers. Brands studied:

Vaseline	Nike sports shoes
Andrex	Lavazza coffee
Heinz Ketchup	Camper
PG Tips	L'Oreal foundation
Ribena	Lynx deodorant
Technics	Irn Bru
Listerine	Persil tablets

Respondents were interviewed before, during and after the period of deprivation, and all kept audio diaries of their experience. Although all respondents had indicated superior product performance as a reason for loyalty before the trial, many concluded during it that the generic alternatives performed equally well and in two cases better – yet all respondents returned to their original brand choice after the study. Interpretative analysis indicated five main types of reason for unusually strong brand loyalties: habit, unique sensory stimuli, inter-generational influence, emotional security and fit with personal identity.

Even non-display brands were shown to be important to personal identity. The study included an Italian woman living in the UK for whom Lavazza coffee – always decanted into a plain Tupperware container kept in the cupboard – served to affirm her 'Italian-ness'. Vaseline was prized as a make-up remover by one woman for its fit with her straightforward, principled image of self. The choice of Andrex for a single, working mother was tied up with both the need to distance herself from her own modest upbringing and her self-identity as a caring mum.

Full results of the research are scheduled for publication in 2006.

More meaning for your money

It is not hard to see why brands with a strong belief should be favoured in the hastening postmodern era. They give you more meaning for your money. They have more colour, more symbolic content, more utility as units in the project of self. Consumers will orient towards these beacons of belief, or steer away from them, but they are far less likely to ignore them. And once a brand is accepted as part of the expression of self, it is that much harder to jettison. These are brands that consumers don't just buy, but join. They are brands that become 'a part of me'.

Strong brand belief also fosters consistency and integrity – two important virtues to counterbalance the drawbacks of postmodern freedom. Feldwick (1991) has shown that, in an ever-changing world, the reassurance offered by consistent brands is 'a vital element in their added value'. And the most recent academic research suggests that brands with integrity can build communities around them, help establish and maintain close personal friendships and even go some way to fill the void created by the demise of traditional social institutions like the Church (O'Guinn and Muniz, 2001). Many commentators have viewed this trend with distaste, but the counter-argument could be made that brands are performing a useful social role. Neither position alters the fact that brands assume a greater cultural significance in our lives than ever – and that brands with a clear belief are best placed to make this a mutually beneficial relationship.

Back to business

You don't actually have to stray into the realms of Quaker morality or societal roles to see the potential of brand belief. Its attractions should be apparent to even the most pragmatic business brains. Belief can help to make a brand less imitable, less fractured, more famous and more loved. Commercial reality and fiscal health, as much as anything else, argue for its consideration as the fulcrum of the marketing effort. At this point we might invoke the notion of the CEO who suddenly recognizes the power of brand belief, who decides that from now on the brand shall have one, and whose sole action thereafter is to send out a rousing all-staff e-mail and to set up a once-and-for-all PR effort to announce the change. (It happens.) But in the complex world of brands and marketing, of course, things are never quite as simple as that.

Note

Unilever 'modern parenting': This brand identity, which was developed by Unilever's David Arkwright in tandem with Pierre-Emmanuel Maire, then at Lowe, is now referred to at Unilever by its slogan 'Dirt is good'.

4 Why passive belief won't do

Brand belief isn't shy. It isn't recessive. It isn't passive. Or at least it is none of these things if it is to reward the investment of time and effort and serve its commercial purpose: to help make the brand *less imitable, less fractured, more famous and more loved*. Belief manifested by a brand must always be active, and in this respect it differs from its human equivalent, in which the degree of display is a matter of private choice. Not all creeds proselytize; not all adherents evangelize. At a strictly personal level passive belief – the kind that is deeply felt but has no obvious external manifestation – can be a richly sustaining influence on a life. It is fine, and perhaps even noble, that its effects may be perceivable by only the individual concerned. But brands are by definition outgoing entities; they are about changing behaviour and motivating people, so brand belief needs to be carried out from the centre into the world. Brand belief isn't just something you have; it's something you do.

In this sense the dynamics of brand belief more closely resemble those of a cause. A cause is always underpinned with belief but never stops there. The aim is somehow to win hearts and minds. Central to the success of any cause, therefore, is an understanding of those hearts and minds in the first place. Also needed is an understanding of how the world works, of how media can be manipulated, of what the trends, ripples and hot buttons in society currently are. A strong ideology, when married with this holistic and continually updated understanding and communicated with energy and imagination, makes for a compelling cause.

So it is with brand belief. The belief (though often less weighty than the kind of belief associated with a cause) must be made active. It must win hearts and minds. It must be kept alive and relevant for people. It must get noticed and talked about. It must come across, not just as a quiet influence working somewhere at a deep level, but as a passion – a word that we might view as signifying the active manifestation of belief.

Everything communicates

Few clichés are more true, or more ignored, than 'actions speak louder than words'. So it is important not to view the communication of brand belief as the commercial equivalent of preaching. Not that this tends to be an issue in reality. One of the most attractive characteristics of brand belief, provided it is sufficiently clear, inspiring and particular, is that it fosters a kind of natural exuberance throughout the business, so that all disciplines seek to find ways to give it active expression. It is a tenet of belief-led marketing that *everything communicates*, starting with the product itself. Look again at Innocent and you see how its communications radiate out from the core: the name, the benefit and the sensorial product experience are tightly linked and mutually reinforcing; the artless simplicity of the pack design signals purity from the supermarket shelf and the palm of your hand; chatty pack copy reminds you of the product difference and rewards you with its offbeat candour; the means of distribution includes the 'hairy grass van', a wit-on-wheels evocation of the natural theme; you are encouraged to engage actively with the company by calling up on the 'banana phone' – a giant fruit-shaped telephone at Fruit Towers HQ; and eventually the same belief-led theme, employing the same characteristic friendliness and wit, radiates outward to ads and PR. Everything communicates; nothing contradicts.

Contrast this with the conventional approach, which views communications as a discrete discipline managed by its own internal experts, in close collaboration with outside specialists like advertising and PR agencies. Not infrequently, this separation shows through as an embarrassing schism, when advertising or PR finds itself at odds with the brand reality as experienced by consumers or the company's own employees. Infamous examples include the Barclays Bank ads starring Anthony Hopkins, which focused on the benefits of size at the very time when the bank was closing branches, and the high-profile rebranding of the British Post Office as 'Consignia', which was accompanied by no change whatsoever in the surly service dispensed in its dismal, queue-ridden branches by an embittered workforce.

It seems that even sophisticated marketers need the occasional reminder that the 'walk' counts for more than the 'talk'. A recent brand audit review conducted by Millward Brown and AC Nielsen on behalf of major fmcg clients was at pains to point out the importance of the product itself in the marketing mix: 'The product is present in more senses and at more occasions than any other element.' Its recommendations included less unfocused innovation, which only served to dilute the brands' integrity, and tighter communications celebrating core values rather than more easily imitable benefits. The report concluded with the injunction that the brands in question must 'stand for something'. Easier said than done, of course, because once you've decided what you stand for you have to be prepared to make that stand every day, in everything the brand does. But this chapter is not about what's easy, it's about what works – and, as our next example shows, few things are as seductive as brand belief communicated by actions, not just words, throughout the brand offer.

Camper: belief made active at every step

Around the world, 6 million feet wear this season's Camper shoes. On some of these feet the left shoe and the right shoe don't match, such are the originality and playfulness with which Camper invites us to share its enthusiasm for that most ordinary and honest of human endeavours: walking.

Camper cares about slowness – it promotes the notion of the 'Walking Society'. It abhors the trend towards speed in modern life, as exemplified by brands like McDonald's and Nike. Instead it invites us to slow down and take in the wonderful world around us, assuming we haven't lost our capacity for the appreciation of the simple joys on offer. For Camper, putting one foot in front of the other isn't just a means of locomotion; it is one of the defining characteristics of our bipedal species, a reminder of our connection with the history behind us and the earth beneath us. 'Contact earth' is one of Camper's much-repeated themes.

The company's home is the Mediterranean island of Majorca. It is still a family business, headed today by Lorenzo Fluxá, a fourth-generation shoemaker. Although Camper is a brand with global reach, the traditional Majorcan way of life provides design inspiration for many of the shoes. Some take their shape from the ancient sailing ships that plied the Mediterranean shores, a wistful reminder of a slower way of life. Others are inspired by the name itself: camper means 'peasant' in Catalan, and it is hard to think of more earthy symbolism than that. The qualities of the peasant way of life – austerity, simplicity and discretion – are reflected in the design rhetoric of the shoes and celebrated on the company's website and in the quirky, give-away booklets you find in its stores.

We talked with Lorenzo Fluxá at the Camper store in London's Bond Street, where the good earth is given over to fashion retailing and commands rent of over £3,000 per square metre. The irony of a brand that means 'peasant' holding its greatest appeal to the urban-chic crowd is not lost on him. Irony is, in any case, a recurring theme in the brand's design repertoire, and Fluxá was clear from the start that his customers would be urban – like the friends from Barcelona who admired and coveted his own, handmade 'country shoes' and espadrilles some 30 years ago. What he is not comfortable with is the notion that Camper is merely a fashion statement. 'When people call us a fashion brand it offends me,' he says. 'Camper is beyond fashion.'

Not everyone buys that. But to those whose challenge amounts to a cynical rehearsal of the anti-global, anti-fashion mantra, Camper provides two answers. The first is the product itself. Camper shoes exhibit qualities not normally associated with the high-churn fashion world: durability, comfort and a kind of friendly sturdiness that befits their purpose; these shoes are made for walking, and not just on catwalks. Many of the designs are classics that are reproduced year after year, with only subtle enhancements, which runs counter to fashion's normal seasonal U-turns. And the use of materials tends towards the traditional and rustic, like natural rubber, canvas and rope, imaginatively recombined in a timeless design aesthetic. The second answer to the anti-fashion brigade was provided by one of the company's chief designers, Marti Guixe, in 2003. His jaunty red and white Camper store bags are emblazoned with the motto 'No los compres, si no los necesitas', which translates from Spanish as 'Don't buy them if you don't need them', a typically full-bodied Camper riposte.

But it seems the world has decided it does need Camper. Last year 3 million pairs were sold, generating around $130 million in turnover. The Bond Street store is now one of over 80 worldwide, in cities as separated as Sydney, New York, Tokyo and Tel Aviv. Opening and refurbishing so many stores puts high demands on capital, which for a relatively small company can result in a short-term strain on resources. Camper's solution is to open its stores slowly, in two distinct phases. First comes the 'Walk-in-Progress' store concept, which is a raw, unfinished space with white walls and products sitting on top of a counter made of piled-up shoe boxes. Customers are invited to write thoughts, messages and ideas on the walls with the red felt-tip pens provided, so that the store gradually takes on the unique patina of the neighbourhood in which it finds itself. Only a year or so later, as funds become available and planning permissions are complete, is the store developed with all the design elements of a fully fashioned Camper interior. It is typical of the creativity of Camper that its solution to a problem should serve imaginatively to reinforce its core belief. Camper stores don't simply open; they evolve: a fine example of the principle that 'everything communicates'.

Figure 4.1 Soft opening: a Camper 'Walk-in-Progress' store

The constituents of cool

More of an issue for the brand is imitation. The very permanence of Camper's designs makes them a relatively easy target for copycats. Fluxá is both sanguine and dismissive about this. 'On the one hand there is the flattery element,' he says, 'but my feeling is that, while they can copy some design features of the shoes, they cannot copy the spirit or the will that is there at the heart of the company.' In this he is right. The young, urban target to which Camper appeals has its antennae finely tuned for integrity and authenticity, the constituents of cool. The strength of Camper's ideological belief, and the passion with which it manifests it through product and everything else, is a force in people's desire for, and willingness to pay for, the real thing.

If belief helps make Camper less imitable, what about the other virtues that we claimed it could confer on a brand: to make it less fractured, more famous and more loved?

Camper is certainly a strongly cohesive brand, and this cohesion owes everything to the heart with which it embraces its ideological stance. Camper believes that, on life's journey, slow is better than fast, and it defines its role in the furtherance of this ideal as making 'the safest and cheapest vehicles possible: comfortable shoes'. Camper, like other belief-led brands, is wary of extension into anything that would dilute its clear reason for being. As Fluxá confides, 'Every week we get offers to put our brand name to watches, bags and clothes but we will never do that just because it could make us some money.'

Is Camper a famous brand? It is certainly more famous than its modest advertising budget would justify, and this fame owes much to the imaginative variation of a consistent theme. In typical Camper style the fame has been slow to come, but shows signs of permanence. Thirty years ago the brand was known in Catalonia; 20 years ago it was known throughout Spain. Its fame is now global, and its appeal extends to the globally famous: Robert Redford, Philippe Starck, Nicole Kidman, Samuel L Jackson and Bruce Willis are all fans, attracted by the cachet of a brand with the courage and wit to translate farmer shoes into urban streetwear.

As for love, the devotion of Camper loyalists would give Harley a run for its money. There are many who have pairs that run to double figures and could not imagine themselves in anything else. Perhaps a quote from the Camper correspondent in our deprivation study will illuminate what it is that Camper so uniquely symbolizes in the fast modern world: 'I buy two or three pairs a year. They are trendy, smart, different. Even when I wear them in meetings, I feel less corporate. I want to be successful in my career, but in a way that I want, broken up with travel and living in different countries. Camper just fits with that somehow.'

Camper is as good an example as you'll find of a company with a strong core belief that is made active in everything it does: name, products, stores, brochures, booklets, website, advertising, PR and, last but not least, its practical contribution to the preservation of the Mediterranean rural world. It is a belief embedded in the company culture, a belief felt with passion and communicated with flair, a belief captured without artifice in its simple, three-word slogan: 'Walk don't run'. This was no adman's line, but was coined by Lorenzo himself. Trenchant, grounded, economical, blunt: a peasant could not have put it better.

A tale of two Co-ops

This full-length case study looks at two brands that approached the end of the 20th century in poor shape and contrasts their divergent fortunes since then. One brand rediscovered and reinterpreted its long-suppressed beliefs; the other was content for its beliefs to remain passive and inert. One prospered; the other foundered. What gives the story extra poignancy is that the two brands are connected. More than that: they are sister brands, born of the same ideology, sharing the same history, related to the same movement, linked by the same roots. They are the Co-operative Bank and Co-operative Food Retail Stores. The bank has become an absolute textbook case of how a brand can seize what it has at the core and apply discipline, imagination, courage and zeal to make it active and relevant for people in the modern context. The stores show what happens when belief is allowed to moulder at the practical level and find expression only in esoteric theoretical debates confined to the upper reaches of the organization. To understand the beliefs in question, it is worth taking a brief detour into the history of the co-operative movement in Britain.

Roots: the Rochdale Pioneers

The co-operative movement was born of need in a time of hardship. From today's comfortable perspective it requires a feat of imagination to get a feel for the lives and conditions of the people who worked in the industrial north of England in the mid- and late 1800s. Whole families toiled for 12 to 14 hours a day at mills and machines in return for wages that would put bread, but very little else, on the table. During the 1840s, the 'hungry decade' of poor harvests, the situation was worsened by the influx of Irish immigrants desperate for work, which served to reduce still further the wages offered. Dependence on the industrial owners was often total; working families lived in jerry-built dwellings erected by the company in order to keep the poor 'fit for work and out of sight', and the only shops from which they could buy their provisions were also company-owned – the 'Tommy Shops', as they were known. The result of this arrangement was the one that always befalls a captive market – it was swindled. Duplicitous practices included the adding of water to butter, sand to sugar and chalk to flour, as well as the more basic cheating at the scales, there being no way to ensure fair weight or measure. In short, those employers whose sole concern was the pursuit of profit – by no means all, but by any reckoning most – contrived to pay the absolute minimum for the hard labour of their workforce, and then ensured that they extracted the maximum back by the daily abuse of a retailing monopoly.

In these circumstances, it is no surprise that the solution of a workers' co-operative, whose aim would be to pool resources and buy and sell produce fairly, presented itself many times to diverse industrial working communities. Most failed, and mostly for the same reasons: arguments about governorship, and the practice of providing credit, which served to weaken both the individual and the whole. But in 1844 a group of 28 Rochdale flannel weavers devised the right formula, which was to become the basis for the progress of the entire movement. Such were the innovation, daring and sheer good sense of their founding principles that they deserve to be noted in full. They were:

- that capital be of the members' own providing and bear a fixed rate of interest;
- that only the purest provisions procurable should be supplied to members;
- that full weight and measure should be given;
- that market prices should be charged and no credit given nor asked;
- that profits should be divided pro rata upon the amount of purchases made by each member;

- that the principle of one member one vote should obtain in government and the equality of the sexes in membership;
- that the management should be in the hands of officers and committee elected periodically;
- that a definite percentage of profits be allotted to education;
- that frequent statements and balance sheets should be presented to members.

In this plain prose can be sensed the foresight and guts of a group that understood minutely the needs of its market – in this case from direct, personal experience – and applied imagination to their fulfilment. The insistence on the equality of the sexes, alone, shows both a pioneering spirit (since it anticipated the universal franchise by some 80 years) and shrewd business sense (since women did the shopping).

The Rochdale Society of Equitable Pioneers prospered and spawned many successful imitators so that, by the end of the century, there were over 400 co-operative societies, with some 600,000 members, commanding an 18 per cent share of the food retailing market – bigger than either Sainsbury's or Asda has now. Some well-off social observers of the time, like Beatrice Potter and Sidney Webb, saw in the co-operative movement the seeds of a better society based on socialist doctrine, but to equate Rochdale co-operation with socialism is weak analysis, since the practical means by which it achieved its ethical ends would delight those of the entirely opposite political persuasion: self-help, self-governance, consumerism of the sort that works backward from need rather than forward from production, and the distribution of profits based on expenditure at the stores – the famous dividend or 'divi' – forerunner by 150 years of the modern loyalty scheme.

There is another, even more important, respect in which the co-operative movement reflected the capitalism from which it emerged: the leverage of economies of scale, which it succeeded in applying to the business of retail for the first time. Through the mechanism of co-operative unions – the joining of funds between many co-operative societies – co-ops could buy in bulk and achieve prices lower than in the independent sector, passing on the savings to customers. Although small and fragmented by today's retail standards – about which more later – the co-operative wholesaling enterprises of the late 1800s were by far the biggest buyers of their day of hundreds of commodities, from custard to soap. The responsibility for the safe husbandry of increasingly large funds led to the founding of the Co-operative Bank in 1876; meanwhile the movement at large gained influence in virtually all aspects of people's lives, adding clothes and furniture retailing, insurance, travel and burial to the list of services provided, thereby creating the omnipresent, cradle-to-grave Co-op that was known to so many by the turn of 1900.

Reality: the loss of relevance in the late 20th century

The high-water mark for the co-operative movement in Britain was probably just after the Second World War when it boasted 11 million members, accounted for 25 per cent of total food retail sales, insured 1 in 10 households, and presided over more burials and cremations than any other funeral director. Decline since then has been steady and marked, reasons for which are to be found both outside and inside the organization. External factors centre on the changes in the governance of society, which undermined the need for the Co-op's philanthropic guardianship. These include the regulation of weights and measures, which ensured that all retailers traded fairly, the introduction of the welfare state and the abolition of retail price maintenance. The internal causes of decline are led by the fragmented nature of the movement in an era of business consolidation, compounded by internecine bickering between societies, and a dearth of high-quality management at the top.

By the time of Thatcher's Britain in the 1980s, with the Labour Party looking increasingly outmoded and the excesses of the unions seen as the cause of Britain's economic trials, the Co-op was viewed more and more as an anachronism. It is at this point that we pick up the diverging stories of the bank and the retail stores.

The story of the bank: 'profit with principles'

In 1986 the banking industry in the UK was deregulated, leading to fresh competition from the building societies, which were able to offer full banking services for the first time. By 1990 the Co-operative Bank had found itself occupying a tiny, uncomfortable space delineated by these newcomers, the big four high-street banks led by Barclays and NatWest, and the smaller regional players like the Yorkshire Bank and

Bank of Scotland with their local but loyal customer base. The Co-operative Bank's share of market – never much to write home about – fell from 2.7 per cent to 2.1 per cent in the five years to 1991 when current account closures exceeded openings for the first time. Along with this quantitative decline came a qualitative drop in the profitability of what accounts remained: in a market where everyone chased the same young, professional, high-value customers, the Co-operative Bank was left with the older, poorer, low-margin end of the spectrum. Consumer research into the bank's image brought more depressing news: the bank was seen as old-fashioned, working-class, associated with leftie political tendencies and 'not really a proper bank' – that is, not credited with providing all the services customers expected from a high-street bank.

The bank's marketing professionals decided that its image needed a shot in the arm from a new advertising campaign and pondered the options for its content. So active was the marketing of the category at the time, and so small was the bank's budget – representing less than a 1 per cent share of voice – that it was not hard to agree on the need for a bold message in order to stand out. The notion of advertising product benefits was swiftly dropped; such messages were ten-a-penny in financial advertising, and although the bank had led some exciting innovations that could make for compelling ads – for example, telephone banking – these were too easily copied by competitors. A message was needed that others could not emulate, and this need focused the team's efforts on isolating 'the Co-operative difference'.

But what was it? The bank's chief executive at the time, Terry Thomas, and his marketing director, Simon Williams, had both for some time nursed a desire to make something of the bank's ethical traditions and now they looked for evidence that this approach might motivate a new, modern consumer. None was forthcoming from research with conquest targets but some crumb of comfort was prised from research carried out among the bank's current customers: although the main reasons for their choice of bank were the normal ones to do with convenience of location, recommendation and family habit, some 5 per cent of customers claimed that they were motivated by the bank's ethical investment policies. This was probably the result of the stance the bank had taken against investment in South Africa in the pre-freedom days, and some vague concept of the humanitarian roots of the co-operative movement.

These findings were not much on which to build a new advertising strategy, but the team concluded that other factors might be at work which could tilt the balance in favour of an ethical stance. One was the growing sense that commercialism under Thatcher had become ever more rapacious and seedy; the other was the theory that the better-educated, professional target that the bank sought to attract would be the very one most open to a radical message. The next step was therefore to research a number of concepts based on ethical investing among undergraduates – the professionals of the future. Frustratingly, it served only to show that even this most informed of groups had no basic knowledge of the cycle of money on which banking depends – that funds held by banks in the form of account balances are invested in diverse ways to produce income, which can then fund interest payments back to depositors. Without some working knowledge of this process, the ethical investing difference would struggle to make sense.

Follow the consumer or follow your belief?

This is the fork in the road. This is the point that is reached by many a team searching to give expression to its most cherished values, only to encounter consumer ignorance or indifference. This is the point at which a team must decide if it is to be a consumer-led brand, and fall in with what is easily accepted, or to follow its beliefs and stand apart. On this occasion the consumer-led approach would have dictated that the bank, with the evidence before it, drop the ethical stance and pursue one of the other options on the table, which included, at the time, changing the bank's name to escape its dowdy associations. Consumers would have voted for that one. But the bank didn't. It decided, instead, to take a 'leap of faith' and make the ethical message hit home. This is not to say that the consumer research was without value – quite the opposite, because, as we saw with Honda in Chapter 2, it is vital to know the level of understanding and interest of your audience before you embark on your cause. For the Co-operative Bank the consumer findings served to leave no one in any doubt of one basic fact: for this approach to succeed, it would have to be about much more than just an advertising campaign.

A series of decisions followed. First, the bank would be clear about what it meant by 'ethical investing', which it defined as the 'responsible sourcing and distribution of funds'. Second, it would not set itself up as the sole arbiter of what was ethical and what was not. Instead, and with great open-mindedness, it invited its 30,000 customers, through the means of an online survey, to express the issues that most concerned them, and invited charities and NGOs like Amnesty International, the RSPCA, the League Against Cruel Sports and Christian Aid to contribute their expert views. This led to a list of companies, industries or countries in which the bank would not invest 'its customers' money'. They included the fur trade, industries that exploited animals, tobacco manufacturers, companies that caused environmental damage, companies with links to armaments supply and countries with oppressive regimes. But it was not enough simply to avoid investment in these areas; the bank would need to refuse to do business with them in any capacity, and so it was that the profitable business accounts of companies on its books that did not meet its ethical criteria were closed. It has become something of a glib throwaway line to quote that 'a principle is not a principle unless it costs you money', but here, for once, was a commercial enterprise, already with its back against the wall, putting that into painful practice.

The bank knew that it had then to find a way both to educate people about ethical investing and to make them care about it. In this effort, the bank's own staff were to be the front line, so every employee went through an intensive training programme to help them explain to customers, both potential and existing, what the policy was all about. The positive responses from customers were the first really encouraging signs that the bank was on to something, and word-of-mouth communication, even in these early days, became an important source of new business.

Only with all this in place did the team get back to where it had started – the advertising. The first burst ran in 1992 in the broadsheet and professional press, and the agency had to tread a fine line between the need for stand-out and the bank's desire to avoid sensationalism. Its solution was to devise a series of little human stories, charmingly illustrated, that parodied the nursery tale 'This is the house that Jack built'. The stories were about ordinary people who cherished some worthwhile personal aim and saved for it with the help of their bank. But the charm was deceptive for there was always a sting in the tail, exposing the bitter irony at the heart of mainstream banking practice: customers' money is often invested in a manner that runs directly counter to the very aims those customers are saving for. A black couple saving to put their daughter through law school, for example, were shown to have their funds in a bank that invested in countries that denied black people legal rights. In this way the ads both explained the normal banking cycle of money and showed why it mattered – before going on to explain the Co-op's ethical difference.

This is the daughter

The Hills sent to law school

Using savings they kept
in their bank

Which their bank
had invested

Abroad in a country

That denies
most of its people

Legal rights.

It happens.
But not at the Co-operative Bank.
Our customers know there are some things
we will never invest in.
Such as countries with oppressive regimes.
Our policy is to invest only in things we
believe to be as sound ethically as they are
financially.
Of course, we still provide all the normal
services you'd expect from a clearing bank with
assets of £2.5 billion, over 5,000 'Link' cash
machines and a full telephone banking service.
The difference is that along with financial
peace of mind our customers receive one other
important benefit.
More peace of mind.

The CO-OPERATIVE BANK

Figure 4.2 One of the first ads to dramatize the Co-operative Bank's ethical difference. Both authors worked on the bank's advertising – Day as Creative Director for over 10 years

From £1 billion to £6 billion in 10 years

The results of the campaign were to reverse the negative ratio between current account closures and openings and turn it into a gain. More significantly, the majority of new accounts opened were from precisely the kinds of professionals the bank sought most to attract. Current account deposits rose by 9 per cent in 1993, some way ahead of inflation, and the bank's 1993 annual report, entitled 'Profit with principles', was able to describe a return to profit for the first time in three years.

The Co-operative Bank still suffered from some perceptions that it was 'not a proper bank', and the next round of advertising, this time on TV and cinema as well as press, succeeded in combining ethical and product messages with surprising power. With this more balanced approach the bank made further gains through to 1996, by which time the ethical position was so well established, and so uniquely tied to the Co-operative Bank, that mainstream advertising was dropped altogether. What had been a dowdy, anachronistic curiosity at the turn of the decade was now firmly established as a cool icon brand, with something important to say about modern life. That 'something' had been there all along as a kind of unwritten code; it just needed a smart and courageous team to give it clarity, substance and meaning for the new consumer, and to make it active throughout the business. The reward, for them and the bank, has been the growth in retail customer deposits from £1 billion in 1993 to £6 billion 10 years on. What a way to end the century, and what a difference from the fate of the stores.

The story of the stores: 'unalloyed tragedy'

The quote is taken from Andrew Seth and Geoffrey Randall's 2001 book *The Grocers*. Carefully researched by authors with an inside knowledge of the industry, and written for the most part in tones of enthusiastic admiration, it takes 300 pages to chart the spectacular rise of Britain's food retail giants. The fate of the Co-op, however, it dismisses in just three, and they are replete with judgements as savage as the one above. They include: 'The Co-op has dropped to sixth place overall and seems to have nowhere to go but downwards.' 'Sales per square foot are stable but at a level around one half of the efficient retailer average figure.' 'Divided policies, for so long the Achilles heel of the movement, appear destined to haunt it to the bitter end.' 'An undeniable death wish attaches to this once great enterprise.'

The Co-op lost market leadership in food retailing as recently as 1985 but its decline had been well under way since the abolition of retail price maintenance in 1964. This change in legislation ended the practice whereby manufacturers set the prices for their goods to which all retailers were compelled to adhere. From that point on, price became a competitive weapon in the quest to build share, and the advantage went to those, like Tesco, Sainsbury's and Asda, that had the discipline to unify their retail portfolios and consolidate their buying efforts in order to achieve better discounts to pass on to customers. The Co-op, fragmented into hundreds of societies, and attempting no such consolidation, never even began to match this buying power, despite its greater overall size.

The result was rapid customer loss, which set in motion a spiral of problems. With its stores struggling to get prices somewhere close to those offered by competitors, but making less despite charging more, investment on infrastructure and staffing suffered. While Sainsbury's and, later, Tesco offered vibrant, well-stocked, well-serviced retail palaces in which to shop, the Co-op was a dreary, sad experience tolerated by the old, the downmarket and those who lacked either the means or the imagination to go elsewhere. Market share was to fall precipitously, from 12.6 per cent in 1960 to 6.1 per cent in 1996. Verbatims from consumer research, conducted in 1997 with current, lapsed and non-Co-op shoppers, illustrate just how bad the situation had by then become:

- 'I was embarrassed to be seen there.'
- 'Co-op is the crappy supermarket up Rose Hill what all the old grannies love.'
- 'It's a bit old-fashioned. And not very much choice. And a bit dirty looking.'

In the decade of the 1990s, when UK food retail sales grew at constant values, the Co-op's sales fell by 15 per cent. Yet this was the very time when the Co-operative Bank was showing the way forward with its new interpretation of long-held beliefs. It would be reasonable to ask why the stores did not attempt something similar – albeit for a different, more mainstream customer base. It would be every bit as reasonable to ask an even more fundamental question: why couldn't they simply get the basics right? In fact, the answer to both questions is rooted in the same problem: an endemic lack of cohesion.

The Co-op's structure is byzantine. It is not really an 'it'; for accuracy, we should be referring to 'them'. Although there is such a thing as the co-operative movement, it is not so much an entity as an idea, a common forum around which all the separate co-operative societies congregate. How many societies in all? Fewer now than the 860 that were operating when retail price maintenance was abolished, but still too many – 50 at the latest count – each with its own separate management team, its own individual way of doing things.

Imagine Britain's food retail scene if the big supermarket chains were structured along the lines of the Co-op. You'd have Tesco Northeast and Tesco Scotland and Tesco East Anglia, say, all with different fascias, different product ranges and different advertising campaigns. Or there'd be Sainsbury's Devon and Cornwall, Sainsbury's Midshires, Sainsbury's Wales and so on, some offering loyalty rewards, some not, some with this recruitment policy, some with that. All the buying would be negotiated separately, too, with some regions joining forces, but others refusing to and going it alone, so that prices would vary widely, but be higher across the board.

In that scenario, Wal-Mart would have walked away with the cream of British food retailing by now, pension funds holding retail stocks would be that much poorer, and Sir Terry Leahy would be plain 'Mr'.

Whatever happened to co-operation?

It is easy simply to ascribe to the supermarket chains the natural advantage of cohesion and scale, but this advantage did not arise without will. Three of the big four – Tesco, Asda, Safeway – have become big through acquisition of smaller regional chains, and the unifying of the various groups has required investment and skill – and doubtless the winning round of naysayers – to pull off. It is an indictment of Co-operative food retailing that it has lacked the determination to do likewise. As Seth and Randall observe, 'They failed, and still fail, to make the one move that might have strengthened their resistance – that of unifying themselves into a single cohesive enterprise with a recognizable strategic focus.'

This chapter is about activating belief. For the Co-op, just one belief needed to be dusted off for it to have fared better over the past few decades – the belief in co-operation. In the 1800s the retail societies were not above working together to pool resources in order to achieve economies of scale. Those early wholesale unions might have been small by today's monolithic industry standards but any one of them was bigger than anything the competition could muster at the time. But when the competition moved on, the Co-op didn't. Its buying effort is still too divided. Only as recently as 2000 have the biggest two societies merged – and even at this eleventh hour with many an 'over-my-dead-body' protest from senior members.

If the Co-operative food retail business can shake off its tendency to operate as a series of jealously guarded fiefdoms, then it has, perhaps, a last-ditch chance of achieving some kind of basis from which to build. Martin Beaumont, chief executive of the Co-operative Group, now by far the largest food retailer and wholesaler in the movement, is realistic about the task ahead: 'The first thing, if you are not an effective retailer for consumers, is to get that right – but that just gets you into the game. There's now a huge amount of effort being put into that issue.'

Parity first, in other words, difference second. But if something approaching parity can be achieved then the business has a rich heritage of values and beliefs that could be reinterpreted to create meaningful difference for today's customers. For example, Beaumont seeks to return to the movement's community roots, with a renewed focus on local, rather than out-of-town, stores. And he looks to build 'an organization that leads the way in respecting customers' concerns and operating with great integrity', citing issues like fair trade and food purity as areas in which the Co-operative Group has already taken the initiative. It is a strategy that deserves to succeed. But, with dozens of regional co-operative societies electing to remain independent, and muddying the water with their own diverse and conflicting strategies, both Beaumont and the movement have their work cut out.

In the end, this pivotal case comes down to the gap between theory and practice. It was a gap the Co-operative Bank successfully bridged, turning carefully considered beliefs into practical reality, making the necessary compromises and painful sacrifices along the way. The stores cared about beliefs and values too, as anyone who has read the co-operative press or attended a co-operative movement conference will attest. The retail society leaders were only too willing to engage with gusto in the many theoretical debates that the subject of co-operation generates – like the long, but ultimately distracting, deliberations on whether or not it is moral to advertise. But while the leaders were talking care and humanity between themselves, the stores were shrieking indifference to shoppers on the street. It is the bank, then, that is the rightful heir to the spirit of those original 28 Rochdale weavers with their objective of improving the lot of their fellow men and women – and their practical, businesslike approach to achieving it.

Belief-led marketing for mainstream brands

It is inevitable that such polarizing analysis should have its detractors, and one who begs to differ is Leslie Butterfield. Since Butterfield worked on the original advertising strategy for the bank, and now advises the Co-operative Group on marketing, his vantage point is as good as any. His critique centres on the vastly different sizes of the two businesses: 'It is one thing to pursue a conviction-led strategy for a relatively small, niche player like the bank, with an upmarket, politically astute target. But for the Co-op retail stores, the size and breadth of the mass-market customer-base makes it harder to be that pointed without alienating significant segments of the audience.'

If true, such analysis would strike at the very core of this book, which seeks to argue for belief-led marketing as a tool for mainstream and niche brands alike. Nor is Butterfield alone in his view. Adam Morgan, in his book *Eating the Big Fish* (1999), reserves the belief-led approach of what he calls 'Lighthouse brands' for challengers, not brand leaders. And Harvard's Doug Holt writes off belief-led marketing as not generally applicable, 'the exception that proves the rule, for one-off brands like Harley and Apple'.

While the pronouncements of people of this stature are not to be dismissed lightly, we cannot help but see a streak of defeatism running through them. None of these marketing experts apparently denies the power of brand belief, yet each seeks to deny it to the biggest brands. But why should such a powerful force be confined to the ghetto of niche, challenger or one-off brands? Aren't there some brand leaders out there that could do with a return to long-lost passion too? Come to think of it, isn't that what leading is all about?

Of course, the bigger the brand, the harder it is to get right, and the more there is to lose; it is one thing to take a 'leap of faith' on Britain's 13th-biggest bank, quite another to do so on a global mega-brand. But this argues only for caution, not abandonment. It argues for a systematic approach that recognizes the volatile power of brand belief and manages it with rigour and skill. We will go on to describe just such a systematic approach in Part 2, which starts in Chapter 6. Before that comes the final chapter of Part 1, in which we introduce the concept of Passionbrands and show why they will be increasingly favoured in the unforgiving global economy.

Note

Some of the information in this chapter is derived from Garnett (1968), Reeve *et al* (2003), Ryder (1994), Trevelyan (1942) and Wilson (2003).

5 Just another brand – or a Passionbrand?

What brands like Camper, Google, Innocent and the Co-operative Bank have in common is their ability to stand for something at once related to, and yet much bigger than, the category they happen to inhabit. They have a view about modern life that is elevated enough to inspire and yet is grounded in the very capability at which the company excels. We call these brands Passionbrands because they ignite passion both inside and outside the company.

The effect of this passion is to promote a kind of virtuous circle. Inside the company it fosters a zest for creativity, a desire to excel, invent and improve, since employees in all disciplines feel motivated by more than just normal commercial considerations. Oxford University's Richard Pascale (Pascale *et al*, 1997) likes to describe employees as 'volunteers who decide each day whether or not to contribute the extra ounce of discretionary energy that will differentiate the enterprise from its rivals'. By harnessing this 'volunteer' employee power, Passionbrands, as we saw with Google, have a tendency to improve their capability faster than category norms.

Outside the company, the passion translates into word-of-mouth buzz that serves to give the brand a vibrancy and salience that can go way beyond the norms for its size. These are brands that people don't just buy, but buy into. Passionbrands also tend to stimulate greater communication between consumer and brand owner. The Co-operative Bank, for example, noticed a marked increase in consumer feedback when it launched its ethical stance, and this dialogue, though confined at first to ethics, was broadened by the bank to help it find new ways to improve customer service. A virtuous circle indeed.

The defining characteristics of Passionbrands

Although Passionbrands vary widely according to their history, category, ownership and size, they all display three defining characteristics:

1. They are brands with active belief.
2. They have confidence rooted in capability.
3. They stay vibrant in an ever-changing world.

We'll review each of these briefly before moving on to the factors that argue for the transition to a Passionbrand identity in an increasingly competitive and complex marketing environment.

Brands with active belief

The Athenians required that their citizens 'leave the world a better place than they found it'. Passionbrands seek to achieve something similar – to make the world a little better than it would be if the brand did not exist. There are two distinct aspects to this: first, to decide in what way the world could be made 'a little better'; second, to ensure that the brand plays an active part in achieving it. Brand belief, then, is the expression of the first of these, knowing that the second is possible.

Crystallizing belief from the wider set of the company's ideological repertoire is no small achievement in itself, and can require much soul-searching and imagination to ensure that it is simple, inspiring, credible and relevant. But, once defined, belief is reassuringly permanent. Capability develops, markets move on, people change, issues come and go, but the brand belief exerts a timeless influence across the board.

The publishing brand Penguin, for example, thrives today by remaining faithful to its original beliefs. Penguin was founded in 1936 by Allen Lane, a young publisher who believed that the joy of literature should be accessible to all. Standing on a railway station, watching his fellow passengers buying cigarettes and magazines, Lane thought,

'What if I can make books for the price of a packet of Woodbines, so that lots of people can afford good-quality writing?' Woodbines – the most popular inter-war cigarette – sold for sixpence, while the typical book at the time cost about 10 per cent of an average week's wages. For the low Penguin price, achieved through the new technology of the paperback, Lane brought authors like George Orwell, Agatha Christie and DH Lawrence within the reach of millions of ordinary people.

Woodbines are no longer popular, but Penguin very much is. Amazingly, it remains the only strong brand in publishing, with a 90 per cent prompted recall. Year-on-year growth is 14 per cent, double the average for the category. Helen Fraser, Penguin's current MD, confirms that Lane's original belief is 'still our view today'. The quality bar continues to remain high, even at the blockbuster end of the business – today's authors range from Salman Rushdie to Nick Hornby – and price typically remains lower than today's most popular cigarette.

Confidence rooted in capability

A US print ad for Budweiser shows a smouldering Latina beauty in a halter-neck bikini top, leaning against a lithe male torso, eyes straight to camera, Bud in hand. The headline reads, 'Confidence is the sexiest thing you can wear.' In eight words it thus manages to convey both a truth and a lie. Confidence is indeed ultimately sexy; truly confident men and women ooze an appeal that can go way beyond their apparent physical charms. But confidence is not something you can just 'wear'. You can't just put it on, the way you put on a shirt, or a halter-neck bikini top, come to that, and people who try to do so are apt to come across as more silly than sexy. True confidence is sexy precisely because it cannot be worn, because it cannot be bought or borrowed, but must come, instead, from within. Confidence is the outer expression of some kind of inner strength.

As with people, so with brands. Confident brands are sexy. They are the ones everyone wants to be seen with, to have close, to welcome inside the project of self. But the confidence is either there or it isn't, and cannot just be added; it must reflect some inner strength. Brands like Innocent and Camper have an unmistakable confidence about them that everyone perceives; it shows in their lightness of touch, their irreverence, their willingness to underplay their hand. Or look again at Unilever's stain-removal laundry brands (Figure 5.1), which have the chutzpah to end their 'modern parenting' commercials with the

Figure 5.1 Dirt is good: the confident 'Splat' brand icon that unifies Unilever's stain removal brands around the world

slogan 'Dirt is good.' In a category where others are screaming 'whiter than white', this is brilliantly disarming.

But in all these cases the brand confidence is rooted in capability. All these brands are very good at something, and have a clear understanding of its importance to people – no matter how trivial the category might otherwise seem. Crucially, they also know their limitations and do not risk blurring their ideological credentials with ill-conceived forays into unrelated territory. These brands stand for something, and they deliver. An inspiring belief backed by great capability breeds confidence – the sexiest thing a brand can have.

Vibrant in an ever-changing world

Passionbrands tend to have a strong sense of their past but they live in the present and welcome the future. These are brands that have a seemingly instinctive feel for the zeitgeist, an eye for the subtle shifts in modern culture, an alertness to economic and environmental trends.

Paradoxically, it is the very robustness of what is at the core that allows for this greater responsiveness to change from outside. Brand belief, with its consistency, its power to anchor values, liberates the brand to respond to changes in markets, culture, competition, legislation, environmental issues and so on, without ever seeming flighty or flaky. Passionbrands move with the times but stay true to themselves. The belief remains fixed; its expression does not.

For example, look at one of the oldest and most famous brands ever: Lux. Since 1928, Lux Soap has celebrated beauty and championed a woman's right to the unselfconscious enjoyment of its rewards. Part of the DNA of the brand is its association with famous Hollywood stars: almost every leading lady in Hollywood has featured in Lux advertising, including Clara Bow, Ginger Rogers, Bette Davis, Rita Hayworth, Elizabeth Taylor, Veronica Lake, Demi Moore, Ursula Andress and Kim Basinger – to scratch the surface of an all-time 'A' list that runs to some 400 glamorous names.

Today Lux is a global power-brand achieving enviable shares in huge markets like India, Brazil and Japan. In 2004 it was successfully relaunched throughout Europe. Behind this momentum is 76 years of consistency at the level of beliefs and values, which has liberated the brand to respond freely at the level of products and associations to changes in what women want from beauty. Lux stays current and vibrant in its packaging, in its products and formulations – which now include shower gels and moisturizers based on more natural ingredients – and in its advertising. Lux has reinterpreted what celebrity means to modern women. Today's Lux stars – like Sarah Jessica Parker, Gisele Bundchen and the Bollywood actress Amisha Patel – no longer simply endorse, no longer dominate every frame of the commercial, but play a cooler, sassier role to symbolize the star quality that this brand believes is there in *every* woman, just waiting to be revealed. Lux has stayed young by changing along with its consumers – but only up to a point; like all really strong brands it knows that, when it comes to the core, a brand must be consumer-leading not consumer-led.

The common thread

There is a common thread, a leitmotif, that runs through these defining characteristics, and through Passionbrands. It is the juxtaposition of steadfastness and dynamism. Brand belief is the rock, the enduring foundation on which the brand is not so much built – that would be too rigid a metaphor – but on which it thrives as a living, exuberant, sensitive organism. Passionbrands are hence both rooted and free, timeless and timely, solid and supple. It is a hugely seductive combination in a volatile world because Passionbrands can offer reassuring consistency (through familiar, unwavering belief) and yet stay fresh and contemporary (through their sensitivity to change and their willingness to respond).

And for brand owners? How seductive is the prospect of a Passionbrand identity? The gains, after all, are not to be made without effort and sacrifice. The integrity of Passionbrands, their holistic meld of idealism and pragmatism, is real, not illusory, and is hard won. On the other hand this is no time for mediocrity, no time to be out there with 'just another brand'. The typical supermarket stocks 30,000 lines; the typical shopping basket implies a rejection of 29,920 of them. A person choosing a new car can ponder more than 268 different models from 53 different marques. No fewer than 45 different airlines will fly you across the Atlantic. Over 100 financial providers will quote you for a credit card. For the UK's average of £150 per head in annual charitable donations, there are 186,000 registered charities that can put it to good use.

It is in this context that the effort and intensity required to create a Passionbrand should be weighed. And perhaps here it is worth reminding ourselves of what brands are for, of why they merit investment, from the brand owner's point of view. It comes down to two factors: to achieve sustainable returns through customer loyalty and, as Doyle (2001) puts it, 'to create the capacity for charging a higher price'. (Doyle goes on to show that this 'capacity' can be used in a number of ways: charge the full premium without losing market share, charge the same as competitors and gain share or charge a modest premium with some share gain.) Passionbrands, by conveying more meaning, by being good at what they do, by reflecting a deep understanding of people and a clear grasp of modern life, are designed to achieve both of branding's generic objectives. They build powerful loyalty and add value, albeit in different ways, for customers, employees and brand owners alike.

A quantitative look at Passionbrands

We wanted to know how Passionbrands – or at least brands that approached the full complement of Passionbrand characteristics – performed quantitatively against other brands in the marketplace. We asked Millward Brown for a view on how to identify them in quantitative terms, and then cross-analyse them in their BrandZ™ database of 23,000 brands around the world. Their first step was to devise a quantitative 'autograph' that would correspond as closely as possible to our definition of Passionbrands. Using measures like quality of bonding, product performance and the degree to which a brand stands for something, Millward Brown built a quantitative identikit of the typical Passionbrand. While this can only ever be a quantitative approximation for what is a somewhat intuitive, qualitative concept to start with, the exercise produced some illuminating findings.

Once the quantitative 'autograph' was agreed, the next step was to enter it into the database to see which brands came out, and to look at whether we instinctively felt them to be Passionbrands.

Passionbrand candidates were:

- Absolut Vodka;
- Adidas;
- Apple;
- Bang & Olufsen;
- Ben & Jerry's;
- BMW;
- Budweiser;
- Burberry;
- Cadbury's Dairy Milk;
- Clinique;
- Coca-Cola;
- Dove;
- Hugo Boss;
- Ikea;
- Mercedes;
- MTV;
- New Balance;
- Nike;
- Pantene Pro V;
- Samsung;
- Singapore Airlines;
- Sony;
- Virgin;
- Whiskas.

This is a candidate list. To call each brand here a Passionbrand without further qualitative assessment would be premature. That said, with one or two exceptions they are clearly very strong candidates. There is no doubt that the overall feeling of this list is that of brands with confidence, momentum and ideological clarity.

The next step was to cross-analyse the candidate brands for various BrandZ™ dimensions to get a feel for general brand strength, likely performance in the market, likely growth prospects and other commercially predictive factors. Some fascinating findings emerged:

- *Greater likelihood to grow market share.* The candidate brands performed significantly better on the metric of Brand Voltage™ than other brands in their categories. As we noted in Chapter 2, Voltage is strongly positively correlated with future share growth. The candidates were assessed as having a 63 per cent chance, on average, of growing share. The average size of the sales increase was assessed at 15 per cent.
- *Capacity to command a higher-than-average price.* Without exception, the candidate brands on the list enjoyed a price premium position relative to their category. On the BrandZ™ Price Index, the candidates averaged 133 against an all-brand average of 100.
- *Greater loyalty.* On the BrandZ™ measure of Consumer Loyalty, the candidates scored nearly double the average of other brands. On measures of both rational and emotional attachment, their scores were significantly higher.
- *Higher 'Brand Magnetism'.* On this metric the candidate brands averaged 58, against an all-brand average of 45.1. They were rated higher on BrandZ™ dimensions of Thorough, Clever and Sensitive, and lower on Unimaginative, Uncaring and Too Predictable.

Even with the caveat – that defining a concept like Passionbrand in purely quantitative terms can only ever result in an approximation – the findings give weight to the view that the investment in a Passionbrand identity is commercially justifiable from the brand owner's point of view.

Culture jammers and Crunch Points: the coming crisis for brands

There is an altogether different kind of reason to contemplate the transition, no matter how arduous, from 'brand' to 'Passionbrand'. Less inspiring, more defensive, it is nonetheless an increasingly vital consideration in a febrile, anxious world. It is this: to be better placed to withstand the assaults and offensives to which today's brands are regularly exposed in the ever-more connected global economy. What is at stake this time isn't just brand growth or price premium or market share. What is at stake is survival: the right of your brand – the right of brands in your category, of brands in general – to exist.

The new challenge to brands surfaces on two planes: the intellectual and the visceral. The former tends to be erudite, predictable, sustained, articulate and promulgated by social commentators in both niche and mainstream media. It is potentially dangerous. The latter tends to be sporadic, socially contagious, triggered by specific events – we will call them Crunch Points – and felt deeply and directly by consumers. It is potentially catastrophic. Either way, as we shall see, the kind of brand you send out into the world is under scrutiny in new and unexpected ways, and will have to justify its existence with new and better answers.

The intellectual challenge to brands

Standard-bearer for the intellectual assault is Naomi Klein, although robust criticism of brands pre-dates her best-selling polemical treatise *No Logo*. Its roots go back at least 100 years to the anti-consumption philosophy of Marx, whose critique of capitalist societies centred on their propensity to create alienation. For Marx, the process by which cash is earned and then used to buy goods produced by others means that workers are 'forced to become consumers – and are further alienated as human beings' (Bocock, 1993). This, he argued, reduces humans to the bestial level: 'Man no longer feels himself to be freely active in any but his animal functions – eating, drinking, procreating, or at most in his dwelling and in his dressing up; and in his human functions he no longer feels himself to be anything but animal.'

The pronouncements of Marx have echoed down the decades in the corridors and lecture halls of the universities in which consumption is part of the syllabus – which normally implies the social sciences. Required texts include those of a whole suite of academics who have taken up the anti-consumption case.

For Baudrillard (2001; Norris, 2004), the consumer society is driven not by the needs and demands of consumers but by the needs of the producers. 'The fundamental problem of contemporary capitalism is no longer production,' he writes, but rather 'the contradiction between a virtually unlimited productivity and the need to dispose of the product'.

Brands and competition create choice, but the sociologist Bauman isn't buying, seeing choice itself as nothing more than a problem for people to agonize over: 'The consumers' misery derives from the surfeit, not the dearth of choices. *Have I used my means to the best advantage?* is the consumer's most haunting, insomnia-causing question' (2000).

Gabriel and Lang, in their study on the multiple roles assumed by consumers in society (1995), supply intellectual gravitas to those who seek to portray the consumer as victim: 'By wanting goods and having such high expectations of them, life is impoverished. People become slaves to the goods, still more to ensuring they get the best deal. In the very act of trying to improve our lives by consuming, we submit ourselves to the forces which exacerbate our alienation.'

Meanwhile, Carroll (1998) explores a different intellectual lineage, taking his theme from Nietzsche: 'The consumerist reflex is melancholic, supposing that malaise takes the form of feeling empty, cold, flat... Consumerism is thus the social analogue to the psychopathology of depression, with its twin clashing symptoms of enervation and inability to sleep.'

These are the ideas that are to be found in dilute form in newspaper and magazine articles on branding and the consumerism it implies. Here, for example, is David Boyle, author of *Authenticity: Brands, fakes, spin and the lust for real life*, taking up the cudgels in a piece in the *Financial Times* (2003): 'Brands are so disappointing to people – and customer loyalty is correspondingly fleeting – because brands are, by their very nature, fake.'

And here is Klein herself: 'What branding is about is identifying through the elaborate cool-hunting market research process what it is we care about and are passionate about as a culture, and harnessing that to sell us something very different. So in a sense it is a betrayal' (Temple, 2000).

But if the case for the prosecution is made with reason and force, the case for the defence, too, is guided by eloquent, expert counsel. It is led by Wally Olins, whose experience in branding goes back further than most, and whose genius lies in landing the point without stretching credulity. While the social argument for brands centres on their utility as instantly recognizable guarantees of quality, making shopping swifter and less risky, Olins readily allows that, for brand owners, they are also tools of manipulation, persuasion and seduction. 'In companies that seduce', he acknowledges in an interview with the *Independent on Sunday* (Sutcliffe, 2003), 'the brand is the focus of corporate life.' His deeper point, though, is that consumers know this, that they understand what's going on, willingly play the game – and enjoy it. Seduction, after all, feels nice.

It is a theme gleefully explored by James B Twitchell in *Lead Us into Temptation: The triumph of American materialism* (1999). Taking a swipe at the academics who cast the consumer as hapless victim, under the ironic heading 'Narcissistic iatrogenic academic obfuscation', he writes:

> I think that much of our current refusal to consider the liberating role of consumption is the result of who has been doing the describing. Since the 1960s, the primary 'readers' of the commercial 'text' have been the well-tended and -tenured members of the academy. For any number of reasons – the most obvious being low levels of disposable income, average age and gender, and the fact that these critics are selling a competing product, high-cult (which is also coated in dream values) – the academy has casually passed off as 'hegemonic brainwashing' what seems to me, at least, a self-evident truth about human nature. We like having stuff.

The problem for marketers

For marketing practitioners, engaged in the everyday exigencies of 'selling stuff', the brand debate, with its thrusts and parries, is not something that warrants a great deal of brain space. There you sit, in a competitive market, trying to shift your lavatory cleaner, say, or launch a new perfume line, or combat bullying retailer tactics; the issue of whether or not your activities are contributing to 'twin clashing symptoms of enervation and inability to sleep' is unlikely to be high on your worry-list. Where marketers do get worried – in fact what really terrifies them – is when the attack on brands gets personal, when the media pick on *your* brand, for some reason, to exemplify what they see as the greater evils of consumer society.

It is a tactic that is becoming more common. The brand victims are chosen in the same way that big cats choose their prey from among the galloping herd: they sense weakness; they smell fear. In a *Times* article on 'Buy Nothing Anti-brand Day' in the US, for example, guess which brands Frank Furedi (2003) name-checks to make a, literally, killer point: 'When demonstrators attempt to wreck a McDonald's franchise or attack a Starbucks they are making a moral statement that is driven by the same imperative that incites Islamic fundamentalists to attack a shop selling liquor or burn down a disco. In their eyes the big brands of the corporate world symbolise evil.'

The Vancouver-based commune of 'culture jammers', Adbusters, likes to embarrass specific brands in this way, listing a 'Dirty Dozen Rogue Companies' bristling with household names on its much-visited website. In recent years its activities have helped to humble both Nike and Gap over stories relating to their sourcing policies. The brand-specific assaults of the culture jammers, like those of the guerrilla film-makers Michael Moore and Morgan Spurlock, bypass the traditions of reasoned debate and present the targeted brands with a threat closer to that of the Crunch Points we cover below.

No brand can be immune from attack in an era in which success itself is seen as grounds for antipathy. But there is a reason why Passionbrands are less likely than conventional brands to constitute easy targets. It comes down to a single word: integrity. The Passionbrand approach demands that the brand is deeply embedded within the organization. The brand belief, with its idea of good at the core, is not something just cooked up by marketing without reference to other disciplines – on the contrary, it is felt and acted upon at all levels in the organization. When the Co-operative Bank embarked upon its ethical banking policy, ethical considerations affected even the choice of toilet paper in the staff washrooms – and it was the staff themselves that did the choosing, based on their own investigations into the eco-credentials of the available options. This greater moral penetration of Passionbrands is not to be confused with the half-hearted results of those trite injunctions, so popular at internal marketing seminars, to 'live the brand'. It has much more in common with the holistic approach of the 'visionary companies' described by Collins and Porras in their classic text, *Built to Last* (2000):

> The essence of a visionary company comes in the translation of its core ideology and its own unique drive for progress into the very fabric of the organisation – into goals, strategies, tactics, policies, processes, cultural practices, management behaviours, building layouts, pay systems, accounting systems, job design – into everything that the company does. A visionary company creates a total environment that envelops employees, bombarding them with a set of signals so consistent and mutually reinforcing that it's virtually impossible to misunderstand the company's ideology and ambitions.

There is nothing to prevent journalists and anti-brand activists – especially those who like cynically to reinterpret goodness as smugness – from taking aim at Passionbrands, but they can expect in return not the meek scurrying and red-faced confusion of brands with something to hide but the robust response of whole organizations that take their commitments seriously. By far the best defence against those who seek to move the brand debate from the generic, to the specific, level – aside from total anonymity, which is hardly a practical brand strategy – is not to be vulnerable in the first place. As the PR consultant Mark Borkowski observes in a *Marketing* story (2004) on Morgan Spurlock's anti-McDonald's film *Super Size Me*, 'The ultimate answer is for companies to clean up their acts.'

The visceral challenge to brands

When terrorists destroyed Pan Am flight 103 over Lockerbie in December 1988 the immediate, and the most tragic, consequence was the loss of 270 lives. Within months a further consequence of the outrage was apparent: the demise of Pan Am itself. The Atlantic routes went to Delta and American, the Pacific routes went to United, and the old Pan Am eventually flew its final domestic flight into Miami on 1 June 1991. Neither the business nor the brand was in sufficiently good shape to withstand the after-effect of an event perpetrated by people, and generated by forces, outside its control. Two attempts have since been made to revive the remnants of Pan Am and keep the name alive. The first, by a former Pan Am executive, ended in bankruptcy in 1996. The second is still in operation, headed by a Pittsburgh airline enthusiast with family wealth. Today Pan Am – once the world's most famous airline, with a fleet spearheaded by 40 Boeing 747s and a network extending to five continents – operates a handful of ageing 727s on three routes to Florida and Puerto Rico out of its base in Portsmouth, New Hampshire.

The loss of an aircraft by an airline, whatever the circumstances, is an extreme example of the phenomenon of Crunch Points: some kind of intervention that causes a critical reappraisal of the brand. Crunch Points can take many forms and arise from unexpected sources. They are no respecters of prestige. In recent years, for example, we have seen Perrier contaminated by benzene, Mercedes overturning its prototype A-Class in an 'elk test', and Firestone being forced to recall 14.4 million dangerously faulty tyres.

Crunch Points do not have to be triggered by big, rare, newsworthy events. Humdrum interventions of a more everyday nature will do the trick. Typical examples include strikes that affect service, bad financial news about the holding company, bad PR about Third World sourcing, a category issue – like the mis-selling of pension schemes – or even, on a less public level, some observed dangerous driving by one of the company's trucks. But whatever their genesis, all Crunch Points stimulate an automatic response: *'What is this brand doing in my life?'*

How that question is answered in the consumer's mind – or how the answer is felt viscerally and translated into action – depends on just two factors: the way the brand handles the crisis at the time, and the underlying store of goodwill felt towards the brand by the consumers concerned. The crucial point is this: only one of these resources can be influenced by the brand owners *after* the event.

That one, of course, is crisis management, and the basic principles are well established and well worth knowing by all who work on the brand. They include: don't hide the truth – especially with the media, who will crucify you if they sense you are not being straight; don't think you can confine the issue to the geographical region in which it surfaced – you can't, so it must be voluntarily opened up wherever the brand is sold or made; assume the situation will escalate and get worse – and be prepared to commit resource to it for the medium and perhaps long term.

But no matter how well the crisis is managed at the time, the brand will suffer some kind of withdrawal from its reserves of consumer goodwill. The withdrawal might be large, it might be small, it might be short- or long-lived, but it will happen; consumers have been given reason to pause in their relationship with the brand, and their goodwill cannot be expected to remain intact. The possible consequences for the brand, therefore, correspond to those of a real withdrawal from a real bank; they can range from a minor depletion of reserves, to being overdrawn for a while, to teetering on the edge of bankruptcy or actually going bust: goodwill gone for good. It depends, of course, not just on the size of the withdrawal, but on the reserves of goodwill that were there in the first place.

It is here that the personality-rich, character-poor, blatantly commercial consumer-led brands are most vulnerable. They might be liked by consumers but the liking does not go deep enough to create the real, heartfelt affection that can help the brand survive a critical intrusion. Reserves of goodwill are unlikely to be great; withdrawals are likely to cause real damage. This might have mattered less in past decades when such intrusions, though possible, were rare. The bad news for brands is that Crunch Points are becoming more common, and there are good reasons why the trend will continue.

More complexity, less control

The first of these reasons is the greater complexity of organizations as markets and technology expand. Peter Drucker, in his essay 'The information executives truly need' (in Drucker, 2003), documents the trend towards structures built on 'partnership rather than control'. In these structures, outsourcing, alliances and joint ventures are necessarily becoming 'the models for growth, especially in the global economy'. With less control over the supply line, with the boundaries of the company less defined and more permeable, and with a wider geography to keep watch over, companies will find problems hitting them from quarters they had not had to consider before.

The second reason is more disturbing than the first: the increase in deliberate, human-created interventions that can affect the brand. In an analogous study in *Harvard Business Review*, April 2003, entitled 'Preparing for evil', Mitroff and Murat look at the major calamities that have hit the world over the past 25 years. The subject matter, which ranges from earthquakes to the WTC attacks, is divided into two broad types: accidental (whether natural or human-created) and abnormal – or deliberately precipitated. Their chilling conclusion: 'The number of abnormal accidents has risen sharply over the last ten years.' As their time line of major crises (Figure 5.2) shows, normal accidents are being increasingly overshadowed by those caused deliberately. Within the subset of the commercial world, too, it is the rise of acts of aggression, rather than acts of God, that is causing the greatest concern. For example, over a 10-year period in the US, five major brands have fallen victim to cyanide tampering: Excedrin, Sudafed, Goody's Headache Powder, Lipton cup-a-soup and Johnson & Johnson's leading drug, Tylenol. All caused deaths.

The third reason for the rise of Crunch Points comes down to connectivity. This time the problem is not so much one of frequency of the underlying problems but their amplification when they do occur. Incidents or ideas that might have caused a ripple 10 or 15 years ago now get swelled into waves and torrents thanks to the internet, e-mail,

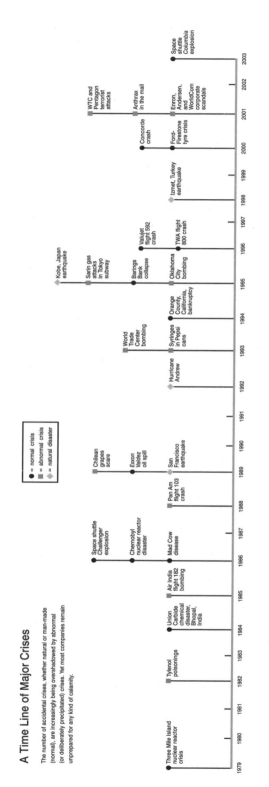

A Time Line of Major Crises

The number of accidental crises, whether natural or man-made
(normal), are increasingly being overshadowed by abnormal
(or deliberately precipitated) crises. Yet most companies remain
unprepared for any kind of calamity.

● = normal crisis
■ = abnormal crisis
◆ = natural disaster

Figure 5.2 Time line of major crises

texting, the increased speed of global communications, and the mass influence of celebrities. The food industry has been a recent victim, hit by Atkins on the one hand and obesity accusations on the other. Atkins became a textbook case of social contagion, turning from a medical fad into an international phenomenon in a matter of months, captivating US and Northern European populations and decimating profits in food brands based on carbohydrates. The obesity issue, originating from health statistic news and books like Greg Crister's *Fat Land* (2003), has snowballed to such an extent that governments are considering punitive legislation – like the British proposal to force food manufacturers to pay for the building of community sports facilities. Hyperactive media, fast global connectivity and ever-more imitated celebrities make Crunch Points out of what would once have been mere irritations.

Trust on trial

Passionbrands, by encouraging denser, deeper relationships and fostering greater trust, offer brand owners better protection from the ravages that can be caused by the growing phenomenon of Crunch Points. With more goodwill in the bank, the inevitable withdrawal is less punishing. A Passionbrand is therefore better placed than a normal brand to pull through when crisis strikes. That, at least, is our contention, and it can be only a contention since, to date, there has been no coincidence of a Crunch Point affecting what we would regard as a fully accredited Passionbrand (although Google's IPO fiasco comes close).

And it would be only fair to point out a counter-argument, supported by academic research, that it is the trusted brands, rather than their more flighty counterparts, that suffer most when things go belly up. When good brands do bad, to quote the title of a 2004 study by Jennifer Aaker, disappointment can apparently be that much greater. This may be so, but to us it misses the point. Of course disappointment might be intensified when it is your most loved, trusted brand that meets a mishap or lets you badly down, but what counts in the end isn't the level of disappointment but the propensity to give the brand another try. With a loved, trusted brand, that propensity is likely to be there, whereas, for the more shallow brand, it might be a case of 'the last straw'. To look at this figuratively, a cold, wet day in summer causes greater disappointment than one in winter – but that doesn't mean you'll be scheduling next year's beach holiday for the winter months. Over the years, summer has been good to you, full of warmth and love; it takes more than one disappointment to break the habits and bonds of pleasure so deeply ingrained. When it comes to surviving a crisis, and winning back lost goodwill, we'll put our money on the Passionbrand.

The end of the beginning

The British Brands Summit of 2004 was, despite the novelty of a live satellite link with New York, a somewhat muted affair. 'Nervousness stalked the hall', reported *Marketing Week* (Benady, 2004), 'as the country's top marketers enumerated the list of crises that brands face.' In addition to the perennial struggle for growth and share, they were 'hounded by pressure groups and regulators, struggling with saturated markets and powerful retailers and confronted with mounting cynicism by consumers'. The solution – proposed by 'speaker after speaker' – was 'to intensify the emotional relationships with customers'.

It's a solution that's not hard to agree with – but it's one that is very, very hard to make happen. Anyone who thinks that intensifying emotional relationships with consumers is easy has not had to do it for a living. It's not about putting a puppet in your ads. Come to that, it's not just about putting belief in your brand. Passionbrands start with an inspiring belief, one that has good at the core, but to get that far is to get no further than the end of the beginning. What really counts is making brand belief active throughout the organization, delivering it with confidence rooted in capability and keeping it vibrant in an ever-changing world. Anything less is not a Passionbrand. It is just tinkering with image.

We have arrived at the end of the beginning of this book. The next seven chapters are about the harder business of making it happen – creating a Passionbrand identity and turning it into reality. The upside is the prospect of better consumer relationships, deeper loyalty, more motivated staff, more sustainable returns and stronger protection against the rigours of a newly hostile world. The downside is the prospect of hard questions, hard decisions and hard work. No short cuts, no one-stop solutions, no 'three easy steps'. We are moving on to *'How'*, always a much thornier subject than *'Why'*.

PART 2

How

6 Creating Passionbrands: the journey starts here

We now embark on the second half of this book, with its exposition of a proven methodology for the creation and maintenance of Passionbrands. The aim of this chapter is to provide an overview of the methodology, introduce the main concepts and models, and address some of the questions that the typical management team will need to ask itself before it embarks on the process.

Methodology overview

The objective is to take an existing brand and, through a process that combines rigour and imagination, arrive at a Passionbrand identity. The methodology is applicable for brands of all kinds, of all sizes, in all categories, including unconventional brands like charities, NGOs, even countries. It is not just for niche players, or challengers, or brands in sexy categories; everyday, mainstream brands will benefit from this approach too.

The methodology comprises two distinct phases: an analytical phase, in which all aspects of the brand and its environment are studied; and a more creative phase, which uses that knowledge to crystallize brand belief and generate the Passionbrand identity.

The process is governed by the model shown in Figure 6.1. It is a four-corner diagram with a key word in each corner: ideology, capability, consumer, environment. The point where these four forces intersect is called the Passionpoint; this is where to focus efforts to create the brand's identity and total marketing offer.

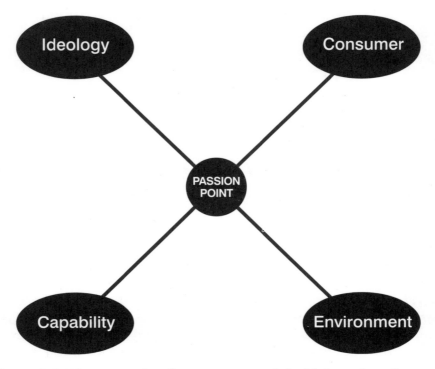

Figure 6.1 The governing four-corner model with its point of intersection: the perfect position for brand identity

The first phase of the process is the rigorous analysis of the subject matter covered by the key words at each of the four corners. The two corners on the left are internal factors, relating to the company or brand itself. 'Ideology' embraces the ethos of the company, and all the values associated with the brand, both current and past, and will include, where possible and appropriate, the foundational beliefs. 'Capability' examines the company's abilities, its 'invisible' assets like the distribution network or trade relationships, its source of authority and its cultural bias – what its culture inclines it to do. It will also be necessary to look at financial capability during this part of the analysis. The internal corners will be covered in detail in Chapters 7 and 8.

The two corners on the right are external factors, relating to the world beyond the company. 'Consumers' will include people who buy, reject or otherwise influence the brand, but the lens will also be broadened to look at people in a much more general sense, to examine behavioural trends, cultural shifts and the trickle-down effect of celebrity. The 'environment' corner covers the entire competitive environment in which the brand sits and is not simply confined to the immediate competitive set. Also analysed in this section are technological, economic and demographic trends, upcoming legislation that could influence the brand and 'crossover potential' – where trends and ideas in other markets or countries might become applicable to yours. The external corners will be covered in detail in Chapters 9 and 10.

Only once the analytical phase is complete is the second phase of the process undertaken: the identification and development of the Passionpoint. At its epicentre will be an inspiring crystallization of brand belief; radiating outward from there, but still tightly grouped, will be the four other elements of the brand identity.

The information uncovered during the analysis is vital as fuel for this second phase, but that is not the same as saying the goodies in the Passionpoint will simply spill out from the analytical findings. There is an undeniable element of creativity in the Passionpoint phase – the requirement to make leaps rather than just build point by point. To those who find the prospect of creative thought daunting we would just say hold your faith. No craft skills are involved, the creativity is structured rather than random, and we offer techniques to demystify the process and unleash the surprising creative energy that is pent up in the typical business team. All this, and more, in Chapter 11.

The result, with dedication, imagination and courage, is a Passionbrand identity. But, of course, it is a long, hard road from identity to reality, from something that inspires on paper to something that performs in the market. Chapter 12 addresses the pitfalls you can expect along that road – with advice on how to overcome them and win round your own people and consumers alike.

Why this methodology?

The internal–external method of analysis is based on the brand audit methodology taught at London Business School on its Brand Management elective. The four-corner model with its intersection builds on this. It has been developed and enhanced by the authors in light of their practical experience and further academic research into what makes great brands. Its power, when used with commitment and intelligence, results from three virtues:

1. *It is holistic and balanced.* This is the biggest and most important difference between this methodology and the tools more typically used in brand management practice. It is also the one that can come as the biggest disappointment, since detail and hard work are involved. You might as well know now that the methodology will not appeal to those who yearn for a heroic, one-stop solution to the mysteries of brand marketing. Nor will it find favour with those – which includes a surprising number of brand consultants – who believe that branding is 'all about' one thing or another: all about consumer insights, or all about innovation, or all about differentiation or killer competence. Branding is not 'all about' any one of these things but is all about all of them and more besides. If branding were a sport, it would be the decathlon. It is this that makes brand management so infuriatingly difficult but, to look at it more positively, also what makes brands so richly textured and attractive.

   The model reflects the integrity typical of Passionbrands. It is deliberately designed to be inclusive, to capture the full diversity of data available about brand, company, consumer, market and world beyond, and to draw themes together at a nexus, in the way that a great city draws people into the melting pot of its centre, where ideas are freely exchanged, developed and fused. By contrast, basing a brand's identity on just one element or another – like a consumer insight, which on our model would occupy a space somewhere just in from the top right-hand corner – is the equivalent of locating it out in the suburbs.

2. *It is rooted in reality.* If you have ever brainstormed brand development, especially if you have done it with the ad agency in tow, you will know that there is a tendency to generate dozens of marvellous-sounding ideas that start with the words 'Why not?' There are, of course, often very good reasons why not, reasons that have stubborn roots in the practicalities of finance, people, culture, resources, technology, distribution, competitor activity and many other factors.

   Passionbrands have a strong practical component. The inspiration that is there at the core, in the form of brand belief, is not just empty rhetoric. It is a call to action, one that will be heeded by the entire business. And action, in real life, is constrained by reality. The methodology, therefore, seeks to gain a thorough grip on all the factors and imperatives that might act as a constraining influence on actions down the road. Chief among these is financial resource, which is why it is analysed as part of the capability corner. Many of the flights of fancy launched by enthusiastic brand teams at brand development brainstorm sessions would be grounded by the most rudimentary understanding of the financial consequences they implied.

This is not to say that the present reality is always accepted as a given forever, but simply that it is recognized up front and accounted for. Probing into the cultural bias of the company, in the capability corner, for example, does not imply the automatic celebration of that culture – since it could be what's holding things back – but is undertaken to forewarn the team of what it is taking on if it seeks to implement sweeping change. To those who find reality a dampener – like the CEO we worked with whose favourite phrase was 'Let's punch a hole in the universe' – we would simply say, 'Get real'; the universe has a habit of punching back.

3. *It is dynamic.* If the first phase of the process is characterized by rigour, then the second is characterized by momentum. This is deliberate. Data, even the high-quality data produced by rigorous analysis, are inert. Without manipulation and method they will just sit there and sulk. Designed into the methodology therefore, in the phase that draws the team with centripetal force from the corners towards the Passionpoint, is the concept of dynamic trajectory. It is a trajectory that moves from information, to insight, and on to imagination.

There is a flow, a direction, an unfolding to this second phase, which has its corollary in the flow of time. Data are always history, a summation of knowledge gained in the past. The trick is to use them to help create the future. The move towards the centre, with its call for creativity and imagination, is also a move from what was, and what is, towards what might be.

The Brand Trampoline

It can help to think of the governing model in a more three-dimensional form, as a trampoline – as in Figure 6.2. Each of the four corners has become one of the trampoline's legs; the Passionpoint is now a small area in the centre of the trampoline, a kind of 'sweet spot', from which propulsion is at once most forceful, effortless and accurate.

When viewed like this it is easy to see how complete each of those four pieces of analysis in the first phase must be – for each has to build one leg of the trampoline. To miss out a corner altogether would result in the disaster that is a three-legged trampoline. But even to skimp a little, to rush, to make false assumptions, could result in a leg that was weaker, shorter or in some way less robust than the others. The result, far from a beautiful exhibition of soaring, controlled propulsion, could be an embarrassing flop (see Figure 6.3).

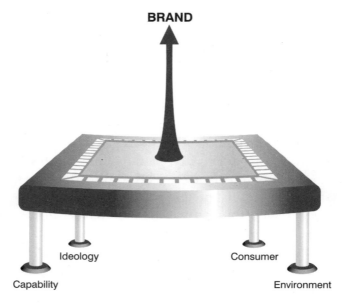

Figure 6.2 The Brand Trampoline

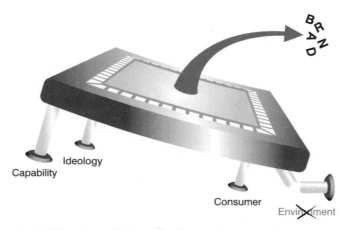

Figure 6.3 The Brand Trampoline with a weakness at one leg – resulting in a misdirected brand strategy

In practice, many brands do exhibit weakness at one or another of these 'legs' and it is worthwhile taking a brief look at the specific kind of brand that results from each specific kind of flaw.

Hollow brands

These are the ideologically challenged brands, all froth and personality on the outside but with nothing substantial at the core. They are the kinds of brands that can prosper in good times, but that do not bear scrutiny when things cut up rough. This is why a brand like McDonald's can have such a hard time chasing back from criticism over health and obesity issues; its salad-plus-fish response looks hollow because it does not seem to emanate from any holistic belief that has the good of humankind at its core. McDonald's has tremendous strengths and yet seems unable to blend them into anything meaningful for people at a deeper level; even the global ad campaign – 'I'm lovin' it' – serves to convey the uncertainty of a brand that is still trying to discover what it stands for.

Question-mark brands

The weakness here is capability. Brands in which belief and capability are unmatched become question-mark brands. The question mark instinctively pops up in people's heads when they are presented with attractive beliefs from a company whose credentials don't seem to fit. Benetton is an example: even if you buy into the ideology so graphically communicated, at some point you must question Benetton's relevance to it.

The no-frills airlines are currently in danger of becoming question-mark brands. They have championed with zeal their ideological stance of freedom of the skies for all – encapsulated best in Wizz Air's slogan, 'Now we can all fly.' But some are beginning to find it hard to deliver; two low-cost European airlines went bust in 2004, profit warnings have been issued by Ryanair and easyJet, share prices are sharply down as nervous investors dump stock, and customers are getting nervous, too, as they begin to feel uneasy about whether their low-cost plane will show up at all. Only credible reassurance on capability will erase the question mark.

Blind brands

No matter how inspiring your belief, nor how strong your capability, it is still vital to maintain a fluent empathy for people. Failure to keep up with how people live their lives leads to a blind brand – a brand struggling to appeal to people it has lost sight of. Look at the recent troubles at Marks & Spencer for a topical example. The company's values and ethos have always been, and still are, highly attractive to consumers, and capability has historically been strong. But through a kind of isolationism, a strange corporate hubris, the brand lost touch with how people live, whom they admire, where they go and what they wear. M&S misjudged the mood of the times, failing to notice how consumers have been influenced by travel and celebrity to want more excitement and zing in their lives. So, perhaps without really wanting to, and with a certain sense of loss, people began to drift away from the brand, feeling that it was no longer 'right for me'.

Irrelevant brands

Irrelevant brands get created when the world moves on and the brand doesn't notice. The weakness, then, is at the environment leg of the trampoline. For example, consider Kodak's slowness to spot the importance of digital photography, which has cost the company dear over the past few years. As the *Guardian*'s business editor observes (Tran, 2004), 'Having misjudged the speed at which digital photography would erode its core business, it now has to catch up with rivals such as Canon, Dell and Hewlett-Packard, and make up for lost time.' Kodak's misjudgement was the result of a kind of group-think: management was so fixated with its existing expertise in film that it just didn't want to see the digital revolution coming. Kodak has now, albeit belatedly, thrown itself into the digital fray, but would have got there sooner, and capitalized on its undoubted technological skills, with a more disciplined approach to the analysis of the competitive environment.

In summary, if you were going to get on to a trampoline and hurl yourself as high into the air as you could, you would want to know that each of the four legs was as solid, well made and well adjusted as the next. The same is true for your brand.

Getting started: team, timing, tips

At the beginning of any process like this it's a case of more questions than answers. Who should be on the team? Should it be a team at all or just an individual? What about including people from outside the company? How long should the process take? Who should run it? Who should do what? Should you set milestones? Which corner do you attack first? Is the order important? Should you work at the level of the company or the brand? How do you avoid getting stuck in the same old debates? What's the best way around conflict? How do you keep from tearing your hair out?

The answer to each of these questions is that there is no single answer; there is a fluidity to most business methodologies and this is no exception. Things can vary according to the nature of the company, the size of the brand and the urgency of the need. But some useful hints and guidelines have emerged through hard-won experience, which you might want to consider before you start.

Someone senior should own the project

A project of this scale needs a champion, someone to signal that this is an organization-wide transformation initiative to create growth. Ideally that 'someone' should be the CEO: there is no surer way to guarantee that the project gets taken seriously throughout the company. If ownership of the project resides at the level of marketing director, there is a danger that it will be seen as just 'something marketing is doing' and it could reinforce the potential within the organization to view marketing as a separate discipline with its own Masonic ways. Alternatively, the board as a whole could share ownership and responsibility but, while this can work well enough, there is nothing quite like the most senior person in the place speaking up for the need at the beginning and the outcome at the end. The aim is to gain emotional commitment from all; a rousing speech from a leader, rather than a communiqué from a committee, is the best way to achieve it.

Team involvement for key stages

In theory an individual working alone, or with a colleague, could undertake the entire programme and devise a Passionbrand identity, which would then simply be reported to the board or project owner. In practice, this would be asking a great deal of anybody, no matter how able, especially in the second phase where ideas need to be generated, challenged and shaped – a cut-and-thrust process that always benefits from multiple input. And however accomplished the final result, the product of an individual or duo is always going to have a tough time gaining acceptance throughout a complex organization. Buy-in is more smoothly achieved when all disciplines are seen to have been involved.

Better, then, to assemble a team and agree the stages at which full-team involvement is crucial. You certainly wouldn't want the full team to be present at every step in the process, especially during the analysis-gathering work, although different sub-groups of the team might be assigned specific tasks at this stage. But, at the very least, the whole team would come together at the initial objective-setting session, the stages at which research and corner-analysis are debriefed, and the stages in the second phase involving the creation and development of the Passionpoint. Team numbers can obviously vary according to size and complexity of the organization – but would normally be between 6 and 25, above which things tend to get unwieldy. What is more important than size, however, is composition.

Cross-discipline teams are better

It is important that the project should not become just a marketing silo. In the end it is the whole organization that makes a brand reality for customers. So if you're in the convenience food business, include your most senior chef; if you're in hotels, include a hotel manager; if you are a Third World charity, include someone who's actually worked on the ground with the poor in a developing country. Apart from anything else, the views of people in these kinds of hands-on positions can be refreshingly direct and often genuinely surprising to marketers who spend so much of their working lives with consumers and advisers.

A neutral moderator can overcome hierarchy

During team meetings, hierarchy should be put to one side. Ideally, people at very different levels of the organization will be represented, and each view should stand on its merits and get its fair chance to be heard. Good ideas and interesting angles can come from anywhere, and the silent hand of seniority should not be allowed to steer the conversation unfairly into areas of its own choosing. This is not an easy one to get right, since everyone knows who the boss is even when that person is not acting like the boss. A good moderator is therefore beneficial – and for this function it might be better to look outside the organization.

Outsiders will broaden perspective

The chief benefit of including outsiders is that they bring a fresh perspective and are not confined by the organization's own 'mental models' – a term evoked by Costas Markides (2000) to describe the patterns of thought that businesses trap themselves into through repetition and routine: 'the way we do things round here'.

Who should the outsiders be? Candidates for inclusion are non-executive directors, organizational stakeholders, important suppliers, respected journalists, researchers who have worked with the organization before or professionals whose expertise relates to that of the business – a dietitian, for example, if the company makes food products. Advertising agency people, designers and so on could be included but never en masse, or the programme will be quickly turned into a communications exercise, and it is far bigger than that.

Identify creatives and mavens

People with a creative outlook are particularly helpful when things get stuck. If the block in the road will not yield to the full frontal assault of linear thought, you'll need their ingenuity to find a way around it or over it or to discover a new road altogether. This is especially true during the second phase of the project.

Creative people are not always found in creative jobs. They could be working anywhere throughout the organization and are identified by their approach to life rather than their titles. Davenport, Prusak and Wilson, writing in *Harvard Business Review* (2003), report on 100 interviews with what they call 'ideas practitioners' – people who act as conduits for new ways of thinking in companies. 'The group was diverse', they note; 'it included, for example, a chief financial officer of a global manufacturer, a chief learning officer for an investment bank, and a chief operating officer of a large US government agency.' The common links were lifestyle – they all read widely and avidly – and an open mental attitude. 'They approach all sources with open minds; they are neither cynical nor overly credulous,' the authors observe.

'We discovered, too, that ideas practitioners tend to value an interdisciplinary perspective, looking to fields outside business for new approaches to solving problems.'

And mavens? The word is from Yiddish and means 'one who accumulates knowledge'. But they are communicators, not just accumulators – people who love to disseminate what they know. Identified by Nebraska University's Linda Price (Price and Feick, 1987) in the context of markets and consumers, mavens also play a role in corporate life. These are the people with good connections and interpersonal skills who stay close to the heartbeat of the organization, picking up on important issues and themes. Their influence going out, as well as their broad-based knowledge coming in, makes them an important part of the project team.

Be clear on roles and responsibilities

The project isn't just talk – there's a great deal of doing to do. Analysis doesn't happen by itself; to get to grips with the capability corner, for example, an individual or team might have to interview people in operations, finance, supply chain and service, and get their heads round a number of financial and legislative issues, including patents, that might affect the organization's ability to compete today and in the coming years.

The moderator should be clear on who is doing what and by when. Roles and responsibilities need to be clearly understood, agreed and noted. Where teams rather than individuals are assigned tasks, the numbers should be kept small to give each team member a sense of personal responsibility and to avoid the difficulties of coordinating too many diaries.

Build internal support through involvement

The aim of the project is a new brand identity and a clear strategy for taking it forward. But that is no more than words on paper until it is implemented – for which you will need heartfelt commitment from the whole organization. As Markides (2000) shows, people are more likely to be committed to something if they feel they have made some kind of active contribution to its genesis.

Simply communicating progress informally, through the members of the selected team, is therefore the very minimum you would want to do to keep people involved. Employee research or an all-staff questionnaire are logical next levels up. But a more creative, dynamic way to gain organization-wide input is to ask for ideas. The Danish retail bank Lan & Spar, for example, encouraged all employees to put forward just one new idea on how to improve the brand; most of these were not usable, for one reason or another, but a few were, and all served the purpose of letting people feel they had an influence in the higher-order issues of corporate life.

Be tough on timing

It is wise to set deadlines for all of the principal stages, bearing in mind the need to build in plenty of time for the formal research exercises. Be aware, for example, that if you choose to use an ethnographic style of methodology, this could take up to three months, so will need to be set up well before the main team-based process begins. Time for reflection needs to be built in after the Passionpoint phase, so that the team can live with the new identity for a while, and then regroup if necessary to voice concerns and suggest amendments. Finally, do set a firm end date for the project – because it will go on forever if you don't!

Example: getting the right team for the TUC

In 2001 the TUC – the representative body for the British trade union movement – embarked on a project to relaunch and reposition trade unionism, in order to make it relevant for the realities of employment at the beginning of the 21st century. The impetus for the initiative had been a fall in membership from over 12 million to just 5 million during the 1980s and 1990s, a reflection of the view that the movement was out of date with nothing to offer for today's working population.

There was considerable sensitivity over the project in some quarters of the movement, where conservatism held sway and notions like branding and image were, not surprisingly, anathema to union leaders. And, right across the movement, opinions on many issues were apt to vary widely and be tenaciously held. The precise make-up of the task force was, therefore, of crucial importance to the success of the project: it needed to reflect this breadth of opinion, to be seen to take account of minority views and to be strongly endorsed at the top in order to have any chance of moving from recommendation to action.

Ownership of the project resided at the very top. John Monks, then leader of the TUC, commissioned the project and, working closely with his deputy and his head of PR, chose the task force to guide it. Seven trade union leaders were on the team, either because they represented the biggest unions or because their unions, though smaller, were more forward-thinking. Outsiders were carefully chosen to balance the group and give it credibility, creativity, impetus and breadth. They included Will Hutton, journalist, broadcaster and chairman of the Industrial Society; Chris Powell, chairman of one of Britain's most creative advertising agencies, and communications adviser to the Labour Party; Richard Freeman, Professor of Economics at Harvard and author of *What Workers Want* (1999); and Nadya Kassan, who represented the emerging view of youth through her work with the National Union of Students.

This was the core team. To manage the project, moderate team sessions and physically implement the analysis and research, an outside marketing team was commissioned, which included one of the authors.

The project took eight months to complete – somewhat longer than would be normal in a commercial organization; this was a reflection of the complexity of the movement and the entrenched views of some union leaders. Its success was in changing the image of trade unionism without compromising ideals. New language, new ways of thinking and new channels of communication were all part of the final matrix. Today, the movement has two new internet brands, attracting people who would not have considered approaching a union before. Membership is rising for the first time in 15 years.

Which level to work at?

Brand belief is a potent force, with many implications. Where should it reside? At the level of the company, or master brand, or sub-brand, or product, or what? Which one of these entities is the best platform for the creation of a Passionbrand? The answer, as with so many questions in marketing, is 'It depends.' In this case, it depends on the kind of brand you are working with, the kind of brand architecture of which it is part and the kind of ambitions for future structure you envision. To some extent, therefore, it is a case of applying your judgement and common sense.

Certain decisions make themselves. In general, for example, it is better to work at the level of master brand rather than sub-brand: there is clearly not much point in lots of relatively small sub-brands having their own brand belief to activate, without some wider form of cohesion. On the other hand, it doesn't make much sense to agonize over the expression of beliefs of a brand owner – like LVMH – that, to all intents and purposes, is invisible to the consumer. Since brand architecture, and the relationship between company, master brand and sub-brands, is at the crux of these decisions, it is worth looking at a few examples to see how the options unfold:

- *Company brand.* This is the simplest structure, characterized by total unity between company (or organization) and the brand as it is perceived by consumers. Hewlett-Packard, the Red Cross and Qantas would all be examples. Brand belief, and the other manifestations of a Passionbrand identity, would, therefore, apply to company and brand alike. It would be impossible for people to draw any meaningful separation between them.
- *Strongly endorsed, linked brands.* Kellogg's cereal brands are an example of this structure. Coco Pops, Frosties, Rice Krispies, All Bran and the rest are all famous brand names in their own right, but are all strongly endorsed by the master brand, Kellogg's, in packaging and communications. The real meaning here, the guarantee of quality, the continuity of relationship, lies in that endorsement. It would not make sense, therefore, to attempt to create a Passionbrand identity for anything other than 'Kellogg's' – the master brand. In this structure, the product brands would simply be varying *expressions* of the core Passionbrand identity and belief.
- *House of brands.* Here the structure is that of a 'silent' brand owner with a stable of separate master brands. Diageo is an example. This £21-billion business is an expert marketer of big-name, premium drinks brands: Guinness, Bailey's, Smirnoff and Johnnie Walker among them. The development of a Passionbrand identity, in a company such as this, would be undertaken at the level of these master brands, and each would be distinct from the rest. Diageo itself, because it is invisible to the consumer and shows all signs of the continuance of this arrangement, would not be a realistic receptacle for brand belief and the other manifestations of a Passionbrand identity.

That said, as you work with the methodology for brands of this type, the wider ownership structure will have implications. So in the capability corner, for example, the financial resources of the owning company, and its relationships with distributors or retailers, would be taken into account.

- *Branded house.* This is like the house of brands structure with a complication – that the brand owner is visible, a brand in its own right. It is therefore the most complex of the structures we are looking at here. Unilever is in the process of moving to this kind of architecture. A brand owner of big, diverse, globally famous master brands like Lipton, Knorr, Dove and Lux, its own consumer presence has traditionally been recessive. This changed in 2004 with the introduction of a new Unilever logo, to appear prominently on packs for the first time, and a meta-identity based on 'vitality'. This structure presents two possibilities: that the Passionbrand identity resides at the level of the meta-brand – Unilever in this case – or that it resides at the level of the master brands – like Lipton or Knorr – with the caveat that each works synergistically with the meta-brand.

These are the principal architectures. Others are of course possible – Aaker, in *Brand Leadership* (2000), gives at least nine, although most are variations of the ones above. Choosing the right level at which to work, at which to tackle the methodology and at which to crystallize brand belief will, therefore, always be somewhat a matter of professional judgement.

Tackling the corners

The analysis of the four corners of the model can take place in any order, or even simultaneously if you have different teams assigned to each. Once the analysis is in, and shared, there is nothing to stop you going back over some of the ground again if new thoughts and issues come to light. The important criterion is that the work is objective, thorough and free from posturing or defensiveness. Illumination is what is required; the more light that shines in for the second phase, the better.

Over the next four chapters each corner will be looked at in detail, taking one at a time. For each of these four corner-specific chapters the format will be the same. We will start with an overview of the subject, then summarize the objectives of the analysis and then describe the kind of output you should be aiming for at the end.

Following that will be a review of some of the best tools and techniques for the analysis of the corner in question. There is nothing didactic about the use of any of these; they are suggestions for getting to the truth, no more than that. Not all will be new to everyone; not all are appropriate for every kind of business. So regard these sections, if you will, as more of a menu than a mantra – but, like any good menu, one with its fair share of interesting specials. The value curve, for example (in the environment corner), is an illuminating way to help you question your category assumptions; service mapping (capability corner) is an elegant method to identify real and perceived gaps in service operations; in the consumer corner both co-operative inquiry and discourse groups can help you gain far richer insight into consumer choices and actions. You'll find these among the 28 different tools and techniques outlined in the four chapters over all.

A journey of discovery

Finally, let us return to the metaphor evoked in the chapter heading: that of a journey. Experience working with teams as they probe the four corners suggests that the metaphor is amply justified, and that mere 'analysis' is too dry a term to describe the sensation of discovery that invariably accompanies the process. For marketers who spend their lives working with the brand at the point where it issues out into the market it is a journey upstream to the source, to the tributaries and half-hidden springs that make the brand what it is. To those whose normal view of consumers is through the prism of focus-group findings, it is like an anthropological expedition to an exotic tribe, a coming face to face with people who seem at once familiar and strange. For those who see in the competitive environment just the biggest rivals, it is like going back into the same landscape with a guide and being shown the camouflaged threats and opportunities that hide in the shadows.

The analysis of the four corners of the model is a journey to the four corners of the brand-world. It is a journey with the power to challenge, provoke and shock but, like any journey of discovery, is not without its delightful surprises either.

7 Corner no 1: ideology

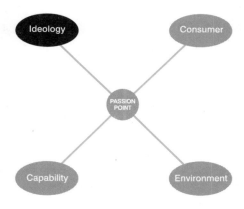

What is meant by 'ideology'? Most of us would intuitively grope for a definition somewhere in the mishmash of ideals, values, ethos and beliefs. The *Collins Compact Dictionary*, the kind of no-nonsense volume that sits on many a management desk, gives 'The body of ideas and beliefs of a person, group or nation'. It is the word 'body' that is instructive, with its sense of unity and coherence. A random mix of ill-sorted or opposing ideas and beliefs can hardly be called an ideology in the same way that one speaks of the ideology of Martin Luther King, or the ideology of Islam, or the ideology of Japan. It is ideological clarity that is impressive, that carries within it the power to change the world – and not just when exhibited by people, groups or nations, but also when exhibited by businesses and brands. The hallmark of some of the most famous companies on the planet (Sony, Hewlett-Packard, Apple, BMW, 3M), ideological clarity is also one of the ambitions of a Passionbrand identity, and a specific aim of the second phase of this methodology. But that is to jump ahead; that is down the line. Before you can work towards tomorrow's ideal, you need first to assess today's reality.

Objective of the analysis

The objective of the analysis is to arrive at an ideological audit of the brand and the organization of which it is a part. In some companies the trail will be easy to follow since the steps will already exist in some kind of visible form – as a written set of principles, a credo, a coherent statement of purpose, a list of company or brand values, and so on. Even so, a note of caution should be sounded, since what is written and what is reality can differ markedly. So normally some inference will have to be drawn from secondary sources – the way the company actually behaves, tacit understanding of culture and mores, unwritten codes and practices, word-of-mouth historical accounts, archived company material. Ideology can be like the body's soft tissue: every bit as important as skeleton and bone, but a lot harder to see on the X-ray.

Output

The output for this corner could be a document, a chart presentation or, possibly, just a single sheet of paper. Whichever of those it turns out to be, the headings should simply be the three below:

- Company or brand history and foundations.
- Current stated values and ambitions.
- Current day-to-day ideological reality.

There are two levels at which each of these headings can be attacked: the brand itself and the organization behind it. It is a matter of judgement where you focus your effort since the balance will vary according to the specific nature of the task you happen to be working on. In many instances it will make sense to look at the subject from both the brand and the company point of view. We will now cover each of the three points in detail, before identifying the tools and techniques that will help you to approach them.

Company or brand history and foundations

How and why was the company or brand created? Was it just something opportunistic at the time, or were there deeper roots and reasons? Often it's a case of both, so the subject will repay some exploration. You're looking for foundational belief, for the original vision, for the thinking that was big enough to create success out of nothing. What was that big idea? What was the founding purpose? What was the need that the brand was created to satisfy? These can be important clues to the underlying ideology that permeates the enterprise even today.

It would be reasonable to ask why this should matter, why events that happened back in the mists of time should have relevance for today's very changed circumstances. The answer is that, deep down, people don't change so much. If the foundational beliefs were strong enough to sustain a brand or company say a century ago, some version of the same belief might well be relevant today. More pointedly, the decline in a brand's fortune can sometimes be traced to the time it drifted away from its foundational beliefs, sensing them to be outdated, outmoded, an impediment to progress.

Kellogg's, for example, was founded in 1906 and became one of the world's most successful brands. But it hit the doldrums in the late 1990s with flat growth and declining margins. What might a review of the brand's origins reveal? What beliefs that were powerful at the beginning could still have relevance to today's world?

Kellogg's has an interesting history. The eponymous Will Keith Kellogg came upon the invention of the cereal flake through a combination of industry and accident. In 1894 he was working as a clerk at the Battle Creek Sanatorium, Michigan, a holistic healing facility where his brother was physician in chief. Their conviction that nutrition was an important component of better health, combined with their vegetarian commitment as Seventh Day Adventists, led them to experiment with new ways to provide a vegetarian diet to the sanatorium's patients. In the process of searching for a digestible bread substitute the brothers accidentally left a pot of boiled wheat to stand and become tempered. When it was put through the usual rolling process each grain emerged as a large, crisp, flat flake.

The sanatorium's patients liked these flakes, or at least liked them better than the dry, dreary fare normally on offer. But when WK Kellogg attempted to sell the flakes on the outside world he found acceptance more limited – until his innovative mind struck on the notion of adding a little malt extract. And so the formula for the success of one of the world's great brands was created: goodness made palatable. Will Keith never lost his passionate interest in nutrition, but he knew that normally healthy people would only continue to eat healthy food if it was combined with freshness and flavour.

Today, when concerns over obesity and nutrition run high, Kellogg's health-based roots and its historical involvement in diet are as relevant as ever. There is an argument that Kellogg's might do better by getting back closer to these original ideals. Certainly, they would feature strongly on any ideological audit for the brand. But on the other hand, you can see how the company would have to ask itself some hard questions about some of its endorsed sub-brands, like Froot Loops, which the American Dental Association accused of being 'no better than candy'. In fact it is not unusual for an ideological audit to throw up foundational themes and ideals that challenge some recent brand practice, and that tension is specifically explored in the second stage of the methodology.

Current stated values and ambitions

Where appropriate, record both brand and organizational values. For most brands, this will simply be a case of noting the values contained in the most recent brand briefing documents. Should values not be itemized in this formal way for your brand, they could be inferred from analogous headings like character, personality, essential purpose and so on. At the organizational level, values should be captured as typically stated in annual reports or the company website.

Ambitions are covered in this subsection because of their potential impact on ideology in the future. A typical example arises when brands contemplate geographical expansion only to discover that their core values don't travel well. Imagine, for example, an ice tea brand operating in Europe and the US with a core value of 'simplicity', dramatized by communications around the theme of 'Live simple', all reflecting the elemental nature of the drink. The brand is ambitious for growth and seeks entry into developing markets like Brazil and the emerging economies of South-East Asia. Trouble is, 'simplicity' is one of those values that is attractive in wealthy societies where it strikes a chord with those who yearn to de-clutter their lives, but is meaningless or worse in developing markets where, for most people, living simply is not a choice but an imperative. Ambitions and values can be mutually antagonistic and, since you will be looking to crystallize values for the long term in stage two of the methodology, it is vital to understand where the brand and the business might want to go in the future.

Current day-to-day ideological reality

An audit worthy of the name should record practice, not just theory, and often there is considerable variance between the two. When companies embark upon design audits, for example, they are often surprised and dismayed by the extent to which the standards so minutely documented in the design manuals are contravened in fascias, advertising, promotional material, even letter headings from head office. Sometimes the audit reveals a geographical skew, with standards rigidly applied close to home and allowed to run riot a hemisphere away.

It is no different with values. At the level of the brand, these can often be ignored or contradicted in the daily activities of hotly competitive commercial life. Inappropriate promotions, the wrong kind of sponsorship associations, a hastily judged line extension, geographical variance – these happen to the best-managed brands, and should be honestly captured by the audit.

At the level of organizational values, it is important to think broadly and ask whether these are applied at all links of the business chain. Journalists, commentators and anti-brand activists are apt to seize upon any divergence between a company's lofty stated ideals and the reality of its arrangements with those who might be less scrupulous.

Starbucks, for example, is proud to display its tenets of global and social responsibility in its outlets. But these have provided a focus for attack by activists who have accused the company of exploiting Third World farmers, albeit indirectly, through the links in its supply chain. In response, Starbucks has initiated a complete review of its relationships with suppliers and has begun actively to cultivate and reward those that can demonstrate environmental and social responsibility. In so doing, it has strengthened its *values integrity* – an important concept for Passionbrands.

Tools, techniques, tips

These are suggestions to help uncover the truth and reach insightful input for the three audit headings. Some of these suggestions are applicable for just one heading or another, while others will help across the board.

Don't ignore obvious sources

You've got to start somewhere. The obvious sources are worth checking to see if consistent themes emerge. So look at recent annual reports and see what the company is saying about itself to a critical investing public. See how this fits with the recent speeches from company leaders. Look at how the company describes itself in PR packs handed out to journalists. Better still, pretend to be a journalist writing about the sector, and call up the company for general information on values and vision and see what you get. The information packs given to new employees can also be revealing, which is why new people can sometimes have more of a handle on what the company's values are at least meant to be than the old hands. Finally, when was the last time you checked out your own brand or company website?

Revisit your current vision and mission statements

They might be vacuous, they might be bland, they might be interchangeable, they might be half-forgotten – but it makes sense to take stock of what they are. And, you never know, buried in there somewhere might be a nugget, a truth, an idea that could be reinterpreted to inspire again.

Seek out the 'living archives'

Talk to people who have been in the company forever – the longest-serving employee, people who knew the founders, people who worked at the place or on the brand when it was in its prime. Or talk to senior industry journalists or venerable commentators with long memories. See what it was that made the company famous, great, special in any way. Then see how that squares with the values and ethos of the company today.

The 5 whys

This is a technique suggested by Collins and Porras (2000) to help crystallize 'core purpose', which they define as 'the organisation's fundamental reasons for existence beyond just making money'. It will help, therefore, in questions about what is really important to the company and how its ethos defines its approach to business.

The idea is as simple as it is powerful. The team starts with a descriptive statement: 'We make X products' or 'We deliver X services', and then asks, 'Why is that important?' five times. In other words, it's an iterative process.

Every time you get to an answer, you probe again with the same question: 'Why is *that* important?' As Collins and Porras conclude, 'After a few whys, you'll find that you're getting down to the fundamental purpose of the organisation.'

Values Integrity Grid

The Values Integrity Grid is a way of plotting your stated organizational values against different links in the business chain. It gives an at-a-glance snapshot of *values integrity* – capturing the reality of where your values are consistently applied and where, perhaps, they are not. For example, a fashion brand whose values included 'freedom' was forced to concede that this value was contradicted in some of the supply-side manufacturing businesses with which it dealt, where union membership and open complaint were ruthlessly suppressed. Ideally, an organization's values should be manifest, or at least free from contradiction, in all facets of business activity.

Assess the delivery of your organizational values by breaking down the main activities of your businesses and recording where and how the values manifest themselves. The values should ideally total no more than five; the business activities will vary according to the type of business and its category. Table 7.1 shows the activities that would typically appear.

BT, for example, has five stated values: trustworthy, helpful, straightforward, inspiring and 'heart' (showing passion and commitment). In order to capture the delivery of those values the team would need to assess their tangible demonstration across the range of business activities. In all probability, not all values would be reflected across all activities, but the team would certainly want to see more ticks than crosses or question marks, and would want to take steps to address the serious lapses.

Examine your current CSR programme

Do the activities seem random or is there some kind of theme? If you sense a theme, does it relate to the company's business purpose or does it stand apart? A CSR programme can tell you how the company wants to think of itself, how it would prefer to be seen by investors, neighbours and the communities it serves – even if that differs somewhat from commercial reality.

Organizational culture framework

Organizational culture features in both of the internal corners of the model, so you'll be meeting it again under 'capability' in Chapter 8. Here, for the analysis of this corner, we are concerned with the ideological texture of your culture – its human face if you like – and the way it affects day-to-day life throughout the organization. The following tool contains a questionnaire to help determine what your culture might be – but goes further than that, to plot four different types of culture against the types of commercial situations to which they are most sympathetic. The insight it gives, therefore, is to show where tensions might exist between your culture-type and the desired human expression of your brand.

The tool was developed by Harvard's Goffee and Jones (1996), and juxtaposes two qualities – sociability and solidarity – within an organizational community.

In their definition, 'sociability' is a measure of 'sincere friendliness amongst members of a community'. High sociability implies a tendency towards compromise and harmony; conflict is avoided. But, as the following shows, there are disadvantages too.

High sociability plus points:

- friendly;
- share ideas;
- like compromise;
- happy places to work.

High sociability pitfalls:

- fear of criticism;
- management can be unsystematic – based on personal ties, not logic;
- can be slow to implement strategic change.

'Solidarity' – the second quality – is defined as a 'measure of a community's ability to pursue shared objectives quickly and effectively, regardless of personal ties'. High solidarity implies an acceptance of constructive criticism, and an attitude that favours solving problems by the best solution, rather than the best compromise. But again, nothing is perfect.

Table 7.1 Values Integrity Grid

Values	Business Activities						
	People	Product	Service Delivery	Suppliers	Partners	Community	Communications
Value 1							
Value 2							
Value 3							
Value 4							
Value 5							

High solidarity plus points:

- orderly;
- focused;
- can move quickly.

High solidarity pitfalls:

- intolerant of weak performance;
- up-or-out culture;
- can be so internally driven that they ignore outside threats

Now, by plotting each of these two qualities on a two-by-two grid you reveal four types of culture – Networked, Fragmented, Communal and Mercenary, each with its own distinct flavour, virtues and limitations (see Figure 7.1).

Goffee and Jones (1996) have shown that each of these types of organization can be effective in particular business situations – but there are also caveats:

- *Low solidarity, low sociability: Fragmented Organization.* Sounds off-putting, but these can be effective organizations. Think hospital consultants, barristers, manufacturers outsourcing piecework, virtual networks – in other words people working largely on their own, without huge reliance on other individuals within the organization. However, 'Working together, for you' is not going to be a believable corporate message.
- *Low solidarity, high sociability: Networked Organization.* Highly sociable, informal cultures. Networked Organizations can thrive where corporate success is an aggregate of local success, and sensitivity to local markets is a critical factor. But loyalty tends to be parochial, between groups of individuals rather than to the organization as a whole, which means that company-wide strategy can be difficult to implement.
- *High solidarity, low sociability: Mercenary Organization.* Mercenary Organizations can be extremely productive, and do particularly well in a highly competitive, fast-changing environment. Long hours, hard work and an exclusive focus on achieving business objectives are the norm. However underperformance is not tolerated and staff turnover can be high. Sharing ideas – and consequently creativity – is not a great feature of this type of organization.

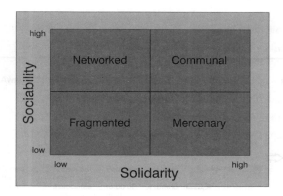

Figure 7.1 Two dimensions, four cultures

- *High solidarity, high sociability: Communal Organization.* Frequently found in start-ups – though this culture can continue to thrive in mature organizations with strong beliefs and values such as religious, political and civic organizations. Often considered 'the cultural ideal', communal cultures are characterized by a strong and universal commitment to business success, equitable sharing of risks and rewards and lavish social events. For commercial organizations they can be difficult to sustain beyond the tenure of the original founders and can be ineffective during periods of growth or change.

What are your organization's 'sociability' and 'solidarity' measures? Decide on whether you are looking at all or part of your organization and focus on the same area for all the questions shown in Figure 7.2. It is quite feasible for a division of a large company to have a different culture from that of the parent.

Use your answers to plot your place on the earlier two-by-two matrix; a lot of 'medium' ticks indicate a company on the cusp of two cultures.

Hang out

When David Bates took over as the new CEO of Krug the thing he did for the first three months was – nothing. No executive decisions, no consumer segmentations, no reorganizations, no rousing speeches. Instead, as Mark Ritson tells it, he 'hung out at the house of Krug, with the ancestors, with the family, at the site of production and he learnt about the nature, the style, the ways in which it was done. The guy imbibed the culture the way you'd imbibe the champagne.'

To assess your organization's level of sociability, answer the following questions:

	low	medium	high
1. People here try to make friends and to keep their relationships strong.	☐	☐	☐
2. People here get along very well.	☐	☐	☐
3. People in our group often socialize outside the office.	☐	☐	☐
4. People here really like one another.	☐	☐	☐
5. When people leave our group, we stay in touch.	☐	☐	☐
6. People here do favours for others because they like one another.	☐	☐	☐
7. People here often confide in each other about personal matters.	☐	☐	☐

To assess your organization's level of solidarity, answer the following questions:

	low	medium	high
1. Our group (organization, division, unit, team) understands and shares the same business objectives.	☐	☐	☐
2. Work gets done effectively and productively.	☐	☐	☐
3. Our group takes strong action to address poor performance.	☐	☐	☐
4. Our collective will to win is high.	☐	☐	☐
5. When opportunities for competitive advantage arise, we move quickly to capitalize on them.	☐	☐	☐
6. We share the same strategic goals.	☐	☐	☐
7. We know who the competition is.	☐	☐	☐

Figure 7.2 What is your organization's culture?

In the end, this is the ultimate source of knowledge: just being there, walking the place, talking with people who work in the company every day, imbibing the culture, the mores, the unwritten codes, the ethics that pervade the organization. If you can find the time, just get out there – to your outlets, factories, service departments, call centres, what have you and, yes, hang out. Hang out and take in. It's a kind of corporate ethnography – and, for getting as close as possible to the day-to-day ideological reality, warts and all, there is nothing quite like it.

8 Corner no 2: capability

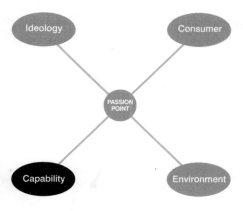

If you are working on a brand right now you will have some sense of your company's capability from the evidence in front of you – the product range or service itself. But this can provide, at best, only a superficial sketch of current status and does not tell you much about underlying strengths and weaknesses, nor how capability could be dramatically improved down the line nor, crucially, how different aspects of capability could be combined more imaginatively to create uniqueness in the market. Capability can lead to leadership – a quality that, as Drucker observes, 'rests on being able to do something others cannot do at all or find difficult to do even poorly' (2003).

Despite the enthusiasm of the academics, ignited by Prahalad and Hamel's 1990 paper 'The core competence of the corporation', capability has become a deeply unfashionable subject in marketing departments. Here the trend of interest has veered inexorably towards the consumer, and it is consumer knowledge, usually in the form of 'insights', that is seen as the most promising source of competitive advantage.

The relative lack of interest in capability results from the common acceptance that a lead can never be sustained for long enough to constitute an enduring advantage, in other words that anything one company can do today another will do tomorrow.

This view is questionable and defeatist. Of course, if it's a case of adding bells and whistles to an existing product line, then a competitor will get there sooner or later if the market looks attractive. But there are many examples of advances in capability that have proved very hard to copy by established competitors. Think counter-intuitively: it doesn't always result from the ability to do *more*; the successful no-frills airlines have given established players like British Airways and Qantas huge problems to overcome by doing *less*. The corporate structures, cultures and existing operational investments of the big airlines make it almost impossible for them to reciprocate in kind.

A similar disregard for accepted industry practice is at work at Zara, the world's fastest-growing retailer. Where other international fashion retailers rely on a network of slow-moving and separate suppliers, Zara makes more than half its clothes in-house. It can design a new line from scratch and get it into its shops in just three weeks, against an industry average of nine months. This flexibility means that its inventories are lower than those of competitors, and its designs are always more current: it produces 10,000 new lines a year and none is in the store for longer than a month. A unique low- and high-tech capability mix has made this flexibility possible. Zara's network of local seamstresses, in 400 co-operatives around its home base in La Coruña, Spain, is directed with the help of advanced, real-time sales data systems that provide instant feedback from the stores. None of Zara's rivals have come close to matching either its speed or its growth; sales are up an average of 27 per cent a year since 1998, through outlets that have exploded from 180, mainly in Spain, to 626 in 44 countries. For Zara, capability does not sit apart from marketing but is a part of it – and a vital part at that.

Another blind spot in current mainstream practice is the tendency to underestimate the 'soft' capability hidden away in areas like database management or trade relationships. If a company has better strengths than its rivals in these disciplines, then they will eventually lead to financial advantages that could be reported to the bottom line or, more pointedly, reinvested in breakthrough innovation. Kellogg's is an example of a business that, under the new leadership of Carlos Gutierrez, has recently improved its capability – not simply by improving its product, but by getting on better terms with the world's biggest retailer, Wal-Mart, with which it previously had frosty, and costly, relations. Capability derives from the total of a company's separate abilities and resources, and the different possibilities for their combination, and these are not apparent from a cursory glance at the end results.

Objective of the analysis

The objective is to provide the raw material for the kinds of decisions you will make in stage two of the methodology. At that stage you'll be looking for ways to improve your end product, and will need to know what the company is really capable of deep down. You will be looking for ways to harmonize capabilities more effectively to offer long-term differential advantage. And because Passionbrands are about activating belief, because they refuse to become – in Klein's memorable phrase – 'all strut and no stuff', you'll need to ensure that belief and capability are aligned.

To do all that, the place to start, in this first stage, is with a frank and considered appraisal of your capability as it stands today.

Output

The final output will be a summary of the capabilities and resources, both tangible and intangible, of the company behind the brand. These will be broken down into subsections as follows:

- *Tangible:*
  – operational;
  – financial;
  – assets.
- *Intangible:*
  – culture;
  – knowledge and relationships;
  – reputation.

This follows the pattern of analysis that would typically be undertaken by a management consultancy such as McKinsey as part of an overall assessment of corporate strengths and weaknesses. It will not, however, take the nine months or so that a McKinsey would require, since the breadth and depth of analysis we propose are adapted to suit the purpose in hand – crystallizing brand identity – and to reflect the normal realities of time and cost.

We will now look at each of the subdivisions of the analysis in turn, before moving on to the tools and techniques designed to help you uncover the truth.

Tangible

Operational

Operations is reality. It is the practical means by which the business keeps its promises to customers. It is lines and tools and processes and schedules and systems and shipments and people. It is organization. It is quality control. It is service delivery. And it is money.

If money were no object, operations management would still be a tough gig, but there would be one less factor to worry about. As it is, the conflicting demands of higher quality, faster speed and the endless pressure on cost make the discipline one worthy of considerable respect.

For those working on brand strategy, that respect should simply take the form of a common-sense understanding of the factors that impinge on brand development. You will want to know, and note, how operations sets and achieves the levels of cost and quality, and what (if any) opportunities exist to achieve an enhancement to either. You will want to learn if there is any spare capacity and, if so, where. You will want to hear the ideas of your operations people for improved efficiency, and how that might affect your brand.

Above all, you will want to understand the knock-on effects of ideas and innovations you might generate down the line, and at least have some kind of feel for their operational practicality. New packaging idea? *But how quickly can the line retool?* A switch to fairly traded raw ingredients? *But what are the current contractual supplier arrangements?* A breakthrough service guarantee? *But how quickly can recruiting be done, and how would you account for the additional cost?*

Operations is a massive subject, so there is neither any hope of nor any point in preparing a full audit for this kind of exercise. But an idea of the basics, a list of the considerations and a note of personnel to get back to when the innovation ideas start to flow are a minimum to work for. It's a way of ensuring that future brand strategy is as practical as it is luminous.

Financial

It will already be apparent that there is some overlap between the disciplines of finance and operations. They are both practical disciplines and, in each case, it is the practical implications for brand strategy that concern us here. The level of financial detail required, therefore, does not equate to a thorough financial audit. Rather, the aim is to generate an overview of the financial health of the company in order to keep any recommendations about the brand realistic and achievable.

The guiding question, then, is 'What are the financial parameters for developing the brand?' For example, is high investment in the brand a realistic option? Does the company have cash? What is the company's borrowing capacity? What is its internal funds-generation capacity? Can the company weather any fluctuations in demand? How fast would a return need to be made? What are the demands of the owners or shareholders likely to be?

Equally, you might need to take a view of the importance to the company of the unbroken maintenance of current revenue from the brand, since improvements that might pay dividends long-term can sometimes involve sacrifices short-term. You'll recall that the Co-operative Bank's ethical restructuring, though eventually very successful, first resulted in a loss of revenue from the closure of profitable business accounts.

Aside from other considerations, ambitious brand plans need to carry the whole organization with them, and that includes the finance director. That person will be greatly reassured to know that financial factors have been sensibly appraised up front.

Assets

'Assets' embraces both physical and human resources. Again, a working knowledge is what is required, rather than a highly detailed breakdown. And again, the point is to understand how the subject might constrain – or liberate – brand development and strategy.

Physical resources include the size, location, technical sophistication and flexibility of plant and equipment, and reserves of raw materials. Location and alternative uses for land or buildings could also be important. All of these resources can influence the firm's set of production or service possibilities and determine important aspects of its cost position.

Crossover between physical and human resources can be an especially important factor – like a first-rate R&D facility with first-rate brains, or a modern call centre with well-trained operatives.

Other important human resources include the sales force, customer-facing staff and people with specialist skills. For each of these you will want to get a feel for levels of training, commitment, adaptability and unionization. For an example of the potential significance of this kind of information, look no further than Zara's network of local seamstresses.

Intangible

Culture

Culture is an amorphous subject with implications for both of the internal corners of the model. Arising from the well of the organization's values, understanding and beliefs, culture manifests itself in behaviour, norms and inclinations. These in turn play a role in shaping the company's capability, which is what concerns us in this subsection of the analysis.

Is the culture entrepreneurial? Is it conservative? Is it far-sighted? Does it favour self-starters or team players? Does it cherish innovation? Is it 'can-do' or is it 'get-permission-first'? Is it goal or process? Is it formal or touchy-feely? Does it like to experiment or does it 'stick to the knitting'?

Understanding these, and other, behavioural traits and biases is another step towards knowing what the brand might be capable of in the future – which developments would be supportable and which would cause discomfort. This can be especially important in service businesses, where radical changes to brands that involve people and behaviour are often best handled through the creation of a new entity – as HSBC did in the UK with the telephone and internet bank First Direct.

Knowledge and relationships

In this subsection you're seeking knowledge about knowledge. What are the company's unique, or special, skills? What exceptional expertise resides in small teams or individuals? What proprietary knowledge exists? Is any of this protected by patents, proprietary technology or copyright? If so, when do these run out? (This is a big issue for drugs companies – and for others too; as an aside here, consider the tale of woe at Lego when, according to one insider, the expiry of their patents for Duplo caught the company by surprise, so that it was not prepared for the rapid entry of other companies, such as Megabloks, into the market. This story, alone, should act as a cautionary note to anyone who feels that all these stages of analysis might be getting a bit superfluous!)

Good relationships with suppliers, distributors and trade and retail channels also imply know-how, since they don't just happen by accident. It takes a certain ability, temperament and experience to build relationships or to develop strong negotiating positions, and, although we might file this kind of knowledge under headings like 'intuition' or 'nous', that is not to denigrate its importance. If your company or brand relationships are particularly strong then you should note, separately, its general skill in this area – since it could perhaps be applied in other ways and therefore be a factor in future brand development.

Reputation

Capability is not just about producing better goods or services, but also about ensuring their acceptance and success in the market. Brand and company esteem is therefore to be regarded as part of overall capability since bold, new ideas are more likely to be taken seriously by both consumers and intermediaries if backed by the right kind of reputation. Your audit should seek to appraise honestly the reputation of the brand, and the company behind it, with customers, partners, suppliers, trade commentators, competitors, bank, local community and, if appropriate, higher levels like government or the civil service. It can be salutary to examine the reality of your brand image with these audiences, as against the desired image contained in your current brand statements.

It is also important to log what we shall call 'brand scars' – events from the past (or present) that have served in some way to injure the brand, leaving behind some kind of negative memory trace. As an example, consider the ill-starred 1999 initiative of the British foods retailer Iceland to go all-organic in its fresh and frozen ranges. This bold and imaginative stroke was arguably ahead of its time and certainly out of step with its relatively downmarket customer base. It failed, publicly and expensively, almost bringing the business to its knees. Clearly, any major new initiative by the business would need to consider this 'brand scar', and probably stay well clear of similar ground in order not to arouse immediate negative comment bent on dredging up the past.

Finally, an estimate of brand valuation should be included as part of this analysis. It will give you a benchmark against which to judge the success of future activity, and is a potent reminder of the sheer value that you are dealing with – and that alone should be an incentive to proceed with both thoroughness and flair.

Tools, techniques, tips

This is a menu of options to help with the analysis. The points are ordered to follow, as closely as possible, the analytical flow outlined above.

Start with interviews

A broad overview of capability can be gained by a series of one-hour interviews with the most senior people in each of the areas described above. They should include the operations director, finance director, head of R&D and head of HR. Decide what you want to learn, prepare a discussion guide and try to encourage candour by ensuring confidentiality.

Service mapping

Service mapping is a useful technique for understanding the operational realities of service companies and identifying where trouble spots might occur. A service map works by visualizing the direction of the flow of processes. Some of these will involve interaction with customers; some will not. For example, in a fast-food restaurant, order taking involves the customer, while washing up does not. The service map captures this distinction by separating types of activity into two zones divided by a 'line of visibility'. Activities shown in the map as above the line of visibility are those that can be directly perceived by the customer; activities shown below the line are those that are invisible to the customer.

Figure 8.1 shows an example service map for an auto repair business. It was generated by first listing each process in the order in which it is performed, then identifying those that involve the customer and those that do not, and then visualizing this information, adding connecting lines to show relationships and direction as appropriate.

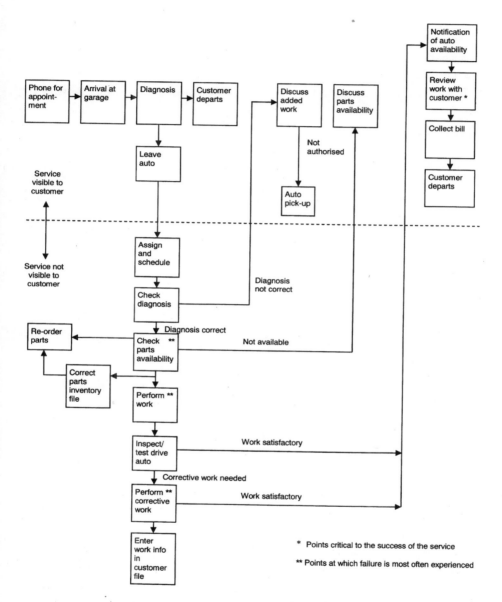

Certain concepts are adapted from G Lynn Shostack, 'Service Positioning Through Structural Change', Journal of Marketing, January 198, pp. 34–43
Source: James L Heskett, 'Service Breakthroughs'. The Free Press 1990

Figure 8.1 A service map for an auto repair business

Service mapping can help uncover potential failure points by showing where processes have too many steps, where operations infrastructure is poorly designed or where there are steps that do not add value to the customer's experience of the service as intended – for example, a fast-food restaurant where an over-abundance of options involves too many loops between waiter, customer and kitchen, slowing down the delivery of the food.

Financial ratios

One way to judge a company's financial health is to look at financial ratios. By relating balance sheet or P&L numbers to each other they provide more insight than raw numbers alone. For example, a firm's current assets and current liabilities as simple numbers contain only limited information but related as a ratio – say 2:1 in favour of assets – they indicate the firm's ability to meet short-term demands from short-term funds.

Financial ratios divide into four groups:

- performance;
- liquidity;
- long-term solvency;
- efficiency.

Performance ratios are worth looking at relative to the sector – as they will yield an objective view on how the company is doing in its class. Liquidity ratios and long-term solvency ratios are useful because they will indicate what expectations you can make about levels of investment – the former in the short term and the latter in the long term. Efficiency ratios can tell you how well particular areas of the business are operating; they are probably the least useful from a brand perspective.

Table 8.1 is a table of the ratios that will be useful in this kind of analysis. In order to generate them you will need your own profit and loss, balance sheet and cash flow statements – as well as those, if possible, of your nearest competitors. Ideally, you will also have the input of your financial director, who will help navigate the different accounting procedures used by different companies and business structures.

Behaviour framework

The most recent research suggests that there are seven primary characteristics that, on aggregate, capture the essence of an organization's behavioural culture. By plotting these on a simple grid and assessing each on a five-point scale, you can produce a composite behavioural picture (see Figure 8.2). Alternatively, if you sense that the organization's behavioural culture is not homogeneous, you can complete the grid for different functions – like R&D or Training – in order to capture the degree of variation and the extent to which it might become a barrier to more effective capability.

Internet sentiment monitoring

What is the prevailing sentiment 'out there' towards your business or brand? How good, bad or indifferent is your corporate reputation? In what direction are opinions moving? Today, it is the internet that will provide the answers – if you know how to look. Vast, dynamic, with tentacles reaching into every kind of subculture and class, the internet serves as both a repository for and an agent of consumer and professional opinion. But its 550 billion documents, most of them unstructured, in multiple electronic formats and languages, present something of a barrier to an informal trawl. As a consequence, internet-based sentiment monitoring has become a highly sophisticated research technique requiring specialized software. Accenture's Sentiment Monitoring Services prototype, for example, uses an advanced 'perception engine' that analyses texts in all formats and languages and interprets the underlying sentiment towards the specified company, brand, product or service with a 90 per cent degree of accuracy.

This chapter, along with the preceding one, has focused on the internal analysis – factors concerned with the brand itself and the company behind it. Over the next two chapters we move on to the external analysis – factors outside the company and, for the most part, beyond its control.

Note

Background information on financial ratios was derived from Doyle (1994) and Pendlebury and Groves (1999). The behaviour framework is based on information from Robbins (1998).

Table 8.1 Financial ratios

Ratio	What it is	Why it's useful	Comments
Profitability			
Return on equity	Net income divided by average shareholder funds.	An indication of how well managers are using shareholder funds.	Average UK ROE is about 18%. Most companies are 5–40%.
Return on assets (ROA)	Trading profit (BIT) divided by average total assets.	Measures the return a firm earns on all its resources.	
Return on capital employed (ROCE)	Operating income divided by capital employed.	Focuses on non-operating sources of funds.	Capital employed is all liabilities and shareholder funds. Generally a better measure of return than ROA.
Net profit margin	Net income divided by sales.	Indicates net profit for every £ of sales.	Will vary across industries. Also reflects business strategy.
Gross margin	Gross profit divided by sales.	Marginal contribution of every £ of sales.	Usually expressed as a percentage.
Operating margin	Operating income (BIT) divided by sales.	Operating profit for every £ of sales.	
Liquidity			
Current ratio	Current assets divided by current liabilities.	This is the margin of safety for meeting short-term cash obligations.	Generally ideal number is slightly more than 1.0.
Quick ratio	Current assets minus stock divided by current liabilities.	More conservative than above.	Ideal is slightly lower than 1.0.
Cash ratio	Cash plus short-term liabilities divided by current liabilities.	Very conservative version of the above.	

Table 8.1 Financial ratios *continued...*

Ratio	What it is	Why it's useful	Comments
Solvency			
Capital structure ratios	Total debt divided by total capital. Total debt divided by shareholder funds.	Measures the proportion of debt in the company capital.	Industry factors and stability of earnings will affect this.
Interest cover	Profit (before interest and tax) divided by interest expense.	Measures the extent to which a firm's earnings cover interest costs.	Generally – the higher the better.
Cash interest cover	Net cash flow from operations plus cash interest divided by interest paid.	Number of times cash flow from operations covers interest payments.	As above.
Cash from operations to debt	Net cash inflow (after interest and tax) divided by total debt.	Measures ability of the firm to meet debt repayments.	
Efficiency			
Stock turnover	Cost of sales divided by average stock.	Efficiency with which firm uses stock.	Need to look at relative place in category.
Debtors' turnover	Sales divided by average debtors.	Tells you the number of debtors turned around.	
Creditors' turnover	Purchases divided by average creditors.	Tells you the degree of credit available from suppliers.	
Fixed and total asset turnover	Sales divided by average fixed assets. Sales divided by total assets.	Tells you the sales generated using either £1 of fixed or total assets.	The bigger the number the better!

	1	2	3	4	5
1. Innovation and risk taking					
2. Attention to detail					
3. Outcome orientation					
4. People orientation					
5. Team orientation					
6. Aggressiveness					
7. Stability					

Definitions:

1. The degree to which employees are encouraged to be innovative and take risk.
2. The degree to which employees are expected to exhibit precision, analysis and attention to detail.
3. The degree to which management focuses on outcomes rather than the techniques and processes used to achieve these outcomes.
4. The degree to which management decisions take into consideration the effect of outcomes on people within the organization.
5. The degree to which work activities are organized around teams rather than individuals.
6. The degree to which people are aggressive and competitive.
7. The degree to which organizational activities emphasize maintaining the status quo in contrast to growth.

Figure 8.2 Behaviour framework

9 Corner no 3: consumer

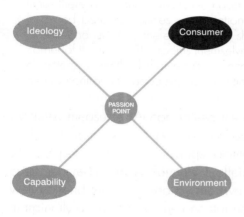

This book opened with a critique of consumer-led brands. It argued that modern marketing practice, with its slavish devotion to consumer whims and directives, was leading brands on a road to nowhere. Thousands of brands, we showed, were suffering from telltale symptoms of malaise: too much similarity, a gradual loss of clarity, little real innovation, *no soul*. How, then, do we arrive at an entire chapter, at the heart of the book, as part of the governing model, dedicated solely to the consumer?

The answer is that Passionbrands are subject to the same commercial forces as all brands, and among these is the consumer. It could hardly be otherwise. A vital stage of the journey towards a Passionbrand identity, therefore, is a real understanding of the real people who exert that force. But there are three big differences between this approach and that typical of consumer-led brands:

1. *Understanding, not direction.* Consumer-led brands look to the consumer for direction. Should the brand do this? Could it be that? What if it communicated like so? Passionbrands do not. They seek, instead, the kind of close-woven understanding that leads to

empathy with people and an intuitive feel for their needs – by far the best springboard from which to imagine ways to serve them better.

2. *Balance, not obsession.* The business guru Tom Peters, in his stage-strutting, virtuoso management seminars, has been known to encourage 'an obsession with the consumer'. Like all obsessions, this one is unhealthy. It leads to narrow, blinkered brand stewardship, and dull, undifferentiated brands. By contrast, the aim of the model is to keep essential forces in balance, so that consumer understanding is one input among others and is used – in combination, not isolation – to guide, challenge, stimulate and inspire.

3. *Depth, not superficiality.* The contemporary approach to consumers, for all its focus and obsession, is characterized by shallowness. Consumers are contacted often, through research groups, about the same things: about the brand, about image, about buying rather than using. The approach we will explore here, by contrast, seeks to look beneath the surface, to sense the underlying currents in the lives of people and their relationships with brands. It will look at what people do, not just what they say. And it will not seek to add weight to commonplace findings by calling them 'insights'. This deeper approach, as we shall see, implies research methodologies, and their combination, that move more slowly but get to the heart.

Objective of the analysis

The objective is *rich description* of the people who buy and use the brand, or who might do so in the future. Rich description starts with the basics – like who your customers are and how they use the brand – and then progresses to more finely grained detail of behaviour, desired identity and the cultural, social and psychological factors that influence contemporary lives.

Output

The output will be a summary or presentation, which should include photographic reference as well as verbal description. Video material, where possible, is also valuable. The analysis should be governed by the following headings:

- *Customers:*
  - the basics;
  - the brand in their lives;
  - consumption in their lives;
  - their lives.
- *Non-customers:*
  - use the category but not the brand;
  - don't use the category.

We'll now look at each of these subsections more closely before moving on to tools and techniques to help you uncover the truth and help you achieve the objective of rich description.

Customers

The basics
You will need to capture the demographics, geographics and psychographics for your current customers:

- *Demographics* are: age, gender, ethnicity, education, income, occupation, marital status, presence or absence of children.
- *Geographics* are: countries, regions, density of population, urban v rural split, climate.
- *Psychographics* are: social class, lifestyle, subculture.

Next, the important numbers. How many customers? How many loyal? What proportion of sales accounted for by which key groups (eg 80 per cent of volume from top 20 per cent of customers, or 70 per cent profit generated in Asia Pacific)?

You should note the relationship between buyers, choosers and influencers – particularly relevant in business-to-business categories. And try to get a view on who your mavens are. Celebrated in Malcolm Gladwell's best-seller *The Tipping Point* (2000), these are the people who evangelize for your brand through their active networks of colleagues and friends; they can account for a disproportionate influence in your brand's popularity and spread.

The brand in their lives
This subsection is about behaviour and motivation. It is important to capture not just what people do but also why they do it.

How and why do consumers choose the brand? Is it simply utility and habit, or is there more to it than that? What is the extent of peer group influence? Is there an inter-generational role – for example, a desire to choose (or avoid) the brand because of familial associations? How much is choice influenced by notions of self and identity – for example, choosing organic products to affirm a self-image of youth and well-being?

The consumption experience: how would you describe it, in its totality? It is important here to focus not just on the choosing and buying, but also on the using, sharing, reflecting and disposing, all of which can influence future brand choice and related meanings.

At what point during the entire experience is the maximum value of the brand released? For example, a pasta sauce could confer maximum value when bought, when displayed, when the aroma is released on opening, when it transforms the dull-looking pasta with its red richness, when it is served and first tasted, or at the end of the meal, in the afterglow of satiety. There might conceivably be two distinct moments of maximum value release – one each for functional and emotional value. Or the same moment might combine both, providing, say, the functional benefit of colour as the sauce pours into the pan and at the same time evoking pleasant emotional identification with a more relaxed, Mediterranean way of life. The Moment of Maximum Value Release can tell you a surprising amount about the real emotional relationship between consumer and brand.

Finally, is the brand part of some kind of informal brand community? Does it promote a set of structured social relationships among users? The classic example is Harley-Davidson, which, as shown in the seminal study by Schouten and McAlexander (1995), was the focus of an extraordinarily robust and supportive social network. The Harley sense of bonding borders on the religious, but weaker affinities based on shared brand usership have been recorded in more everyday categories from cosmetics to alcoholic drinks.

Consumption in their lives
Start with the category and its place in the lives of your customers.

Is it a category that people buy every week (like soft drinks), a couple of times a year (like suncare) or once in a while (like cars)? Is use of the category characterized by promiscuity (like shampoos), inertia (like banks) or comparatively strong loyalties (like newspapers)?

What about emotional feelings towards the category? If you imagined a spectrum that runs from the utilitarian, at one end, to the hedonistic, at the other, where would your category sit?

It is important to understand how new people enter the category and, conversely, why they might leave. Is it governed by life-stage? Is it status related? What is the influence of peer group, or celebrity?

Once these baseline category facts are in place you should widen the lens a little to look at consumption in a more general sense, since ideas and trends can exert influence across permeable category boundaries.

This is best tackled by thinking about two important, related concepts in consumption theory: Brand Constellations and the Diderot Effect. In different ways, these concepts converge on the desire for harmony and symbolic consistency in people's lives.

The Diderot Effect is named after an 18th-century French philosopher, Denis Diderot, who noted how the gift of a new dressing gown altered his perceptions of the study in which it hung (McCracken, 1988). Whereas his previous 'ragged, humble wrapper' had been harmonious with the poor bric-a-brac that filled the room, the new 'imperious gown' put its surroundings to shame. Diderot found himself gradually replacing items in the room so that they matched a common aesthetic standard that the gown had set. The Diderot Effect is a powerful and frequently overlooked factor in modern consumption with implications for brand design; a new set of towels in a bathroom, for instance, could start a process that raises the aesthetic thermostat sufficiently to expose the previously unnoticed flaws of an inelegant bubble bath pack. Tim Clark, of Emirates, has explored its use to positive effect. Noting the raised levels of appreciation for good interior design, driven in part by the popularity of TV programmes like *Changing Rooms*, he shunned the 'bureaucratic style' of the standard aircraft cabin interiors offered by Boeing and Airbus, and commissioned a designer of luxury yacht interiors to create something more daring, eclectic and contemporary for the Emirates fleet.

Brand Constellations take the theme of harmony a step further, to the symbolic level, and describe a tendency to favour products from diverse categories that serve to promote symbolic consistency. A brand constellation for a young, professional girl-about-town living in the UK, for example, might include Evian, Café Rouge, Top Shop, Nokia, iPod, Maltesers, Adidas, Nurofen and Ikea. As part of the analysis for this corner you should look at the kind of constellation of brands among which yours would sit – from the consumer's point of view, of course; it is not a wish-list!

Their lives

Now we move beyond the brand, beyond the category, beyond consumption, to look at the lives of your customers in a more general sense. Clearly, though, some structure needs to be imposed here since 'people's lives, in general: discuss' is a theme too broad in scope to be either useful or manageable.

As ever, it pays to think first about the purpose the information will eventually serve. It is to help identify ways to improve the brand's value and appeal to customers that might not be evident through a study of consumption practice alone. Experience has shown that the most fruitful way to achieve this objective is to divide the analysis into three sectors: life habits, life themes and life projects.

Life habits means the routine (or, quite conceivably, lack of routine) that typifies the day-to-day lives of your customers. Here, techniques like audio or video diaries can be highly illuminative. The aim is to capture the 'life in the day' of your typical customer (or, should the 'typical customer' be hard to pin down, of a representative sample of customers). Seemingly irrelevant details and candid observations can all count; don't be afraid to record them. Even though it is hard to know what will be useful at the outset, the richness of the material can be inspiring when you're looking for breakthrough thinking in stage two of the methodology.

Life themes are the social and cultural influences that affect your customers and help shape their desires. These are the prevailing winds by which modern life is buffeted, and a knowledge of their direction and force is a vital part of understanding how people navigate their lives. Be prepared for considerable variation according to where your customers live. In Northern Europe, for example, life themes for young adults might include the all-pervasive influence of technology, an increasingly competitive career ladder, too little time and the issues of longer-lived parents. In Asia Pacific, life themes for the same group might include inter-generational tensions brought about by much newer patterns of personal freedom, the conflict between a new individuality and an ancient urge to conform, and the social and practical problems of chronic lack of living space.

Life projects are the roles and identities that your customers choose in their lives. They will tend to be multiple, aspirational and complex, sometimes played out simultaneously and frequently in conflict. To be a good mother, a successful lawyer, a supportive friend, a caring daughter, a better tennis player – these are all life projects, and they will be in constant flux, to be intuitively weighed and balanced, with trade-off, compromise, pride and guilt their natural accompaniment. But if the reality of life projects is messy and often frustrating, the desire that underpins them is the most interesting thing you can know about your customers. It tells you not so much who they are but *who they want to be*.

Non-customers

Why study non-customers? Primarily, because they always outnumber customers, often by a considerable margin. Logically, therefore, issues, trends, movements, subtle changes, sweeping innovations are more likely to be spotted outside your customer base than within it. As Drucker (2003) observes, 'The first signs of fundamental change rarely appear within one's own organisation or among one's own customers.' Costas Markides (2000), in his book devoted to strategic innovation, suggests that thinking about non-customers can result in 'a new customer segment that is emerging because of changes in the industry, or an existing customer segment that other competitors have neglected, or even a segment that has been created from the existing customer base through more creative segmentation'.

Non-customers matter; they can sometimes be as indicative of future brand strategy as any other single factor, so an understanding of who they are and what motivates their choices can repay dividends. For the purposes of this analysis, there are two subsets of people to consider: those who buy the category but not the brand; and those who don't buy the category.

Use the category but not the brand

Some of these people will simply be outside the target for your specific segment of the category. But what about those who are very much inside your desired target group and who still do not choose the brand? Understanding why could provide a valuable early warning system for brand health and could do it before current customers walk and join the non-customer group.

For example, in the early 1990s Motorola enjoyed world leadership in the market for cellular handsets. Perhaps if the company's marketers had understood more about the motivations of the small but increasing numbers of people choosing Nokia, they would have been able to respond more quickly to the subtle changes in the dynamics of the market that eventually propelled Nokia to the number one slot.

Don't use the category

Understanding more about why people don't buy into the category can be a springboard for real strategic innovation.

For example, Enterprise Rent-A-Car is a company that owes its success to the identification of a new group of customers who, until the existence of Enterprise, were simply not in the car rental market. During the early 1970s, Enterprise, at that time a car-leasing firm, realized that there were opportunities for car rental in local towns. So, rather than slugging it out at the airports for the attention of the business traveller alongside Avis and Hertz, they set themselves up in local towns where people lived and worked – offering a free pick-up service as part of the deal. As a result, people rented cars when they might not have done: when their own car was being repaired, for the weekly shop, for viewing real estate, for family days out. By the mid-1990s Enterprise had become the biggest car rental company in North America, and now owns the world's largest private vehicle fleet.

Tools, techniques, tips

What follows is a menu of options to help you reach better answers to the questions raised in each of the subsections of the analysis. We'll review research techniques first and then move on to tools and frameworks to help you probe the way consumers make choices in your category.

Mix research methodologies

This is the most important advice of all. Any research technique is subject to bias and will suffer shortcomings of one sort or another. This means that no one methodology should be relied upon in isolation to provide robust data. The academic ideal is triangulation: a mix of both qualitative and quantitative methodologies of different kinds so that the findings of one can be balanced and cross-checked with those of the others, allowing truly significant themes to emerge and to be validated with a high degree of confidence.

Five qualitative techniques for richer research

Focus groups have their place. But for richer findings, sharper detail and greater rigour, try combining them with one or more of the qualitative method-ologies below. The last two of these are currently at the leading edge of academic research into consumption behaviour.

Market-oriented ethnography

Ethnography is a technique that gets up close and personal, putting researchers in the midst of the social and cultural life that is the subject of their study. Originating in the social sciences, made famous by the anthropolo-gists Sir Edward Evans-Pritchard and Margaret Mead, the ethnographic method starts with a deceptively simple question: what's going on? And it seeks the answer, not in what people say, but in what they do.

Market-oriented ethnography (Arnould and Wallendorf, 1994) typically implies four to six weeks of observation, in the appropriate real-life context – homes, offices, hospitals, streets – with video running much of the time, care-fully logged and time-coded by the researchers. A period of adjustment is usually allowed, in order to reach a point where the presence of the video is ignored and ceases directly to affect behaviour.

The observation is not aimless; it must ensue from some kind of ingoing theory and an understanding of commercial objectives. (Ethnography is often used to check out how well the hypotheses derived from other research actually play out in the field.) What it produces at the end is rich, actionable discoveries that might not have been uncovered by standard techniques alone. There is nothing quite like the detail, the low-down earthiness of well-conducted ethnographic research, and this candour, together with the under-lying patterns identified by skilled interpretation, can often make for the most illuminating and challenging debrief of a marketer's career.

Ethnography can be used in many commercial and not-for-profit contexts. The Kansas-based specialist Ethnographic Research Inc has documented a wide range of successful uses over recent years (Ritson, 2003):

> Ethnography has been used to discover why injection drug users share needles (it isn't part of the 'culture' of drug use; it is because needles are expensive and hard come by). Surveys could not get there. Ethnography has been used to document mothers' needs and convince marketers and product designers of the importance of potential profits to be had by developing diapers that kids can put on alone. Ethnography has revealed the complexity of baking in India and the importance of texture, smell and storage in selecting and using flours for the family hearth. Ethnography has helped uncover what doctors think they

are saying to their patients, and what patients actually are hearing their doctors say. It has been used to discover the range of faces that should be put on greeting cards for US Latinos. And it is being used every day in the design of office systems, furniture, new food products.

Ethnography Lite

If a full-on ethnographic study is ruled out by budget or timing realities, you can still take advantage of techniques that owe their existence to the ethnographic school. Audio diaries, video diaries and accompanied shopping trips all make use of established ethnographic concepts, since they all record behaviour in its appropriate setting, and capture, in all their richness, the sights, sounds and spontaneous feelings of people in real-time, real-life contexts.

Nor should the value of simple empirical observation be underestimated. It might have saved Wal-Mart some embarrassment when it first launched in Brazil. As *The Economist* (2003) relates, 'The aisles in its stores were too small because it hadn't noticed that shopping in Brazil was a family outing, so aisles needed to accommodate grandma and the children as well. The aisles were widened.'

Depthnography

With a little imagination, you can devise depth-interview research exercises that relate specifically to your market but meet ethnography half way, so that interview and in-context observation are combined. The technique is based on the phenomenological interviewing methodology used by Susan Fournier of Harvard and first described by Thompson, Locander and Pollio (1989).

For example, a fashion brand wanted to know more about how women chose clothes. The researchers visited the homes of women and asked them to 'talk them through' each garment in the wardrobe – relating the story of how and why it came to be bought, when and where it was worn. It revealed a depth of understanding that could never have been achieved out of context since the clothes themselves prompted each woman's memory and allowed her spontaneously to recall significant practical and emotional details that would have remained subliminal in any other setting. As well as providing this more finely grained understanding of the motivations behind fashion choice, the technique also served to provide the researchers with a better visual image of the women's lives, homes and general appearance and the way they stored and cared for clothes.

Co-operative inquiry

Co-operative inquiry challenges one of the most fundamental aspects of conventional qualitative research: the notion that some kind of 'we' studies some kind of 'them'. Instead, this fledgling methodology seeks to close the separation between researcher (traditionally the active agent) and respondents (traditionally the passive subjects). The result is 'active subjects', fully aware of the objectives of the research, and fully participating in the exploration of their own behaviour and the extrapolation of meaningful conclusions. Underpinning this radical thinking, developed by the academics John Heron (1996) and David Reason (1988), are both practical and moral considerations: it is a way of avoiding the artificiality of conventional research methods and of dismantling the power-based relationship implied by the practice of treating people as mere objects of scrutiny.

Co-operative inquiry breaks with the terminology, as well as the methods, of conventional research. Subjects are called 'co-researchers'. Together they form an 'inquiry group'. In its purest form, the methodology demands that the inquiry group sets its own research objectives through discussion. A group of peers – health workers is the classic case – might meet to decide what issues merit their combined involvement. In most commercial contexts this is impractical, so the methodology described here is a slightly more dilute form than that espoused by Heron and Reason.

Typically a researcher will work with an inquiry group of between three and six people, will have an embryonic idea of the objectives of the research and will discuss these with the group in the initial meeting. This discussion might yield modifications to the objectives if it is felt by all that the outcome will be improved in some way. Imagine, for example, a researcher seeking to understand more about the way people deal with personal finance, and their emotional interface with the financial category. The objective might be modified by agreeing to include only certain sorts of financial transactions as meaningful, or perhaps by separating them into two subject areas, the serious and the everyday.

Once the objective is finalized, the researcher and the group work together to agree the best way to generate behavioural data. It might be agreed that diaries are kept, video-logged, friends interviewed. Timings would then be agreed and rules of contact between co-researchers established.

Throughout the live research period, the co-researchers would be actively seeking to make sense of their own behaviour in relation to the objectives they have helped to refine. It is this that yields the principal benefit of the methodology, since self-awareness is heightened through involvement; results show that when there is a clear point to behavioural reflection it is done with a surprisingly penetrating honesty.

The group meet on the agreed day to share their experiences and explore the motivations that guided their behaviours. The researcher's role will be to prompt, listen to and capture these responses – but not to lead them in any particular direction. The findings would be documented by the researcher but the main points would be first circulated among (or discussed with) the group so that all co-researchers could suggest modifications, themes and ideas. A final draft would then be written up and shared.

Co-operative inquiry is still in its inception, and its commercial application has been developed as recently as 2004 by one of the authors – Edwards – as part of research into consumption habits. But already its virtues are apparent: more penetrating glimpses into human behaviour that derive from the committed engagement of intelligent people with an objective they understand. As people become more aware of standard market research techniques, and more savvy, cynical and disingenuous in their response to them, co-operative inquiry will be well placed to become one of the seminal qualitative methodologies of the future.

Discourse groups

Discourse groups work a little like focus groups but with one important difference: they capture naturally occurring speech, with all its asides and overlaps, rather than the carefully ordered exchange that results from the direction of a moderator.

In discourse groups the researcher welcomes people into a room where there is some stimulus material laid out, and sets them some kind of task. The purpose of the task is simply to provide the impetus to get people talking and give them an initial angle from which to proceed; it is not necessarily important in its own right. For example, the stimulus might be new product concept boards and packs, and the task set might be to put them in order of likely success. What is of interest is not so much the final order, but the dialogue that the task provokes.

The researcher then leaves the group alone for an agreed period of time to interact with the stimulus, and with each other, totally un-monitored. There is no two-way mirror, and the group should be reassured of that if necessary. The aim is to generate, and record, spontaneous reactions, and naturally occurring speech, no matter how random and incomplete.

It is precisely this lack of control that gives the methodology its unique flavour. There is no moderator bias. People react and return to the stimulus in the manner and the order that occurs naturally, and if there is any bias at work it is their own. There is no careful guidance. If items are ignored then that, in itself, is considered valuable information – more valuable than the persistent probing of a moderator to wring out some kind of reaction, come what may. The 'problems' of dominant and recessive individuals within the group are accepted as more reflective of real life, and the way people defend or alter their positions according to the personal dynamics in the room is considered of value in its own right.

In analysing the data, the methodology draws on the tenets of discourse analysis (Elliott, 1995, 1996) – an interpretive technique derived from psychology – which searches first for the inconsistencies in what people say and then looks for the deeper patterns that nonetheless hold true. The tenor and tone of the speech are seen as important, and exclamations, inflections, sighs, yawns and gaps are all noted.

There are practicalities to consider in the use of discourse groups. You need to have multiple microphones to pick up all speech as people move about the room. You should aim for 'rich stimulus' in order to provoke stronger reactions – items that people can pick up, manipulate, open, smell. And you should allow for a high tape-to-transcription ratio, since all conversational asides and nuances are captured.

If you mix this methodology with normal focus groups you will almost certainly gain a richer understanding of what people really feel about the stimulus. For example, in research conducted by the authors into a new banking product, a transparent credit card was shown in both focus and discourse groups. In the former, the respondents sought to make sense of the card and articulate what they thought it was meant to imply – openness, clarity and so on. In the latter they simply reacted at the visceral level – along the lines of 'I *love* that! I *must* have one of those!'

Which reaction really counts? Both – which is why the mix of methodologies is the real lesson here.

Five steps to better qualitative interpretation

1. Transcribe the tapes.
2. Listen to the tapes with the transcription in front of you, marking it for intonation, enthusiasm, sarcasm and other aspects of language and communication that would not otherwise be apparent from the transcription but would affect meaning.
3. Code the data into conceptual themes. You can do this either by highlighting passages in different colours or through a cut-and-paste process on the PC.
4. Now read through the data again, this time theme by theme.
5. Leave the work for a day or two and see which themes stick in your mind, and then return to the transcription and consider what relevance each theme has to the objectives of the research.

Don't ignore old-but-good quantitative techniques

There is a temptation in consumer research to go for the newest fad, but this natural desire for currency can mask the power of techniques that have stood the test of time. In the quantitative sphere, for example, conjoint analysis is still the most useful tool for determining with accuracy the relative importance people put on product or category features, including price. By forcing respondents repeatedly to trade off pairs of values, and assigning weightings to each as it goes along, it can capture the optimum combination with a high degree of confidence. The technique is therefore useful in looking at new market segmentation or calibrating product features.

Brand relationship typology forms

As part of a research initiative that explored the nature and meaning of people's relationships with their chosen brands, Susan Fournier (1998) developed a typology of different consumer-brand relationship forms (see Table 9.1). Understanding and defining the type of relationship your different consumers have with your brand, and with competitor brands in the category, can generate insight and help shape strategy.

Customer choice chain

What are companies competing for? They are competing for choice – for customers actively to choose their brand and to keep on doing so. But choice is not a simple matter; it is not like an on–off switch. Instead, a process is involved – a chain of activity with the aim of moving a person from ignorance of the brand, at one end, to committed advocacy, at the other.

The customer choice chain, developed by Lars Finskud (2004), is a fact-based visualization of the seven stages that link those two extremes (see Figure 9.1). But to view it as a natural and inevitable flow towards advocacy is, of course, misguided since the natural pull – the inertia force – is backwards, down the chain, not forwards along it. Rather like the blood in your leg, which must be continually pumped upwards though muscular action to combat the natural pull of gravity, and checked by valves in your veins to prevent backflow, the propulsion of customers along the choice chain only results from active effort and must be shored up at every stage. But marketing resources are finite and the profile of relative strengths and weaknesses for each brand is different: one brand might have great awareness, for example, but weakness in converting users into ambassadors; another might be far less well

Table 9.1 Brand relationship typology forms

Relationship form	Definition	Example
Arranged marriages	Non-voluntary union imposed by preferences of a third party; intended for long-term exclusive commitment, although at low levels of affect.	Adopting a husband's preferred brand of packaged food or toothpaste.
Casual friends, buddies	Friendship low in emotion and intimacy, characterized by infrequent engagement and few expectations for reward.	Household cleaners.
Best friendships	Voluntary union based on reciprocity principle; endures because of continued provision of voluntary rewards.	Performance products for enthusiasts – such as sports equipment.
Kinships	Non-voluntary union with lineage ties.	Inherited brand habits such as household medicines.
Flings	Short-term, time-bounded engagements of high emotional reward but devoid of commitment and reciprocity demands.	Holiday of a lifetime, trial products.
Secret affairs	Highly emotive, privately held relationship considered risky if exposed to others.	Treats of all kinds – designer lingerie.
Committed partnerships	Long-term, voluntarily imposed, socially supported union high in love, intimacy and trust and a commitment to stay together even in adversity.	Male relationship with sports car marque.

Table 9.1 Brand relationship typology forms *continued...*

Relationship form	Definition	Example
Marriages of convenience	Long-term, committed relationship precipitated by environmental influence of circumstance rather than deliberate choice.	Retailer choice because of location.
Compartmentalized friendships	Highly specialized, situationally confined, enduring friendships characterized by lower intimacy but higher socio-emotional rewards. Easy entry and exit.	Low-priced cosmetics.
Courtships	Interim relationship on the road to a committed partnership.	Baby nappies, wipes.
Dependencies	Obsessive, highly emotional attachments cemented by the view that the other is irreplaceable.	A long-established skincare brand.

Source: Adapted from Fournier (1998)

known but convert a higher proportion of informed consumers into quality perceivers. The value of the framework is to help you define which points will disproportionately repay expenditure of resources and energies: to identify the leverage points, if you like.

To do this you will need numbers for each stage and, ideally, numbers for your competitors too. If you imagine 1,000 potential consumers, how many are aware of the brand? Of these, how many make it into the next box – 'informed'? And then so on, up the chain.

It quickly becomes apparent that mere awareness is no guarantee of success. For example, Figure 9.2 compares customer choice chain data in fast foods in Canada. Harvey's wanted to know why its relatively high awareness level – 886 out of 1,000 – yielded just 105 'committed customers' at the other end of the chain. By comparing statistics at all points in the chain with McDonald's, Harvey's identified where its weak spot was:

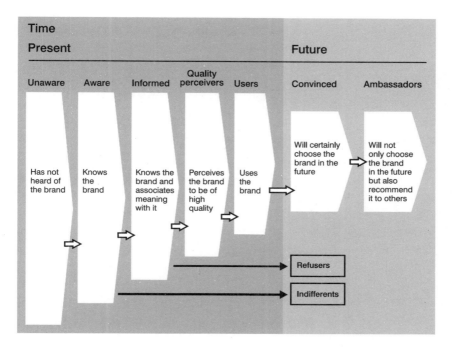

Figure 9.1 The customer choice chain

in converting 'quality perceivers' into 'users'. Although its base of 'quality perceivers' was high, compared with McDonald's it did far less well moving them along into the next box. For Harvey's, which had been considering opening more outlets to increase its reach, the data led to a new strategic focus: a redeployment of resources to improve the 'values fit' in the young adult segment in order to stimulate greater usage.

The customer choice chain is not dissimilar to the Millward Brown Brand Pyramid™ concept that we looked at in Chapter 2 (and both are related to the classic AIDA motivational model). Either of these tools can be a real eye-opener into what is really going on in the way customers perceive, use and choose your brand – and the points at which your brand might have something to learn from its competitors.

And on that appropriate note – choice and competition – we move on to the final corner of the model: environment.

Note

Background information for this chapter is derived from Arnould *et al* (2004).

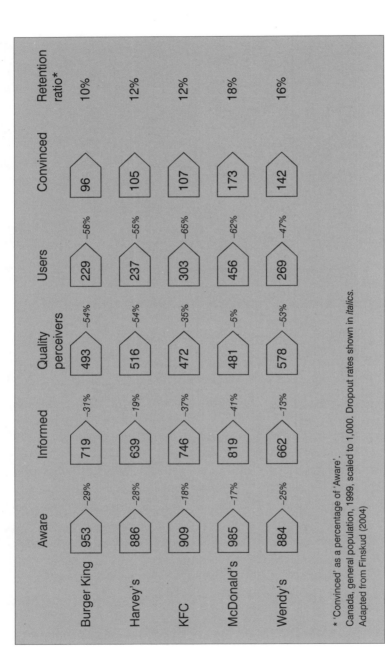

	Aware		Informed		Quality perceivers		Users		Convinced	Retention ratio*
Burger King	953	−29%	719	−31%	493	−54%	229	−58%	96	10%
Harvey's	886	−28%	639	−19%	516	−54%	237	−55%	105	12%
KFC	909	−18%	746	−37%	472	−35%	303	−65%	107	12%
McDonald's	985	−17%	819	−41%	481	−5%	456	−62%	173	18%
Wendy's	884	−25%	662	−13%	578	−53%	269	−47%	142	16%

* 'Convinced' as a percentage of 'Aware'.
Canada, general population, 1999, scaled to 1,000. Dropout rates shown in *italics*.
Adapted from Finskud (2004)

Figure 9.2 Comparing customer choice chains in fast food

10 Corner no 4: environment

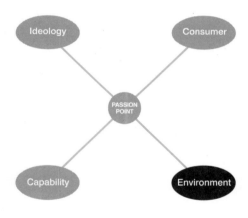

This chapter is about context. It looks at the broad environment in which your brand must earn its living. It is the most dynamic of the corner-subjects so far, the most prone to sudden change and therefore the hardest to pin down. But it matters. A brand can have terrifically attractive values, backed by superb, proprietary capability, fused with a good understanding of consumers and still fall victim to a force that comes out of the environment, seemingly out of the blue, and decimates shareholder value in a matter of months. Look at Polaroid for an example of all of that. Like Kodak, it was tripped up by a new technology and missed the signals that pointed the way to the digital revolution. Its fall, if anything, was even more dramatic since the category it dominated – virtually owned – shared with its unbranded, unconsidered rival the distinguishing feature of instant imaging. The lesson is that competition can come from directions other than the competitive set, and that even total dominance of a category can be of little comfort when there are predators that can devour the category itself. This is why the analysis of this corner is designed to consider both micro (within category) factors and macro (general environmental) factors that might affect future brand strategy. None of this is to imply that the analysis is all geared to defence; it might be a jungle out there but it's always worth keeping in mind that jungles are profuse environments with rich opportunities for the swift and aware as well as mortal dangers for the un-evolved.

Objective of the analysis

The objective is to gain an overview of all the factors in the competitive environment that might affect the success of your brand – from competitor activity to upcoming legislation. Since the competitive environment is in constant flux and since you will need to project forward in the second phase of the methodology, some sense of prevailing trends, as well the documentation of current facts, is required.

Output

The output should be a summary or presentation, complete with appropriate photographic and video material, governed by the following headings:

- *Micro:*
  - the category and its assumptions;
  - the immediate competitive set;
  - category hotspots and warning signs.
- *Macro*:
  - the Big Five factors;
  - macro hotspots and warning signs.

We'll now look at each of these subsections in more detail before reviewing the tools and techniques that could help you with the analysis.

Micro

The category and its assumptions
As ever, basics first. How do you define the category in which your brand operates? What are the main strategic divisions within it? The female bath and body-care category, for example, can be divided into

three broad segments: 'everyone/everyday'; 'premium' (sometimes called 'mastige', a somewhat unattractive elision of 'mass' and 'prestige'); and 'luxury'. Each of these broad sections can then be plotted on an axis of 'cosmetic' and 'natural' so that the best way to view the category as a whole is with a simple grid (see Figure 10.1).

It is likely that a grid along not dissimilar lines will be possible for your category and, if so, this of course should be captured for the analysis. The space occupied by your brand on the grid can also be plotted.

Next, make a note of the prevailing 'category assumptions' – the generally accepted success factors without which it is tacitly agreed that no brand in the category can prosper. Then – much harder, but tremendously useful for the second stage of the methodology – probe which of these might be open to question, might be challenged by a brand determined to gain leadership by doing things differently.

The academics Kim and Mauborgne (2004), famous for the development of the value curve (about which more below), point to the Belgian cinema market in the 1980s as an example. In a hard-pressed industry, with movie-going in steep decline owing to competition from videos, satellite and cable TV, the factors necessary for mere survival, let alone prosperity, were seen to be self-evident: the conversion of existing city-centre properties to multiplex formats with smaller viewing rooms, combined with an expansion of food and drink services and increased showing times. All of the cinema operators that had survived the industry shake-out adopted that formula.

But these category norms were eventually challenged with spectacular success when Bert Claeys opened Kinepolis: the world's first megaplex. This massive, specially commissioned, 25-screen, 7,600-seat centre on the outskirts of Brussels offered movie-goers a radically superior experience. Seats were oversized and there was so much legroom that people

	Everyone/ everyday	Premium	Luxury
Cosmetic			
Natural			

Figure 10.1 The main strategic divisions in the female bath and body-care category

could pass without anyone having to stand up. Screens were colossal and sound systems more powerful and sophisticated than anything offered before. With ticket prices at the same levels as those of competitors, the new concept won a 50 per cent share in its first year, growing the market into the bargain. Kinepolis is now by far the dominant force in the Belgian cinema industry, and the concept has been rolled out success-fully into other markets in Europe and Asia. The assumption that Claeys had challenged was the need for city-centre locations. By abandoning that one category norm and locating each megaplex outside the city, Claeys was able to achieve the lowest cost structures in the industry and thereby fund an irresistible cinematic experience.

The immediate competitive set

First, a general overview. (This is the kind of updated data that should be at the fingertips of any good marketing department.) How many competitors are there? How concentrated? How differentiated? How dynamic?

For each competitor brand, what are the size, market share and growth trend? Which brand is the most recent new entrant? Which brands have most recently disappeared?

Next, a who–what–how strategy for each competitor – *who* are they targeting, with *what* products or services, and *how* do they deliver their offer to customers?

Example: a who–what–how analysis for the UK internet bank Smile

WHO: 25+ young professionals
serious about money
plan for the future but still want to be seen as
fun and young

WHAT: internet-delivered banking services; personal
accounts only

HOW: internet only; no other channels
low charges – achieved through simple structure
accessible, non-banking language
easy-to-use interface
strong use of colour, wit, topicality
credibility and structure through backing by
Co-operative Bank

You should make baseline observations of each competitor's marketing implementation: proportion of resource devoted to each communications discipline, amount of NPD activity, extent of price promotion, and typical distribution pattern.

Try to summarize strengths and weaknesses of each competitor today. Then try to look forward: what would you say is the future strategy for each competitor? What likely new entrants could there be, with what strategies? Where are the threats to your brand most likely to come from?

Category hotspots and warning signs

These should start to emerge from the analysis of the subsections above. Hotspots are areas of unusually intense activity or change within the category – a flood of new entrants into one strategic sector, for example, or the rise of one type of format at the expense of others. This has happened recently in the yoghurt market, with the rapid growth of probiotic and drinking yoghurts; it almost certainly points the way to a future based on health rather than sweetness. Warning signs, conversely, would include the demise of brands from a strategic sector. Or it could include shrinkage of the category as whole, resulting, perhaps, from an unexpected change in consumer behaviour. It is precisely this kind of mundane, easily available data that could have provided early warning to both Kodak and Polaroid of the advance of digital photography. Sales of film were on the slide well before either company took action to confront the new technology.

Macro

The Big Five factors

The five macro factors are demographics, economics, socio-politics, legislation and technology. Anyone who's done a PEST analysis (politics, economics, social, technology) will have confronted something similar but, while that stalwart of MBA programmes is designed for overall corporate strategic planning, our five factors would be studied as they relate specifically to the brand and its future. Clearly, the relative importance of each factor will vary according to the nature of the category that your brand happens to inhabit; socio-politics, for example, is particularly important to charities and NGOs; demographics is particularly important to brands with single, age-specific targets, like mothers of young children. Nevertheless, to suit our purpose here, it will be more vivid and practical to view each of the five factors through the lens of a constant category, and to that end we have chosen, based on recent, personal experience, the European yoghurt market as a kind of running example throughout.

Demographics

How could demographic trends affect your brand? By 2015, for example, a quarter of the EU population will be over 60. In 2025, China will reach its projected maximum population of 1.5 billion. By 2030, over 60 per cent of the world's population will live in cities. By 2050, whites will be a minority group in the United States. None of these changes is that far off, yet any might have an impact on future brand strategy.

How might demographics be important in our yoghurt category example? Europe's rates of childbirth – the lowest on the planet – and an ageing population are both significant factors. The projections call into question the traditional focus on children as the natural target for yoghurt – since there will be 3 million fewer children in 2008 than there were in 1999 – while opportunities for health-preserving product niches present themselves at the other end of the human lifespan. The projected increase in single-person households could also be a factor, as yoghurt, with its neat pot format, is easily presented as a single-person snack.

Economics

You should study those economic factors that will affect expenditure on your category in the markets in which you operate. At the broadest level this would be GDP growth, but usually more relevant are levels and projections for personal disposable income (PDI) and employment and salary trends.

In many European countries, low interest rates, a buoyant housing market and stable employment have ensured that PDI levels have remained high. Projections are upbeat. In the UK, for example, a PDI index figure set at 100 for 1998 is projected to rise to 133 by 2007. For the yoghurt category, this kind of continued, broad-based prosperity might signal a chance to develop the indulgent, or even luxury, end of the spectrum.

It can help to look at historical, as well as projected, economic patterns. Long-term trends – those that started some years back and seem to persist despite short-term ups and downs – can sometimes expose new areas of opportunity for brands. The United States, for example, has seen the gradual emergence of a new 'mass affluent' class over the past three decades. Figure 10.2 shows how, in 1970, household income levels were skewed strongly towards one end of the spectrum. A huge proportion of households brought in virtually the same, modest amount of money. Past that hump, the numbers of households earning at greater increments fell off a cliff. Market offerings in many categories, therefore, saw a polar split between the very basic and the very expensive – a $2 toothbrush at one end, say, and a $1,000 tooth-whitening procedure at the other.

By 2000, however, the curve lines on the graph had smoothed out. There is still a peak at one end but, beyond it, there is now an attenuated slope, indicating that each incremental income bracket is populated by more households than before.

P&G have developed three successful products specifically designed to appeal to this new mass affluent class: the Swiffer, the SpinBrush and Whitestrips. Each is strategically designed to recognize both the willingness of these consumers to pay for a more refined offer and their continued inability to make the leap all the way to the really expensive end of the market. The Swiffer, for example, at $25, sits somewhere between a $5 broom and a $90-a-day maid. Whitestrips teeth whiteners and the SpinBrush both cost many times more than the $2 toothbrush but many times less than whitening procedures or cosmetic dentistry.

Socio-politics

What socio-political issues might affect your brand? A review of governmental agenda items and important consumerist lobby group themes can all repay efforts. Our yoghurt team, for example, would record government initiatives on health – like the UK government's 'health4schools' scheme – and monitor lobby-group action aimed at curbing obesity and controlling the sugar content of foods; a knowledge of government's attitude to advertising, especially to younger people, would also be important. This information could be helpful not only in shaping the offer of any single brand, but in determining where new usage of the category might come from: a switch from biscuits to yoghurt as an acceptable, everyday children's treat, for example.

Legislation

All recent and upcoming legislation that relates to the category should be noted. Our friends in the yoghurt world, for example, are battling,

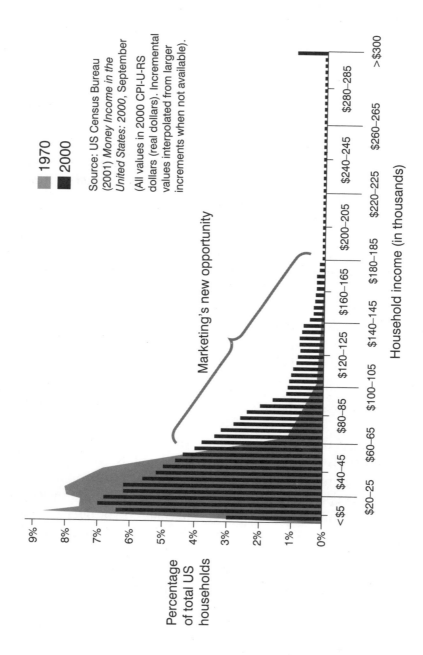

Figure 10.2 The emergence of mass affluence

as we write, with proposed EU legislation that would compel the product sold on UK shelves to be called 'mild alternate culture heat-treated fermented milk'. (Imagine getting *that* into a snappy slogan, or working it into your TV ads: 'Thanks, mum! My favourite mild alternate culture heat-treated fermented milk!') The reason for the proposal is that the UK yoghurt industry uses a different bacterium from the one used in mainland Europe.

Whatever your brand, any proposed move into new categories or new geographies should automatically be accompanied by a thorough review of the legislative complications involved. And beware the traps that the trend to outsourcing is starting to create. For example, the manufacture of many beauty-care products is outsourced and the responsibility for conforming to new legislation can sometimes fall into a hole between the parties; at least one brand has recently fallen foul of new EU legislation that has drastically cut the permitted levels of certain fragrance ingredients in products used on the skin.

Legislative change is not, of course, all about the downside. Changes in the law can also provide big opportunities. These are sometimes well-signposted changes – such as the deregulation of the airline industry, which paved the way for the new, low-cost carriers – but sometimes less obvious legislative change can also lead to entrepreneurial initiative. For example, changes in pension legislation in the UK, scheduled for 2006, will allow residential property to be held as part of a pension fund for the first time. This could pave the way for financial services providers to create buy-to-let packages designed specifically for this new market. The overall message is that the study of an apparently tedious subject can lead to surprising new angles in brand strategy and product development.

Technology

Technology can be the trickiest of the Big Five. Technology moves at such a pace that it can be beyond the scope of any team to monitor all its possibilities for brand enhancement. Or the problem can be the other way around, when exciting developments based on new technology seem all too apparent, seem so obviously to promise a bold new future, only to disappoint in reality, usually through failure of uptake.

A few years ago, for example, many were predicting that digital printing would signal the demise of traditional paper-printed products; instead of buying a newspaper, it was thought, you would arrive at a news-stand and plug in your 'eBook' to download the news, which you would then read comfortably off its neat little screen on the bus. Well, here's a digital dream that didn't fly. WAP, similarly, failed to live up to its early hype, and has only recently started to recruit users with applications like the download of ring tones and Java games.

Predicting which technologies will capture the imagination of a fickle public is notoriously tough. The best approach to the analysis, therefore, might be the humbler one of looking at the kinds of problems or issues your category needs to solve and then looking out at technologies in other categories that might have 'crossover potential' for yours. To come back to our yoghurt example, one of the current issues in that market is the need to find ways to break out of the pot-and-spoon format, in order to achieve the street-cred necessary to attract more young adults. Looking at new technological solutions for product delivery in other markets might give clues. The current boom in drinking yoghurts was itself initiated by a technological advance in the production process that allowed for a longer shelf-life and solved the problem of product separation in the bottle.

In many markets, technology can also be important as a secondary influence – where innovation outside the category has a knock-on effect on demand within it. The battery industry, for example, is currently riding high, with a 20 per cent volume growth between 1999 and 2003, thanks to the popularity of new technologies like digital cameras and digital video cameras. Within a market like this, a grasp of technological trends is vital, since it can tell you where to focus your efforts: button-cell batteries, for example, will grow with the increasing proliferation of remote car-locking systems.

Macro hotspots and warning signs

The aim is to look beyond the category for forces that could have an effect within it. Macro hotspots might include, for example, the rise of ethical consumerism, which according to the latest report is now worth £25 billion in the UK alone. According to Charles Middleton, managing director of a bank that invests exclusively in businesses with social, environmental and cultural aims, 'There are very few industries in which there is no possibility of bringing some environmental and social ethics to bear.'

Health trends can also repay careful observation, irrespective of the category of your brand. Allergies, for example, are a medical hotspot, with the incidence of asthma, eczema and hay fever all doubling in rich, Western societies over the last 10 years. P&G, alert as ever, has been smartly off the blocks to respond to the trend. In 2004 its Ariel Non Bio became the first detergent to offer consumers allergy-free washing after securing the seal of approval from the British Allergy Foundation.

Macro warning signs include the rumblings of international affairs that could have implications for the brand. Of growing concern, for example, is the degree to which provenance can become a liability following military action. Clearly, US brands have become vulnerable on this dimension since the 2003 invasion of Iraq. In an analysis on 30 December 2004 the *FT* explored the prospect of the subtle tarnishing of US brands in the minds of millions of ordinary consumers: 'If the American dream played such an important role in the growth of iconic US brands,' it asks, 'what happens if significant numbers of consumers begin to think the US is a bit of a nightmare?' Country of origin is not something any brand can alter, of course, but there is no doubt that the dial of nationalistic pride can be turned up or down. HSBC, for example, is a brand that presents itself as a citizen of the world, rather than highlighting either its origins in Hong Kong and Shanghai or its current incorporation in the UK. Similarly, as Figure 10.3 shows, some US brands are – for better or worse – perceived to be a great deal less American than others.

Techniques, tools, tips

As with the other corners, this section should be viewed as a menu of options. The aim is to help you reach better conclusions to the analysis of the subsections above.

Some thoughts on defining the category

The problem of category definition can cause (often unnecessary) agonizing and has been explored at length by Levitt, Markides and Drucker, among others, who tend to attach great significance to the amount of scope that the definition offers. The classic cautionary tale is that of the US railroads, which missed the coming revolution in road and air transport by defining their category as, simply, 'railroads' rather than, much more presciently, 'transport'. The trouble with examples like this is that the benefit of the broader definition is only really evident with hindsight. In a fluid modern world where

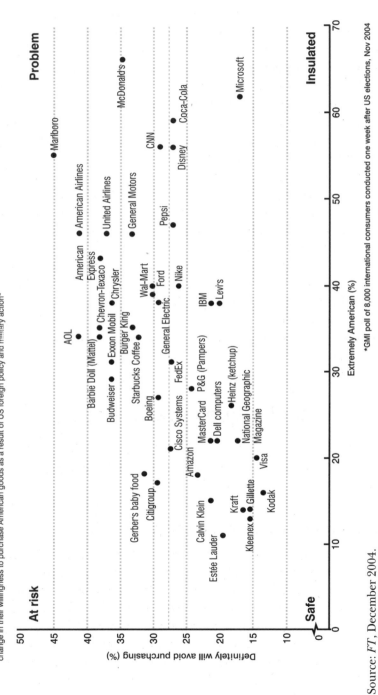

Source: *FT*, December 2004.

Figure 10.3a International attitudes towards US brands

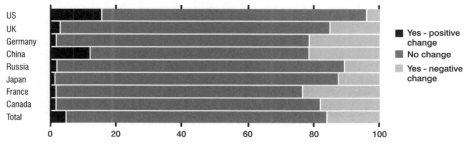

Source: *FT*, December 2004.

Figure 10.3b International attitudes towards US brands

competition might one day come from almost anywhere, these cautionary tales can paralyse attempts to do a necessary job with clarity and speed.

So don't deliberate for too long. Common sense dictates that the way forward is to apply two simple criteria: the category definition should be broad enough to reflect the realities of consumer choice and narrow enough to make comparisons with competitors both possible and meaningful.

For example, The Sanctuary is a UK brand that makes a range of indulgent spa products to be used in the home. It could therefore, quite properly, define its category as 'premium home spa', in which it would find itself competing with other spa brands like Dead Sea Magik and Nirvana. But the reality of consumer spending decisions makes this too narrow because The Sanctuary competes for bathroom pamper-spend with non-spa brands – like Origins, Korres and Boots Natural Collection. At the other extreme, The Sanctuary could equally justify the definition of its category as 'female discretionary self-pampering expenditure', along with products as diverse as magazines, chocolate and lipstick. This reflects the reality of consumer choice since money earmarked for a personal treat is not necessarily destined for a predetermined sector. But the definition is too broad to be practical, offering little scope for meaningful comparison with genuine competitors. If The Sanctuary spent its time watching the chocolate market it could miss important developments closer to home.

So The Sanctuary sensibly defines its category as 'female bath and body-care'. This, as we have already seen, can be broken down into six strategic groups, and The Sanctuary's offer can be mapped in one of these: premium/natural. This gives The Sanctuary a way to prioritize finite marketing time. It carefully monitors, first, its own strategic group, and then the category as a whole – and, of course, keeps an occasional eye on developments that might come from outside to threaten the share of treat-spend attracted by the category.

If you want to read more on the issues and implications of how you define what business you're in, the most practical academic source is Markides, *All The Right Moves* (2000).

Value innovation and the value curve

Value innovation is a way of looking at the assumptions made by your category – the category norms, if you like – and asking yourself which of them could be challenged in order to create a dramatic leap in customer value. Developed by Insead's W Chan Kim and Renée Mauborgne, the process begins with four questions:

1. Which of the factors that our industry takes for granted could be eliminated?
2. Which factors could be reduced well below the industry's standard?
3. Which factors should be raised well above the industry's standard?
4. Which factors should be created that the industry has never offered?

It is the first two of these that are counter-intuitive, and especially no 2. It is by no means an obvious step, when embarking upon a programme of improvement, to first ask yourself how you might dramatically *reduce* the standard of certain factors well below industry norms. And yet it is precisely this probing that allows managers to liberate resources for dramatic gains in areas that customers value more.

The Accor Hotels case quoted by Kim and Mauborgne in their original 1997 paper (republished 2004) is still the most inspiring example of the technique in use. It starts with the problems facing the French budget hotel category in the mid-1980s: stagnation and overcapacity. At that time there were two distinct segments in the industry. At the cheap end were the no-star and one-star hotels. Room rates were 60–90 francs per night, and people came just for the price, putting up with poor beds, poor sound-insulation and dubious hygiene in the resigned acceptance that you get what you pay for. In the next tier up were the two-star hotels with an average room rate of 200 francs per night. These hotels attracted customers by offering a better sleeping environment but charged, for the privilege, a much higher price.

Accor's managers began by identifying what customers of all budget hotels wanted, irrespective of their final choice: a good night's sleep for a low price. This is a key concept in value innovation: to shoot for the mass, to look for the unmet needs that will unite large groups of what were previously considered disparate customer-segments. In this respect, it is an anti-niche tool.

Having identified what all customers wanted, Accor then had to work out how to give it to them – which in practice meant looking at which generally accepted hotel features could be reduced or dispensed with in order to fund the elimination of the sleep–price compromise. If you think back to those original four questions, this is the process that combines the first two – looking at how an industry currently *over-serves* its customers. In this case it led to the creation of an entire new hotel concept: Formule 1.

In a Formule 1 hotel there are no costly restaurants or appealing lounges. Many other features are reduced to *well below* the standards of one-star or even no-star hotels. As Kim and Mauborgne tell it:

> Receptionists are on hand only at peak check-in or check-out times; at all other times there is an automatic teller. Rooms are small and equipped only with a bed and bare necessities – no stationery, desks or decorations. Instead of closets and dressers there are a few shelves and a pole for clothing in one corner of the room. The rooms themselves are modular blocks manufactured in a factory, a method that results in economies of scale in production, high quality control and good sound insulation.

By these measures, Accor halved the cost of building rooms and reduced staff costs from 25–35 per cent of room sales – the industry average – to 20–23 per cent. These savings facilitated the provision of the things most customers really value. Formule 1 offers levels of quietness and bed comfort well beyond those offered by the two-star hotels, yet charges a price only marginally above that of the one-star hotels.

The extent to which a value innovation deviates from category norms can be graphically visualized in a value curve (see Figure 10.4 for Formule 1's value curve). If you were to plot your current brand offer against that of its category you would probably find that the two curves are closely aligned. This is because, in most categories, rivals compete by offering slight improvements on the accepted dimensions of price and quality, but don't challenge the shape of the curve itself. By contrast, focusing your efforts on seeking a fundamentally new and superior curve can be one of the most effective ways to make a dramatic leap in competitive appeal to a broader body of customers – a point that Kim and Mauborgne amply demonstrate in their conclusion on Accor:

> The company has not only captured the mass of French budget customers but also expanded the market. From truck drivers who previously slept in their vehicles, to businesspeople needing a few hours' rest, new customers have

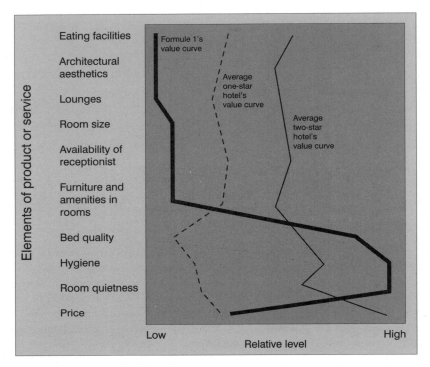

Figure 10.4 Formule 1's value curve

been drawn to the budget category. Formule 1 made the competition irrelevant. At the last count, Formule 1's market share in France was greater than the sum of the next five largest players. Accor has already built more than 300 Formule 1 hotels across Europe, Africa and Australia. The company is now targeting Asia.

(Adapted from Kim and Mauborgne, 2004)

Take advantage of government sources

Don't forget that much of the commercial and demographic data you need can be accessed, usually quickly and often without cost, from government sources. In the UK, for example, the Department of Trade and Industry (DTI) is an authoritative source of a wide range of commercial data, broken down by sector, and including details like regulatory guidance, trade associations and environmental legislation. The Office for National Statistics (ONS) holds census data broken down by region, age, ethnicity, religion, numbers of single-person households, numbers of dependent children, numbers of pensioners and so on. Better still, it cross-analyses the data so that you could explore, for example, the number of single-person households in England and Wales occupied by a 20- to 30-year-old working woman. Not all countries are as well served in this respect, but many have at least one good source – like the ones below (the French, German and Japanese websites are all available in English):

- France: www.insee.fr;
- Germany: www.destatis.de;
- Japan: www.stat.go.jp;
- United States: www.census.gov;
- UK: www.dti.gov.uk; www.statistics.gov.uk;
- for quick links to all national government sites: www.gov/main/ www.stat_int.html.

Look abroad for pointers

Sometimes, looking at how your category performs in other countries can stimulate ideas for change closer to home. We've already seen, for example, how the Co-operative Food Retail stores in the UK have struggled to shake off their dowdy, downmarket image; yet in Italy and other southern European countries the Co-op is a thriving, mass-market success. The name, logo and fascias are the same – but something about the formula is working better in those markets than in the UK. Looking at what is done differently (fresher fruit? better locations? superior service? centralized buying?) could yield useful insights on strategy for the UK team.

Talk to trade gurus and journos

Sometimes business teams can be so caught up in their own brand-world that they fail to perceive important category hotspots and warning signs. This can be particularly true of service, or business-to-business, categories where new ideas and trends are more masked than they are in, say, fmcg where the evidence is there for all to see on the supermarket shelves. Often, trade gurus, trade journalists and headhunters, with their finely spun networks and frequent contacts, can be the most informed and up-to-the-minute sources of valuable information: what's coming round the corner and why, which initiatives are making an impression and which are drawing flak. Court them; they love to talk.

We have now reached the end of the four corner-analysis chapters and, with it, the end of stage one of the methodology. There is still work to be done, of course, but it's a different kind of work, with a different kind of focus: a focus on creativity, imagination and fusion. We now move on to stage two – and the Passionpoint.

11 Marketing imagination and the Passionpoint

On 19 June 2003, in his regular column for the UK trade magazine *Marketing*, Professor Mark Ritson offered the opinion that the big management consultants were struggling to make sense of brands. 'Despite enormous investments and acquisitions,' he wrote, 'there is growing acceptance within the client world that management consulting companies "don't get the branding thing".'

Why should this be? The top management consultancies would excel at stage one of the methodology under review in this book. That process of analysis – so vital for understanding the conditions necessary for brand success – would be meat and drink to the likes of McKinsey, Accenture, Boston Consulting and Bain.

The problem is that great branding cannot be achieved through analysis alone. You can't analyse your way to becoming the kind of seductive, fascinating, multi-textured, familiar-yet-surprising, trusted and respected, valued and loved entity that we call a great brand. Brands just aren't created, or maintained, that way. They are not the kind of problem for which there is always a single, deductively reasoned solution.

This means that there inevitably comes a point where analysis must be put on hold and a more creative phase cleared for take-off. Analysis might indicate the emergence of a new 'mass affluent' class; but it will not invent the Swiffer. Analysis could uncover the problems of the Co-operative Bank in the late 1980s; but it could not have provided the ethical banking solution. Analysis might have proved to you that the ordinary working person in 1936 yearned for cheaply priced literature;

but it could not have arranged for the Penguin paperback. Marketing intelligence must yield, at some stage, to what Levitt (1983) aptly called 'marketing imagination'.

The relationship between these two forces – marketing intelligence and marketing imagination – can be made vivid with a simple diagram. Imagine you are at ground level with your brand and you want to take it to the high peak. You move up the hill of analysis until the peak is tantalizingly close. But between that point and the top there is suddenly a deep chasm (see Figure 11.1). The chasm cannot be crossed by the step-by-step process that has got you all the way up to this point; only a big, daring leap will get you across.

The edge of that chasm is where you are now. It will take a leap of imagination to cross it. If there is anything about brands that the management consultancies don't 'get', then this is probably it. The management consultancy culture is to move forward always with intelligence, reason and certainty, always with answers that can be checked, corroborated, refined; it would strain every fibre of that culture to make that audacious, breathless leap.

Later in his *Marketing* column Ritson hypothesized that consultancy's loss might be advertising's gain, that advertising agencies might 'again inherit the world', that they might 'regain their place at the top table' to

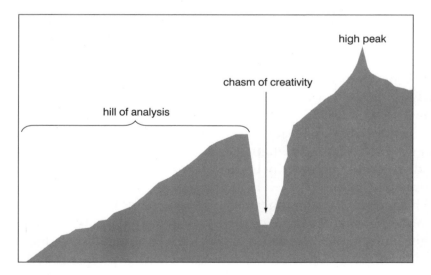

Figure 11.1 The relationship between analysis and creativity on the journey to brand greatness

partner marketers in the quest for brand greatness. This is doubtful, to put it kindly. Agencies have plenty of imagination; they specialize in creative leaps – but they'd never make it up the hill of analysis, never reach the take-off point, in the first place. The numeracy isn't there; the rigour isn't there; the sheer patience isn't there. And the creativity of ad agencies is tethered, not unreasonably, to the subject of communications in general and advertising in particular. Discipline-specific creativity is not what is required at this stage.

The curious thing about marketing imagination, it emerges, is that it is extraordinarily difficult to outsource. The natural focus of the specialist brand consultancies, for example, tends towards the analytical, particularly the study of consumers, and their brand-bull's-eye and brand-onion diagrams often go no further than a hint towards potential creative outcomes. The big design consultancies like Landor come closest to combining analysis and imagination in appropriate proportions but, even here, the creativity will be skewed towards their specialist discipline.

The ultimate source of marketing imagination must, therefore, be the brand organization itself. Often managers will say at this point that theirs isn't a particularly creative industry, that their teams tend to be untrained in the ways of imaginative thought. There are two kinds of answer to this. The first is that, without marketing imagination, no company will prosper for long and no brand will make it beyond the status of a second-rate player following in the shadow of the leaders. Marketing imagination is, as Levitt (1983) argued, a necessary part of the competence of any organization, irrespective of the category it happens to occupy. The second answer is more inspiring: there is almost certainly a pool of untapped imagination in your team, and the process through which we shall steer you in this chapter is designed to help release it. So let's look now at how you make that all-important transition from stage one of the methodology – analysis – to stage two – creativity, imagination and the Passionpoint.

Stage two overview

The corners are done. The analysis is in. That's the good news. The more sobering reality is that there is still a complete stage of the methodology to go, with all the energy, input and soul-searching that it implies.

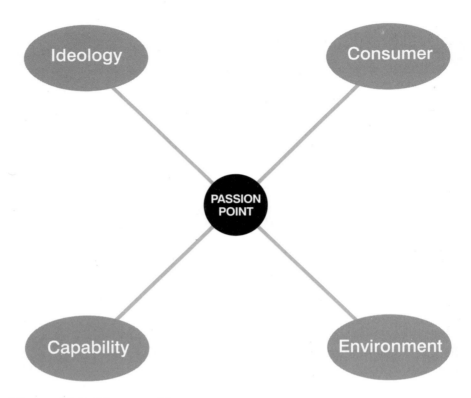

Figure 11.2 The transition to stage two

But stage two will have a very different kind of feel from stage one. It's a time, as we have indicated, for creativity and imagination; but it's a time for courage too – the courage to look deep down into the information in front of you, deep down into the soul of the business, and ask yourself what you really want for your brand, what heights you really want to scale, what sacrifice you are really prepared to make in order to create something of which you, your organization and the world beyond will feel proud. It's a time for reason and passion to meet – and to make something extraordinary out of the union.

None of this is to suggest that the process is random, a free-for-all debate with no clearly defined edges or objectives. There is a very definite shape to the process, a strong spine of order, and its governing principle is that of dynamic trajectory. As Figure 11.3 shows, dynamic trajectory ensures that you and your team move, by degrees, first from information to insight, then on to imagination – and finally on to inspiration, with the crystallization of brand belief itself.

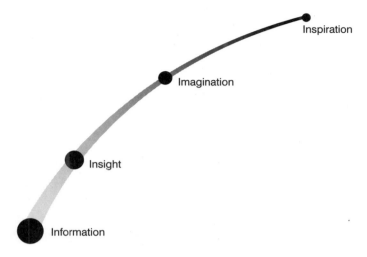

Figure 11.3 The line of dynamic trajectory, which guides the team from the four-corner analysis to the Passionpoint

Throughout the remainder of this chapter we will take you along that line of dynamic trajectory, identifying the way-stations along the route that will guide you from the debrief of the analysis at one end to the Passionpoint at the other. The chapter will close with a recent practical example.

How to begin

The first thing to note is that the opening session of stage two definitely calls for the assembly of the full task-force team. As this might be the first time that everyone has been together since the initial gathering prior to stage one, it would be as well to open with a reminder of what you have set out to achieve – the creation of a Passionbrand – and what that means:

- A Passionbrand is a brand with the courage and imagination to stand for something at once related to, and yet bigger than, the category it inhabits.
- A Passionbrand is a brand with active belief and the confidence and capability to help bring about its fulfilment.
- A Passionbrand is a brand that is consistent at the core and yet always fresh and vibrant in an ever-changing world.

● A Passionbrand is a brand with high values integrity – a brand deeply embedded into the organization of which it is a part; it is not simply a marketing concoction.

With this reminder in place, the rest of the session would then be devoted to debriefing the analysis of the corners. So at this stage, on our line of dynamic trajectory, we are still very much at the 'information' end.

But the debrief will lead, of course, to discussion, debate, perhaps even vigorous dissent. This should be encouraged – since it forces people to engage with the data and awakens their faculties for insight – but should be sufficiently controlled so as not to get out of hand. The moderator's skill here will be in capturing the dissenting voices yet keeping the debrief presentations moving. In reality this opening session is likely to last a full day and, in any case, it is no bad thing to build in a pause between this outpouring of information and the insight sessions that will follow. Not all the information can sink in right now anyway; in all probability some of it never will; but it is there, and in all but the most rigid of minds it will be starting to exert an influence on the imagination. The value of information in the creative process is often underrated by those unfamiliar with the way ideas are formed – which explains why so many managers, when briefing creative specialists, are still seduced by the notion of the open brief. As any creative professional will tell you, there is virtually no harder place to start than that; ideas are not simply dreamt up, conjured out of nowhere, but emanate, in a mix of both conscious and subconscious manipulation, from some kind of basis of truth or substance or at the very least contention. Great art always starts with a blank canvas, never with a blank mind. The information might seem unwieldy right now, it might give you that sinking feeling as you try to take it all in, but wait; let it sift; it will play its part in unexpected ways as we make progress.

From information to insight: capturing themes and tensions

The next session asks the team to reflect on the corner-specific analysis and to capture themes, on the one hand, and tensions, on the other. In any creative process, themes and tensions are important springboards for invention. They are both expressions of *connection* – the lifeblood of creative thought – even though, in a yin-and-yang sort of way, the kinds of connections they describe are the inverse of each other: themes are about a coming together, tensions about a pulling apart. Perhaps it is easy enough to see why the discovery of a theme is important to creative thought; but of the two it is tension that is usually the more potent. It is the very desire to resolve tension, without resorting to insipid compromise, that unleashes ingenuity – as we saw in the Accor Hotels example in Chapter 10.

So engage with enthusiasm, try to cover the full sweep of the data you are holding, watch the videos again perhaps, look at the photographic evidence again, strive to see beyond the superficial – and get all the apparent themes and tensions down. Then take a break. Because there are some soul-searching questions coming next.

From insight to imagination: the Passion Questions

We are still at the insight phase on our line of dynamic trajectory but, as we progress through this section, we will be moving gradually – imperceptibly, even – on to imagination. The task is to answer six questions. But they are not the kind of questions that will yield to linear thought alone. They are questions to which, in a strictly rational sense, there is not necessarily a single correct answer. Answers must also *feel* right, must appeal to both instinct and emotion and to a kind of unspoken sense of destiny. That does not mean, however, that the head is not engaged. If that were so, we might as well have dispensed with the entire analysis stage altogether. Rather, these questions are specifically designed to engage head *and* heart, to pit your instincts, ambitions and desires against realities, numbers, constraints, and to encourage answers that will be forged with passion and tempered with intelligence.

To achieve this, each of the Passion Questions is specifically framed to link two different corners of the model. Since there are six ways to combine two of anything from four of anything, there are six questions to pick up the six pair-combinations possible in our four corners. Each single question, therefore, forces the team back into two different corners of the model, forces them to confront the conclusions and contradictions contained in that analysis, and to emerge with an answer – perhaps an answer that will mount a challenge to the very assumptions of the analysis itself. Question no 3, for example, asks, 'What should we stop doing now in order to stay true to our values?' In so doing, it forces the team back into the two internal corners of the analysis, to examine capability – and with it all the many things the company does to be commercially successful – and to juxtapose that reality against the stated list of values that the ideological audit has uncovered. Invariably, on this one, something has to give: either an activity or a value is dropped or modified; it is a rare brand that does not require, at the very least, some fiercely honest introspection.

In theory, you can approach these six questions in any order. But experience shows they are best tackled in the order given here – for a reason that, to make things more interesting, we'll reveal at the end of the section.

Question no 1: What are we good at that's good for people?

This question is designed to push the team deep into the capability and consumer corners. It is a question that is really two questions. What are we really good at? And why is that important to people?

Some pointers here. What you are good at does not amount to a list of your current products or services. They are manifestations of a deeper competence and it is that deeper competence that should be expressed. You're looking for what your business can do really, really well – perhaps could do even better in the future, given the right conditions and commitment. That said, a eulogy of expertise won't count either unless you can show how it really matters for the people who end up as your customers, which means you've got to look hard at the evidence in the consumer corner – how people lead their lives, what they want for their futures – and ask how the thing you do especially well can make a difference. Raise the stakes. Take inspiration from the way Unilever highlighted the real significance of its expertise in stain-removal, in a low-key, everyday category, with its 'modern parenting' approach. Probe your capability hard and describe with guts and flair the real significance it assumes in people's lives. What is your company's deep purpose? How does your brand improve lives? Why does it have a right to exist? You are taking the first tentative steps towards revealing your brand belief.

Question no 2: Which values will we still hold when the world moves on?

This question connects the ideology and environment corners. It is quite normal for the ideological audit to have thrown up a fairly long list of values at the level of both the brand and the organization behind it. This is one of two questions to help you probe those values and narrow the list down to those you would defend to the end. Ideally, by the time we get to the Passionpoint, there would be no more than three. By projecting forward and imagining how the future competitive environment might look, in perhaps 5 or 10 years' time, it forces the team to consider which values are for all time and which are merely serving a convenient purpose for now.

An excellent example of this process at work is cited by Collins and Porras (2000), who tell the story of a high-technology company debating its core values. The management team had included 'quality' on the list, but the CEO wanted to test how serious they were about that decision:

> The CEO asked, 'Suppose, in ten years quality doesn't make a hoot of difference in our markets. Suppose the only thing that matters is sheer speed and horsepower, not quality. Would we still want it on our list of core values?' The members of the team looked around at one another and finally said no. Quality stayed in the *strategy* of the company, and quality-improvement programmes remained in place as a mechanism for stimulating progress; but quality did not make it to the list of core values.

The same group of executives then wrestled with leading-edge innovation as a core value. The CEO asked, 'Would we keep innovation on the list as a core value, no matter how the world around us changed?' This time the management team gave a resounding yes. The managers' outlook might be summarized as 'We always want to do leading-edge innovation. That's who we are. It's really important to us and always will be. No matter what. And if our current markets don't value it, we will find markets that do.' Leading-edge innovation went on the list and will stay there. A company should not change its core values in response to market changes; rather, it should change markets, if necessary, to remain true to its core values.

Question no 3: What should we stop doing now in order to stay true to our values?

This question links ideology and capability. It forces the team to examine its most cherished values in the light of commercial reality – in light of all the things the company does to survive, thrive, meet those shareholder demands. Principles-versus-profit is therefore one inevitable turn for the debate to take. Imagine, for example, a big foods brand with 'healthiness' as a stated core value – but with a sub-brand or product line open to criticism on health grounds. (You'll remember that we speculated on this kind of tension when we looked at Kellogg's, and its endorsed Froot Loops brand, in Chapter 7.) In order to stay true to the core value, in this example, the sub-brand would need to be dropped or modified. But that decision itself could not be possible without scrutiny of the knock-on commercial effects implied, which would include the ability of the company to withstand the short-term loss. The financial analysis, which was part of the capability corner, is obviously germane here.

The seriousness with which a Passionbrand upholds its core values often implies sacrifice. Recall, for example, how Innocent had to accept less margin in order to offer smoothies that matched its ideal of purity. Other factors that might need to be reviewed in order to maintain values integrity include supply chain, partners, joint ventures and hiring policy.

But this is not to imply that, in the tussle between values and current commercial practice, it is always values that win. A company might decide that it cannot afford, or simply will not countenance, changing the activity that the adherence to values demands. Fine. *But then the value has to be dropped or modified.* The point is that contradiction between values and practice cannot be tolerated. High values integrity is part of the definition of a Passionbrand and this question is designed to help ensure that it is achieved, one way or another.

Question no 4: How is our industry currently letting people down?

This question links consumer and environment and is by no means as simple as it might seem. It is not confined to inquiring what consumer 'unmet needs' might be, or what consumers are demanding of the category but failing to get; fact is, if consumers are actively asking, then at some point a brand will find a way to deliver. The question has a deeper purpose: to look at how your industry quietly, perhaps unthinkingly, dare we say even cynically, mis-serves people in ways of which they are not yet aware. Nobody was asking for ethical banking before 1992, until the Co-operative Bank showed how standard industry practice was letting people down by investing their funds in ways that they themselves would never countenance and would be horrified by if only they knew. The launch of Innocent, implicitly if not overtly, showed that people were being let down by an industry that was content to sell drinks that seemed 100 per cent pure and natural but were not. The smoothies industry norm of using concentrates was accepted practice – so accepted that Innocent had a tough job over-coming it – but nobody had deemed it necessary to ask whether consumers would find it acceptable if they were let in on the secret.

Every industry has its secrets, its accepted norms, its nod-and-a-wink deceits and illusions that, since no one notices, no one complains, are deemed OK by all. Water is injected into pre-packed chicken breasts; ice tea contains a great deal of sugar but virtually no tea; the shelf-life of bag salad is achieved through a process called modified-atmosphere packaging, which has been shown to destroy vital nutrients. How can any of this be wrong when it's all standard practice?

Occasionally these practices become notorious, as the industry is caught at it by the media or by a watchdog and is made to recant and cringe in the glare of public disapprobation; the 'mis-selling' of pensions in the UK in the 1990s is an example. But more often they amount to no more than accepted tricks of the trade, too insignificant to be picked up on the radar. And since nobody is making a fuss, where is the incentive to change?

The answer is that, if your industry is found wanting and people are left unknowing, what more incentive do you need? So take an honest look at the category norms and assumptions outlined in the environment corner; then look again at what people want for their lives, the things they really care about; then simply note the ways in which the former undermines the latter. Simply note for now – but be prepared to challenge accepted practice when we come to look at future capability further on.

Question no 5: How might our historical ethos be reinterpreted for people today?

This question links the ideology and consumer corners. It looks at the values associated with your brand, along with the roots and ethos of your organization – and plots them against today's life, as lived by today's consumers. The aim isn't to allow consumers to dictate what those values should be; this would result in a consumer-led brand, open to all the vicissitudes we have already identified. The aim is to ensure that the expression of values and organizational ethos – in everything the brand does – is framed with relevance for modern life.

Cast your mind back to the example of the Co-operative Retail stores. When the movement was founded in 1844 its most potent values were those of honesty and fairness. The practical expression of those values, through reassurance on fair weight and measures and an undertaking to supply 'the purest provisions procurable', was right for those times, when people were prey to cheating and fearful of what they were really getting for their money. Today no retailer adds sand to sugar or chalk to flour, but that does not render the original core values moribund. Quite the opposite: consumers are as concerned as ever about what goes into food – just in different ways. As we outlined in Chapter 4, while many in the Co-op's leadership are stuck in the past, the more enlightened management at the newly merged Co-operative Group is steadily reinterpreting long-held values and ethical roots. The result is the most honest food labelling in the industry, with fat and sugar content boldly displayed on pack fronts and shelf strips, along with a well-publicized stance on GM and the championing of fairly traded and organic foods.

Question no 6: What is our future credible capability?

This question actually links all four of the corners of analysis. Capability is obviously involved, since the aim is to imagine how the organization might be able to develop its capability in the coming years. But that deceptively innocent word 'credible' hints at the wider task: to explore future capability in light of imagined future consumer needs, the projected future shape of the market, and deeply held organizational values. There is a world of difference between what the company could conceivably do in theory and what it could credibly expect to succeed with in practice – what consumers, retailers,

suppliers, intermediaries, the competitive environment and the organization's own employees would support. All four corners are
therefore necessarily involved.

The question is deliberately open-ended, explicitly framed to solicit
ideas. But there is a condition: for every idea generated that implies a
development at the periphery, you should generate two at the core.
Teams, confronted with an exercise like this, are often only too happy
to imagine exciting new extensions, bold new territories, new
peripheral initiatives; it's often much harder, and usually much less
fun, to imagine meaningful improvement in capability at the core –
that familiar heart of the business that everyone lives with every day
and can tend to take for granted. But Passionbrands are always strong
at the core; it is that inner fire that justifies the use of the word 'passion'
in the first place. And breakthrough invention at the core is the most
transformative power in marketing. The Belgian cinema operator Bert
Claeys didn't elect to turn his city-centre cinemas into bowling alleys or
shopping malls, or engage in any number of other fringe ideas that
might have suggested themselves in a hostile commercial climate; he
innovated at the core, invested in the Kinepolis concept and trans-
formed not just his own business but an entire market. Unless your
core capability is so defined by a technology or process that it is in
danger of becoming bludgeoned by circumstances – the recent fate of
Kodak and Polaroid – core must take precedence over fringe. But even
here, for these troubled brands, the recognition that it is expertise in
imaging, not simply in 'film', that defines their core capability serves to
remove the caveat. A Kodak breakthrough in imaging will always be
more credible than a Kodak adventure into PCs or watches or some
other distant market zone.

Even those ideas you do generate that seem peripheral at first
should be explored in terms of core strengths, to see if there is a way to
re-frame them so that they can invigorate the heart rather than frolic
on the fringe. Porsche's venture into the SUV market, for example,
was initially framed as a challenge to its engineers in core terms: to
develop a 4x4 that performed and handled like a sports car. Some of
those engineers were taken off the company's racing car programme
to work on the project, ensuring that the very best talents were
engaged. The result was the beautiful and successful Cayenne. That it
is popular with Porsche loyalists, either as a second vehicle or as a first
family car when their 911 days are over, is testament to its credibility as
a core, not fringe, development.

There are many ways to come at future credible capability, not all of them sweeping or revolutionary, and if the team gets stuck you might want to consider some of the thought-starters outlined here:

- *Format.* Is there a more convenient format in which your product could be offered? In 2003, the *Independent*, an upmarket British newspaper, broke with the traditions of the category to offer its paper in a choice of broadsheet and tabloid formats. Sales rose by 9 per cent and later one of its rivals, *The Times*, flattered by following suit.
- *Style.* Nokia, Swatch and the iPod have shown that adding fashion and style to technology can send brand share soaring and, at the same time, grow the market.
- *Product specification.* It isn't just a question of what you could add to make a more attractive product, but also what you could remove. The budget airline model is predicated on the removal of traditional service elements. The removal of traditional outlets like shops, offices or branches can also pave the way for a more streamlined or cheaper service – as the successful telephone or internet banks, like First Direct and Smile, have shown.
- *Geography.* Future credible capability for your brand might simply mean opening up ambitious new markets in which to develop your current activities. Ikea has been extraordinarily successful in spreading a consistent, tightly controlled formula around the globe.
- *Ingredients.* Is there a reason to consider fresh, fairly traded or organic ingredients for your product? Are there other ways to break the accepted norms for your industry – the ones that conspire to let consumers down?
- *New segments.* Could your product be modified to target new kinds of customers? By 2000, sales of nutritional supplements made by US specialist EAS had flattened out at $155 million. Two years later they had surged to $270 million, with increased margins – achieved by targeting new segments outside the brand's traditional base of avid bodybuilders and athletes. Suitably modified supplements were now aimed at less zealous, but much larger, groups.
- *Speed.* Could you revolutionize the supply chain so as to get product developments out there faster than all your competitors? This is what Zara has achieved with its three-week turnaround from design to hanger, against an industry average of nine months.

- *Focus.* Is there a case for dropping some or all of your minor products or services in order to specialize in the major one? An advertising agency brand, for example, might consider dispensing with the through-the-line activities, and 360-degree communications, in order to devote all its focus and talent to creating really great advertising.
- *Small but multiple improvements.* Could you embark on a programme that would see product improvements and new ideas hitting customers on an unusually frequent basis? This strategy has helped Emirates achieve its reputation as the most innovative airline in the world. A continuous stream of ideas and both a policy and a process of rapid implementation are the vital ingredients.
- *Price.* Could a radical reshaping of your offer, or the way your product is created, give you a massive advantage in price? This is how Accor achieved its dominance of the budget hotels sector with its Formule 1 concept. Porsche, too, achieved cost savings by sharing basic-level components for its Cayenne with VW's Touareg.
- *Personnel.* Is there a star out there – star designer, engineer, software genius, say – who could help make your brand more attractive for customers? LVMH owes much of its recent growth to its policy of attracting the most talented designers in the business, like Marc Jacobs and Ozwald Boateng, and giving them a great product canvas to work on.

This is by no means an exhaustive list and, of course, whatever the start points chosen to stimulate creative thought, the resulting ideas must always be evaluated against projected consumer needs, projected market conditions and your own organizational values. How far into the future should you look? For most industries it is best to project three to five years: much beyond that and it gets too hard to call; much closer and you are likely to be describing the reality today.

We have reached the end of the Passion Questions. The significance of the order, incidentally, is its faithfulness to the idea of dynamic trajectory: the questions are more closed at the beginning, so more accessible to insight alone, becoming more open-ended as they progress, requiring more original thought. The team, therefore, learns to flex its creative muscles gradually, as it moves from question to question, arriving at no 6 fit, supple and ready for the inventive leaps it demands.

From imagination to inspiration: the Passionpoint

The Passionpoint is the crystallization of a Passionbrand identity. Its purpose, once captured and agreed, is to *inspire action*, to show everyone who works in the organization, at any level, what the brand is for, what it believes in, what it's good at and what it sets out to achieve in the world. Anything the brand does in the future – and Passionbrands are all about doing – will emanate from, and be judged against, the five statements you commit to paper now.

So it is not the work of a moment. But on the other hand, the Passion Questions should have helped you close the gap between analysis and its ultimate distillation. They should have helped you glimpse your brand belief, should have served to reduce and refine your values, should have sharpened your view on the market and revealed what is special about your core. Or, conversely, perhaps not; perhaps they have merely persuaded you that a Passionbrand identity is not for you. It happens. Not every brand in every category can justify certain sacrifice against uncertain gains, and the Passion Questions are designed to flush out those for which the fit will never be right. But, assuming you have reached a point where you want to commit, or at least to proceed a step further, let's look at the Passionpoint more closely and reveal what its five elements mean (see Figure 11.4).

At the centre of the Passionpoint is brand belief. Radiating out from there are the four elements that combine with it to codify a Passionbrand identity. The position of these four is significant, reflecting the relationship of each to a single corner of the governing model. Idealized self is positioned at the top right because it is a way of describing the consumer; coming context relates to the environment; extraordinary core is about capability; and forever values is placed top left, to reflect the position, on the model, of ideology.

Each of the elements in the Passionpoint needs to be defined for your brand in such a way that they make a cohesive and inspiring whole. The order in which you tackle them is not important and, of course, you might want to visit each more than once and refine each in relation to the others, in order to achieve the cohesion that is so vital to success. We will now take a brief look at each of the elements in more

Figure 11.4 The Passionpoint, with its five elements

detail, give an example of a completed Passionpoint and answer some frequently asked questions. The chapter will close with a recent case to illustrate how the process works in practice.

Idealized self

This is not a description of who your customers are, but of who they want to be. It is the self they imagine in moments of reflection, the self they aspire to, the self they believe, often against all evidence, that they could become. It is not to be confused with the fantasy self, which is the stuff of very pleasant daydreams and which, for most people, is no more than a diversion, a mini-movie to watch in the mind, of which their alter egos are the star. The fantasy self is entertainment; the idealized self is desire.

The Spectrum of Self is captured in Figure 11.5. Nobody wants to make the journey backwards, from actual self towards worry-state self; everyone makes the mental journey from actual self to fantasy self, but usually in daydreams, rarely in reality. The journey most people really want to make is a shorter one, from actual self to idealized self. From tired working mother to an attractive woman in control. From single, slightly awkward young man to single urban guy with a bit of edge. From 55 in years to 45 in looks. The role of a brand is to help them, in any way that it can, both practically and symbolically, on that journey. Your description of the idealized self in the Passionpoint, therefore, needs to be worded to reflect the potential role that your brand plays in this personal drama.

Coming context

Brands don't operate in a vacuum, so no brand identity makes sense without a reference to context. But context changes as markets change, as competition develops, as issues explode, as trends evolve. Coming context does not, therefore, seek to describe today's situation (unhelpful), or tomorrow's detail (impossible), but the swelling themes that exert a deeper influence, the ones that will give shape to the market and to society in the not-so-distant future. You should aim for a statement that combines demographic, competitive and cultural insights in such a way that its relevance for your brand is clear.

Extraordinary core

It is neither easy nor credible to apply real passion to half a dozen different things at once. Passion implies focus. This is reflected in the

Figure 11.5 The Spectrum of Self

capability of Passionbrands, which tends towards the single and central rather than the varied and dispersed. Better to do one thing superbly well than many things tolerably well.

What is your brand's extraordinary core? The aim is not a florid description of standard capability, but a simple description of extraordinary capability. This was the point of the call for invention in the last of the Passion Questions: to ensure that your core capability will be clearly better than, or clearly different from, that of any other brand in the market. That market, of itself, might not be remarkable, but the tangible offer of the brand within it must be. There is nothing special about banking, for example; but there is something very special, utterly unique, about the *ethical* banking of the Co-operative Bank. And that difference is right there at the core: ethical *banking*, not some vague fringe notion such as 'ethical corporate citizenship'. It should go without saying that extraordinary core can never be something as insubstantial as *'our unique personality'*. It should be a real capability that manifests itself in real benefits and should be fused so tightly with your values that other brands might achieve parody but never parity. Google with its PageRank display, Zara with its three-week turnaround, Camper with its peasant design aesthetic, Innocent with its 100 per cent pure juice smoothies: in all these brands the extraordinary core is there for everyone to see, but hard for anyone else to emulate.

Forever values

The aim is ideological clarity: a short list of values that relate strongly to one another and exert a unifying influence on the identity as a whole. It is especially important that values and brand belief be mutually reinforcing. Brevity will help this cohesion. The list should be potent yet spare: three values, simply stated, strongly felt. Values you will hold forever. Values you will cherish, even when the world moves on. Be particular; be pointed; don't be afraid to use words outside the accepted business lexicon. Look at Camper's encapsulation of the values of the peasant way of life: austerity, simplicity, discretion. It is a beautiful combination, the one that Camper lives by, and you just *know* it is for real: no focus group in the world would either suggest, or endorse, a word as pungent as 'austerity'. It has to come from the heart.

Brand belief

Brand belief is the brand's take on the world; it is a view on what would make the world a little better and how the brand can help make it happen.

A Passionbrand is a brand with the courage and imagination to stand for something at once related to, and yet bigger than, the category it inhabits.

These are the phrases to recall when you attempt the crystallization of your brand belief. You are seeking to express the brand's deep purpose in language that elevates it from the commercial and parochial to the human and universal. The aim, remember, is to inspire. The statement should therefore not feel too cramped by the ceiling of commercial activity. A statement like 'We believe that people deserve the best shoe craftsmanship and the finest materials at a reasonable price' will get heads nodding but will not set pulses racing. But on the other hand there is no inspiration without connection. A lofty statement about the world that is completely unrelated to the brand's sphere of activity amounts to no more than corporate hubris. 'We believe in the freedom of all humankind' would be justifiable only from a brand with something to contribute thereto – and it would take quite a brand to justify that one. The aim, when crystallizing brand belief, is to sense both the sky above and the ground below. *Inspire and connect.*

The brand belief for Camper, for example, might be expressed as follows: 'Camper believes that, on life's journey, slow is more rewarding than fast.' This statement succeeds on both criteria. It inspires by evoking concepts of stature and scale – but it connects because the relevance to Camper's commercial sphere is self-evident. It doesn't actually mention shoes – belief statements are more powerful if they don't refer to the product – but the connection not just with footwear but with the comfort and durability of Camper's shoes, with their rustic design aesthetic, and with the values of the peasant way of life, is strongly evoked.

Camper is still a young business, led by passionate founders and guided more by instinct than a formal statement of identity. But based on Camper's prolific communications, and our interviews with Lorenzo Fluxá, we can extrapolate a completed Passionpoint for the brand (see Figure 11.6). The extrapolated Passionpoint for Camper is summed up in a three-word brand idea – a concept that will be explored fully in Chapter 12.

Camper: The Walking Society

Figure 11.6 An extrapolated Passionpoint for Camper, summed up in a three-word brand idea

Frequently asked questions

What do we expose to others?

The point of a Passionbrand identity is to inspire action and ensure cohesion, which means that it will need to be communicated to people throughout the organization and beyond. But what exactly do you use to effect that communication – just the Passionpoint, or the answers to the Passion Questions, or the analysis itself, or the raw data or what?

Since the Passionpoint is the crystallization of the new identity, this should be the basis of all communication and briefing – within the organization and with suppliers and partners. You'll notice that the statements in each of the Passionbrand elements are deliberately epigrammatic, so that the complete identity can be quickly seen at a glance. But this means that the first time it is presented to each new audience it will almost certainly need a little more flesh on the bone. Each of the elements can therefore be presented together with a sidebar that captures, bullet-point style, the *essential* points needed to promote a fuller understanding. In Figures 11.7 and 11.8, for example, are the extraordinary core and coming context elements for Camper as they might look with this additional sidebar information.

The answers to the Passion Questions should be kept as workings in the margin – to be exposed if necessary when the task-force team is challenged to justify the conclusions captured in the Passionpoint. The four-corner analysis and the raw data behind it are, of course, valuable information and should be kept and regularly updated as part of the measurement and maintenance phase that will be described in the

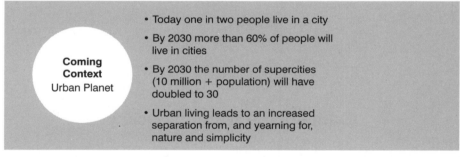

Figure 11.7 Coming context element for Camper, with sidebar

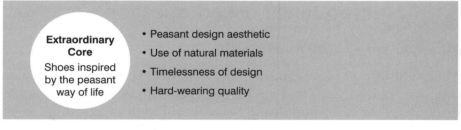

Figure 11.8 Extraordinary core element for Camper, with sidebar

next chapter. But this, too, might need to be presented in the event of a significant challenge to the new identity, in order to show that all the necessary homework has been done. This is particularly true of financial and operational analysis in the capability corner.

What's permanent and what's temporary?

Brand belief and forever values are permanent, a fact that should be taken into sober consideration when they are first framed. The other elements, because they each reflect in some way a dynamic and fluid entity, are subject to modification over the years. It is important, however, that the initial statements for these elements be captured at a sufficient level of depth to preclude frequent meddling. A well-conceived statement of extraordinary core, for example, might remain unchanged for decades even though its manifestations, through specific products and services, might be in constant flux. Similarly, the statements of idealized self and coming context should aim for the deep themes and should avoid the lure of fashion or reference to temporary phenomena. By these means the Passionbrand identity will display the qualities of durability and consistency without succumbing to ossification.

Whatever happened to 'essence'?

The problem with the concept of brand essence is passivity. The word itself has etymological roots in being rather than doing – from Latin *esse*, 'to be' – and this is exacerbated by the tendency, in brand essence statements, to favour expression by means of a single *noun*. 'Brand Essence: Care'. Fine – but what is anyone supposed to *do* about that?

Brand belief, by contrast, evokes an arc of connection between the brand and the world; it awakens a cause, inspires action, and for this reason alone is preferred to essence as the statement at the heart of the brand. But this is not to say that your current, single-noun statement of brand essence is lost to the world forever. If it is sufficiently strong to have survived the Passion Questions unscathed it will no doubt find its way into the eventual statement of brand belief – where it will team up with energetic verbs, worldly adverbs and charismatic adjectives to lead a life of far greater action and adventure than it did when it sat there as essence, just kind of *exuding*, all on its own.

What about 'personality'?

This will come as heresy to most people in marketing and everyone in advertising but – there isn't one. Brand personality is a chimera, a will-o'-the-wisp, a get-out clause for brands trying to hold themselves together when everything else about them seems to pull in diverse directions. Personality isn't up to the job. As captured in most 'brand personality' statements, it amounts to little more than a pasted-on smile, or a single set of clothes, for the brand to wear, come what may. These statements usually comprise a list of adjectives – vibrant, confident, carefree – that doesn't come near to capturing the subtlety and empathy that a real personality implies. In real life, personality is not so fixed; someone isn't just 'vibrant, carefree and sunny' all the time – when they are bearers of bad news, for example, or engaged in weighty tasks; in real life, personality is an outer manifestation of deeper values, and its precise expression varies according to context. It would be very disconcerting if it didn't – and that is true, too, of brands.

The curious thing is that brands like Innocent and Camper, brands without fixed personality statements, are the ones whose expression of personality seems to be the richest, the most three-dimensional, the most like personality in real life. These brands are too grounded, too confident, too interesting to be held to a neat set of words. Ironic one minute, curious the next, angry, intelligent, wise, hilarious, iconoclastic, wistful, zany by turns, they behave in a way that is always in accordance with both the context and their own deeper character. Variation at the surface reflects consistency at the core – at the level of values and belief. That is why they engage us so ingenuously and yet always come across as one brand. If you want your brand to be more expressive as well as more cohesive, do yourself a favour: kick out its tightly prescribed personality and forge cohesion with something deeper.

Practical example: The Sanctuary case

The Sanctuary is the spa products brand that we encountered briefly in Chapter 10. It competes in the UK bath and body-care sector and is unusual in its market for its real spa provenance. The Sanctuary Spa was opened in 1977 in London's Covent Garden as 'a little oasis for women'. Men were not admitted. A combination of naked bathing, an atrium pool over which Joan Collins was photographed soaring on a swing, and live koi carp in the lounge served to imbue the spa with a fame beyond its size. In 1998 a licence to create products using The Sanctuary name and trademark was sold to an entrepreneur with no previous experience in consumer goods. Under the guidance of a trade marketing expert, products were formulated based on the treatments offered at the spa, and six lines were launched through the leading UK high-street chemist, Boots, in early 1999. By 2001 the range had grown to 34 lines, achieving £8 million at retail, and the management realized it was at a crossroads. Among the growth options under review were extensions into areas as diverse as haircare, self-tan and male grooming. It was at this stage that the need for outside specialist expertise was recognized, in order to determine brand identity, brand potential and brand limits. The project was undertaken by the Ingram Partnership and involved both of the authors.

Themes, tensions, questions

One theme that caught the imagination of the group following the stage one debrief was the significance of *time*. It came through strongly first from looking at the detail of the consumer corner, in the section on 'life habits'. Sanctuary loyalists tended to be working mums, which in practice meant they had barely a moment to themselves from one end of the week to the next, between looking after kids, caring for the home and holding down a (usually part-time) job. They yearned to be the calm, assured person that a less hectic life would permit. The theme was amplified in the environment corner. Demographic projections indicated a growth in the number of working mums in the future, which implied the emergence of a whole new time-constrained cohort. Social trends, which included the proliferation of activities for kids requiring a parent to drive and supervise, implied an ever-shrinking reserve of personal time for these women.

The most important tension involved the capability, environment and consumer corners. A clear factor in both The Sanctuary's capability and its place in the competitive environment was its provenance as a genuine spa brand, with long-standing spa credentials; this was its ultimate source of authority and its real claim to competitive difference. The tension arose because this, surprisingly to the team, was not an important factor in why women bought the brand, and even when examined in depth proved to be not especially motivating.

The subsequent process of probing and questioning revealed numerous new angles and several blind alleys but served, in the main, to reinforce the importance of time to consumers and provenance to the brand. The breakthrough came with the attempt to forge a connection between these two concepts, which involved a deeper exploration of what spa credentials really meant. The result was the rediscovery of *spa ritual* as the brand's extraordinary core – more meaningful than simply *authentic spa products* because of its added dimension of time. This, as we shall now see, was a pivotal step for the case, resulting in a strongly cohesive Passionpoint and a compelling brand belief.

Creating The Sanctuary Passionpoint

In its definition of idealized self, The Sanctuary was able to aim for higher-order emotional territory than is normally available to bath and body-care brands. This was justified by the notion of spa ritual, with its potential significance to women as a structured way to put some 'me-time' into their week. The sidebar in Figure 11.9 shows the current reality of the women's lives and, by implication, the nature of the personal journey on which the brand would be a partner, offering practical, emotional and symbolic support.

In coming context (see Figure 11.10) the team isolated the relevant demographic, social and competitive trends, and summarized them under a single banner: complexity. They showed that women's lives would become more complex – so 'me-time' would become more precious; meanwhile, the market would become more crowded and fractured – so a bold claim to difference would be vital, especially for a brand with a low share of voice.

By focusing on ritual as its extraordinary core (see Figure 11.11), The Sanctuary distanced itself from mainstream brands seeking to muscle in on the spa phenomenon. The Sanctuary's deep knowledge of the mysteries of spa ritual, combined with authentic treatments and advice on how to create a real spa experience at home, promised both the enhancement of beauty and the enrichment of time.

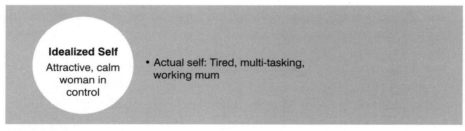

Figure 11.9 The Sanctuary's idealized self element, with sidebar

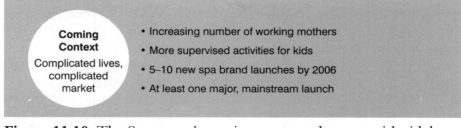

Figure 11.10 The Sanctuary's coming context element, with sidebar

Extraordinary Core
Products and advice rooted in a deep understanding of rituals of the spa

- Existing Mande ritual range
- New combination treatments with ritual themes
- Time-change treatments: eg self-heating sugar scrubs

Figure 11.11 The Sanctuary's extraordinary core element, with sidebar

Ritual was already at the heart of some of The Sanctuary's most successful products. The Mande range, for example (a body soufflé, an exfoliating scrub and a super-foaming bath soak), was based on an Indonesian pre-wedding beauty ritual. It was decided that future capability should focus on ritual-led concepts. Each would be designed to enrich a single hour that a woman might get to spend to herself, offering psychological, spiritual and beauty benefits. Product concepts based on the Tanaka beautifying ritual of Myanmar, and the Balinese spice ritual of Boreh, were scheduled for launch in 2005.

Among The Sanctuary's original list of values were two linked concepts, 'progressive' and 'innovative'. These were dropped in view of the projected upsurge in new product development that an increasingly competitive market would imply. It was agreed that if The Sanctuary tried to outstrip the market on these dimensions it would eventually contravene a deeper value – authenticity – which was more sacrosanct to the brand.

The three forever values (see Figure 11.12) now served to define brand limits and guillotine inappropriate new product ideas. Cosmetics and electric massagers were dropped because they would not be found in a real spa – and could therefore not be upheld as authentic. The proposed shampoo range was dropped since shampoo is about efficacy, not pampering. Instead, a heat-scalp treatment was developed for which the pampering

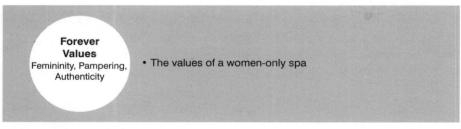

Forever Values
Femininity, Pampering, Authenticity

- The values of a women-only spa

Figure 11.12 The Sanctuary's forever values element, with sidebar

value could be held intact. Finally, a men's range, long mooted for the brand, was recognized for what it was: a step too far for a brand so firmly rooted in femininity.

The statement has scale (see Figure 11.13). Here is a brand with something important to say about modern life: women these days are devoting too much time to others, not enough time to themselves. The Sanctuary provides a reminder of the value of time spent alone, and why it can be so good for a woman's sense of mental and physical well-being. The argument would be that this, in turn, is also good for the woman's family and all those she comes into contact with, allowing the headroom to evoke newsworthy, societal themes.

But connection is there too. The Sanctuary, with its spa heritage, is a credible entity to champion such a belief. One hour to oneself in a busy, modern home is hard to come by – but the one place you can go and lock the door is the bathroom. By championing a woman's right to that hour, by creating products that enhance her health and beauty while she takes it, and by showing her how to make the most of the spiritual side of the ritual, The Sanctuary provides a practical, not just symbolic, agency for its belief. It is a 'little oasis' still – but now, in a woman's hectic day, a little oasis of time.

Figure 11.13 The Sanctuary's brand belief element

The Sanctuary Passionpoint

A brand identity like this (see Figure 11.14), for all the rigour and insight involved in its creation, is still just words on paper. People don't buy words, they buy brands, which means that the journey that began way back in Chapter 6 isn't quite over yet.

Figure 11.14 Full Sanctuary Passionpoint, without sidebars

12 From identity to reality: six guiding principles

It's exciting to have been part of the creation of a new brand identity but the moment passes with the recognition that the people you really need to excite are consumers. And of course, they won't see your Passionpoint, with its crisp identity statements and its inspiring brand belief. You can't gather consumers together and give them a presentation, and they'd doubtless be nonplussed even if you could. The only way to engage, impress, excite and inspire them with your new identity is through the brand itself. It is through contact with the brand that consumers perceive its meaning, its difference, its value, its passion. Day after day, in dozens of different ways, your brand is out there making its own presentation; the point of this chapter, with its six guiding principles, is to help you ensure that it's as powerful as it can possibly be.

Principle no 1: Get the order right

The implementation of a new brand identity involves numerous steps, and one of the commonest errors is to leap too far ahead too soon. For example, in late 2003 the UK utilities giant British Gas trumpeted a major new service initiative, called 'Doing the right thing', in a £50-million advertising campaign. Six months later, embarrassed by the problems of trying to live up to its promises, it finally got round to telling its own staff. Reporting on the belated launch of its £2-million internal communications campaign, *Marketing* (2004) asked, 'Has British Gas got it back to front?' It then proceeded to answer its own question by suggesting that an 'inside out' approach would have been preferable, whereby 'internal communications leads to cement patterns of behaviour in the organisation, before being backed by heavyweight advertising'. As Figure 12.1 shows, British Gas started precisely where it should have finished. It did the wrong thing, as so many have done before, such is the urge to communicate a bold new identity to the consumers at whom it is ultimately aimed. It is an urge to be resisted, and simple logic will show why.

The diagram plots the four major blocks of activity in the implementation of a new brand identity; within each of these, as we shall see later, are many smaller steps. The diagram splits into two symmetrical halves. First comes the internal process, in which communication precedes product development; then comes the external process, in which product reality precedes communication. This is the flow of action – the order in which things are *done*. But the logic for the order is seen when you think backwards, starting at the end and working out what already needs to be in place before you can tackle each stage. Before you can communicate your changed product to consumers it must exist, in all its facets, and must be as close to perfect as you can get it – or they will punish you for letting them down. But before it can be perfected, before it can even exist, your own people have to design it, provide it, ensure that it is backed up with the necessary service and after-sales care. But before they can do that with intelligence and commitment, they must understand the need for it, their individual importance to it, and its place in the success of the brand. The order of doing is fixed by this reasoning.

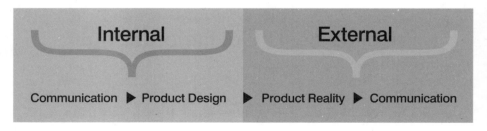

Figure 12.1 Implementation: the four major blocks of activity

The Co-operative Bank is a textbook example of the process of *thinking backwards but doing forwards*. You'll recall that management started at the end of the spectrum, by thinking about how to differentiate the bank in a new advertising campaign; this led to thinking about how the bank could make a meaningful difference to consumers' lives; this led to the ethical banking concept, which in turn led to consideration of the role of everyone who worked at the bank in providing it.

That was the thinking. But in the implementation of the new strategy – in the *doing* – the bank was fiercely disciplined in reversing the order. As a first priority, management communicated the new ethical concept to its employees. It counselled their views, met their challenges and sought their ideas before doing anything else. Together with them, and with specialist outside advisers, it then created the fine detail of the ethical offer, ensuring its integration into every aspect of the brand. An important part of this was the training of every member of staff, so that no one at the bank was unprepared for customer questions and concerns. The new concept was encountered by consumers first at the level of the product, which gave the bank a chance to assess reactions and fine-tune the details of the offer before getting on its soapbox. Only at the end of the process did it launch the new identity to a wider public with a high-profile advertising campaign. By this time it already had a strongly committed workforce fully engaged with the new identity, and had made subtle improvements to its initial product and service offers.

The idea that advertising should follow, rather than accompany or precede, the introduction of the new product itself is sometimes challenged by those who argue for the need to create excitement in order to gain trial. But for most brands, and for service brands especially, there is a stronger argument for getting the new product out there for a while, ahead of the fanfare. First, as we have just seen, it gives the product a chance to develop, to go 'live' for a contained audience, allowing management to rectify any flaws before the glare of publicity exposes them. Second, it takes advantage of the dynamics of 'Saatchi's Law'. Coined by Lord (Maurice) Saatchi, this states a simple but important truth: *Satisfaction equals performance minus expectation.* The hype of publicity, by boosting expectation, leaves a more slender margin in which satisfaction is to be achieved. Conversely, a slower burn, letting the product ease into the lives of loyalists, getting feedback and improving, before launching a well-judged publicity campaign, serves not merely to satisfy but to delight. Expectations are not raised but product performance is. Passionbrands like Google, Innocent, Camper and the Cooperative Bank all keep advertising to minimal levels compared with peer brands, and all work harder on exceeding the expectations of customers at the point where it matters most: the product.

Principle no 2: Understand, inspire and encourage your employees

Internal marketing is in vogue at the moment, the stuff of articles, seminars and speeches. But how different is it, in practice, from its forebear, internal communications? Is it just the same, often quite dull, thing in a fancier guise? Or is it as sophisticated, calibrated and creative as its glamorous cousin, consumer marketing?

Certainly, a new brand identity needs to be marketed, not merely communicated, to the people inside the organization. And the start point, if we are to take the word 'marketing' seriously, is the realization that your own people do indeed form a market, and that the defining feature of markets is choice. Employees are people with choices. They can choose to work inside the organization or to take their skills elsewhere. They can choose to give their all or to do enough to get by. And they can choose whether or not to take on board the new identity: whether to embrace it, improve it and play their dedicated part in it, or to pay lip-service to it and ignore it, perhaps even work against it. This choice needs to be recognized, and the reasons that employees might go one way or the other need to be understood, which means that, before you can think about communicating the new brand identity, you have to know your audience.

Understand them

Are they suffering from initiative fatigue? If so, how do you convince them that this time it really matters? Is there emotional commitment to the organization's current values, or is there a wall of cynicism to climb? Is there a sense of unity in the company, or is it balkanized, with different departments pulling different ways? Does a subculture of resistance exist? If so, why? Who are the influential people, the ones that inspire the people around them, for good or bad? Some of this crucial information should have been uncovered during the internal analysis phase, but you might still need to commission specific internal research: groups, depths, intranet questionnaires, depthnography and co-operative inquiry are all candidate techniques.

Targeting

Can you really communicate with everyone in the place as a homogeneous team, or should you target specific groups first and work from there? The Co-operative Bank targeted, initially, 20 of its middle managers for training in the new ethical banking concept. It then trained them in the skill of training others. With their help it took the new identity both up and down the organization, spreading understanding gradually to all levels of staff. Or perhaps your research will show that the organization breaks into totally different kinds of groups, each requiring specifically targeted communications initiatives.

Inspire them

When you come to the communication itself, it needs not only to explain the new identity – that is the minimum requirement – but to inspire emotional commitment to it, and to encourage action in support of it. Every person needs to know exactly how he or she can make a difference to the success or failure of the brand, and should leave the presentation wanting to play a part.

The fusion of clarity and persuasion is as tough to get right internally as it is for consumers, and you'll need to invest real money, time and effort in the communication phase. Don't be dull. This is not a time for memos, e-mail or PowerPoint. Neither is it the time for a sermon. An imaginative combination of short talks from charismatic leaders to set the agenda, multimedia shows to generate emotional appeal, and interactive sessions to make people feel involved is a reasonable minimum aim. Don't let the magnitude of the moment deter you from the use of humour or candour. These can be a great deal more effective than punching the air and calling for the extra mile. Colin Mitchell, a senior partner at Ogilvy & Mather, New York, cites an example of the power of wit, blended with style, in a paper on internal marketing in *Harvard Business Review* (2002):

When Volkswagen relaunched its brand with the 'Drivers Wanted' advertising campaign, the company also created a film to explain the brand vision to staff and dealers. Forgoing the usual speeches and beauty shots of cars, the film took the form of a whimsical journey of two young people setting out on a Saturday morning to do some errands, inter-cut with slogans that captured the new spirit of the brand.

It was a fantastic piece of work and so sweetly got the brand feel right – with its captivating music, cool humour and off-beat casting – that it became the basis for the first commercials in the television campaign. Here, then, is an example of an organization demonstrating its strength of intent: it takes its own staff seriously enough to create not just another 'mood-tape' medley, but a bespoke film of sufficient quality eventually to become scaled down for a national US consumer campaign.

Demonstrating with action is always a good follow-up to communicating with words. For example, if your new identity is all built on the concept of innovation (and many are) you need to become more innovative in the way the company behaves – or your staff won't believe you mean it. The UK media planning specialist PHD, for example, has long enjoyed a reputation for pioneering in its business-to-business sector. In 2004 it recommitted itself to that value in a major new internal initiative. But actions accompanied the words. Pioneering ideas unveiled at a presentation to 200 staff included a holiday exchange programme whereby staff could buy and sell holiday entitlement, a new contract on which there were no set hours of work, and a high-tech drop-in centre for clients – not just its own but those of competitors – to use whenever they pleased. To underscore the way it wanted its employees to behave, management first changed company behaviour. In attractive businesses, with well-paid, already motivated staff, this will be enough to stimulate the extra commitment that can make so much difference. Sometimes, though, employees need a little more incentive than that.

Encourage them

Much has been written on the power of an attractive ideology to galvanize otherwise truculent employees and get them behind the brand. And there is evidence that some people will even sacrifice material gains in order to work in the right kind of organization. As

Bergstrom *et al* (2002) observe, 'Employees may be willing to accept somewhat less in terms of benefits and compensation in exchange for being aligned with a brand they feel connected to.'

Yes, they may, but don't bank on it. People have lives to lead and families to support and they can't go down to the supermarket checkout and spend a bit of ideology. Money talks, and there is no shame in management putting its money where its mouth is to offer incentives for commitment to the company's ideals. And here it is vital to note that the people who affect brand perceptions the most are often the ones who are paid the least: sales staff, service staff, people who work in call centres, people who work in factories, people who deal with complaints.

Ritz Carlton, for example, inspires its 24,000 service staff with the motto 'We are ladies and gentlemen serving ladies and gentlemen.' But it reinforces this ideal with an incentive scheme that rewards the right kind of service. Chambermaids, whose income might be 0.1 per cent that of the CEO whose strategy they are daily implementing, can get up to an extra $500 plus a luxury weekend away for such initiatives as noting customer preferences as they service the rooms.

Quality Bicycle Products, based in the suburbs of Minneapolis, includes as part of its vision statement a commitment to protecting the environment. It underlines that commitment with dollars. Employees who live within 10 miles of the company are paid $2 a day extra if they get there by bicycle, bus or as part of a carpool. Small incentives can mean a great deal to people on modest incomes – and small changes in daily behaviour can make a great deal of difference to the brand.

Principle no 3: Remember that everything communicates

In marketing industry parlance the term 'communications' normally refers to a narrow range of media-based activities: advertising, PR, direct marketing, digital and sponsorship. It is convenient, of course, to have a collective term to distinguish this kind of discipline from others such as pricing, packaging, product design, service strategy, distribution strategy and brand architecture. But convenience shouldn't be allowed to obscure an unalterable truth: everything communicates, whatever it happens to be called and whether it is intended to or not. A surly sales rep will imbue the brand with a little surliness no matter how much you are spending to tell the world it's cuddly. A long queue at check-in will say 'neglect' no matter how brilliantly your ads say 'care'. A beauty product found in the discount pharmacy will exude the opposite of exclusivity, notwithstanding its star-studded PR launch. In the minds of consumers your brand exists as an ever-shifting image whose pixels are made up of the thousands of experiences – lasting or fleeting, trivial or deep – in which some aspect of the brand was a part. But there is as much potential for clarity as there is for interference. If everything communicates, then everything the brand does is a chance to press home your new identity. It is a chance you must seize.

The start point is to enumerate all the different ways in which your brand touches people's lives. Conventionally, this task is approached by means of a list or a table – pack design, call-holding message, company vehicles and so on – but the drawback with this even-handedness is that it fails to capture how it all feels from the consumer's point of view. A more illuminating way to go about it is to put the consumer in the picture, literally, as in Figure 12.2.

Here we imagine a person surrounded by the different kinds of stimulation and contact that a given brand might imply. Brand contacts are now grouped in zones according to their potential vividness: contacts at the centre are felt more intensely than contacts further out.

Closest to the consumer is the Zone of Intimacy. Here brand contact is voluntary, sensory and direct. The brand is there because the consumer wants it to be, and its sensorial qualities – taste, colour, fragrance, feel, sound, weight, atmosphere – are strongly perceived and noted, subliminally if not consciously. 'Intimate' means exactly that: the product might well end up inside the person (drink, snack, analgesic); or the person might well end up inside the product (hotel, aircraft, car). Whatever the precise conditions, there is a vividness to these self-selected, intimate brand contacts that is stronger than those in either of the other two zones.

One step outwards is the Zone of Discovery. Here the brand is not expected to be part of the moment and contact comes as more of a surprise – when the brand pops up as part of a magazine article, say, or a branded vehicle parks in the neighbourhood, or an impromptu mention is dropped into the conversation by a colleague or friend. In the Zone of Discovery the mind is open and the guard is down; contact

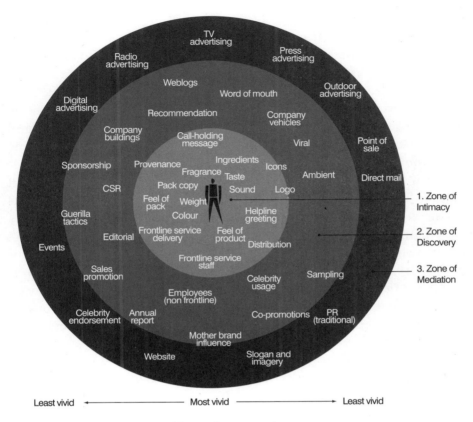

Figure 12.2 The zones of brand perception

might be less direct than in the Zone of Intimacy but is made vivid – for good or ill – by virtue of its very surprise.

Farthest from the consumer is the Zone of Mediation, in which the brand is perceived indirectly, through a medium. This is where we find advertising, direct mail, brochures, sales calls and most of the ordnance of classically defined marketing communications. In the Zone of Mediation the mind is rarely open and the guard is invariably up. Contact is made diffuse not just by the intervention of the medium, but by the lack of interest, or even cynicism, felt by the consumer towards yet another commercial message. There is still scope for vividness, but it is much harder to achieve than in the other two zones, requiring creative and media ideas of sufficient ingenuity to penetrate the haze of indifference.

Most marketers spend most of their time in the Zone of Mediation – if not in absolute then certainly in relative terms. Getting brochure design right, putting the finishing touches to a commercial, building a better mailing list, struggling for more display space in store: these media-based activities take up a disproportionate amount of finite marketing resource. This is a norm that is well worth breaking. In the task of disseminating your new identity, through everything the brand is and does, priority should follow the order of vividness. Start in zone one – the Zone of Intimacy – and work out from there.

When Porsche's engineers designed the Cayenne, they ensured it had the 'rorty and sporty' Porsche sound, to emphasize the purity of its pedigree. This is zone one communication. When Zeev Godik launched his Gaucho Argentinian steak restaurants in Europe, he built them around big, open kitchens, with heroic hunks of meat on display, both as reassurance on quality ('We have nothing to hide') and as theatre (to emphasize the carnal, macho nature of the experience). This is zone one communication. When *Saga Magazine* wanted to shed its one-foot-in-the-grave image and portray its over-50 readership as active, sexy and sorted, it put Mick Jagger on the cover – and pretty much repositioned an entire cohort. This is zone one communication with a great eye for zone two, since it got people talking. In the quest to spread the word that your brand has changed, the product is the ultimate prophet. At the very least you could take a leaf out of Innocent's book and devote as much time and talent to pack copy as you currently do to advertising copy: it's hundreds of times more likely to be read.

Principle no 4: Make at least one big symbolic gesture

In 1994 Tony Blair became the leader of a political party that had been out of power for 15 years, having suffered four consecutive general election defeats. Associated with heavy industry, class warfare and dyed-in-the-wool socialism, the Labour Party was considered by many to be unelectable, despite the self-inflicted wounds of the governing Conservatives. Blair signalled change first with words. Labour became 'New Labour' – which would work for a 'new Britain'. But he knew that neither this nor the pledges to pursue modern, market-economy policies would be enough to dispel the deeply felt reservations of a suspicious electorate. What made people sit up and take notice was a big, symbolic gesture. In the face of bitter opposition from activists, Blair sacrificed the infamous 'Clause 4' of the party's constitution, which stated Labour's traditional commitment to state-owned industry. Blair proved willing to take the party to the brink of civil war in order publicly and symbolically to shed this last vestige of old-style socialism. In the next general election, in 1997, having now spent 18 years in opposition, the Labour Party won by a landslide.

If you are not courageous, a new brand identity can come and go without anyone really taking much notice. Words, even words backed by the many daily actions and changes in behaviour that the new identity demands, can be drowned out by competitor activity, market complexity, consumer inertia, events. But a big gesture can strike drama into the process, like lightning on a balmy summer's night, which can make the news unforgettable. The right kind of gesture will send the same powerful message to employees and consumers alike, will be contentious enough to capture the attention of the media and will be all the more credible for including an element of sacrifice.

Principle no 5: Be consistent and cohesive

Anyone who works in marketing will know that this common-sense twin objective is infuriatingly hard to achieve. A strong brand belief is an enormous step in the right direction but alone is no guarantee of success; you will still need all your powers of vigilance and persuasion to ensure that the brand is both consistent over time and cohesive across disciplines.

Entropy is the enemy, but you can expect friendly fire from some of the forces on your side. Creative partners can be especially problematic. Inspired by your brand belief, each of these – advertising agency, digital agency, design house, promotions team – will devise a brilliant creative idea. Each of these ideas – with the right kind of guidance and input – will reflect the new identity. But each of them will be different. It is as though there were some kind of unwritten code at work that prevents creative convergence. The faculty of different creative luminaries to interpret the same brief in utterly diverse, curiously incompatible, ways and to combine this genius with a reluctance bordering on the maniacal to share work and adapt ideas from others is one of the mysteries and miseries of modern brand stewardship. The telltale word – and everyone in marketing has heard it – is 'interpretation'. It sounds wonderfully free, marvellously expansive – and it is; but it is the death-knell of cohesion.

But while the creative services industry remains fragmented, you will have this issue to deal with. So what are your objectives? You want to allow for enough flexibility in creative expression to avoid formulaic banality, but you need to ensure enough commonality to come across as one brand. One way to achieve this is to take responsibility first for the development of a single *brand idea*, which will then be used to brief each of the different creative partners.

A brand idea is a bridge between the brand belief and its ultimate, detailed creative expression in all the various communications disciplines. It must capture the Passionbrand identity in a soundbite, and is intended, unlike the elements of the Passionpoint itself, to be shared with the outside world. Captivating, motivating and brief, it should be the single thought, the slogan perhaps, that will hold everything else together. But the word 'slogan' shouldn't imply that it is the province of the advertising agency; a brand idea must be a media-neutral solution.

The Sanctuary, for example, generated a strong brand idea by working closely with its media planning agency, Naked Communications, which was able to take a helicopter view of all its eventual applications. You'll recall that The Sanctuary's Passionpoint reflected the importance of time to its consumers. The brand believed that 'Every woman needs and deserves to take at least one hour entirely to herself every week.' This was captured, in a brand idea, as 'Your perfect hour of Sanctuary'. This phrase, which became the brand's slogan, was the focal point of the brief for all creative partners. Everyone involved on the brand had to show that their creative solutions dramatized the 'perfect hour' in some way. A big, single-minded idea like this is more obviously unifying than a range of different creative themes that happen to converge on the brand belief. But although 'the perfect hour' is tight enough to ensure cohesion, it is not so closed that it precludes imaginative variation. Here are some of the creative expressions that it led to:

- *In products:*
  - one-hour ritual sets;
  - candle with one-hour markers;
  - special gift pack designed as an hourglass, with different products in each end (eg salt scrub and sugar polish).
- *In store:*
  - slogan on shelf-display;
  - 'menu cards' for one-hour home-spa treatments;
  - free take-home door hangers: 'Do not disturb... for just one hour';
  - 'Happy Hour': name for Sanctuary three-for-two promotions.
- *In collateral materials:*
  - give-away one-hour CD of relaxing, drifty music;
  - one-hour read, free with pack;
  - mini-hourglass, free with pack.
- *In events:*
  - National Women's Day: men advised to give women one-hour pamper treat;
  - slogan as theme for The Sanctuary stand at The Vitality show, which also offered free lifestyle/time management consultants.
- *In PR:*
  - commissioning research on the importance of 'me-time' in women's lives, linking to a national stress charity;
  - developing a competition with a leading magazine to find the woman who most deserves her 'perfect hour' – the prize... her perfect hour!
- *In sponsorship:*
  - sponsoring the quiet coaches in trains;
  - weekly, one-hour Sanctuary radio show with blissed-out sounds.

And, of course, it was expressed in advertising like that shown in Figure 12.3.

A strong brand idea is not an easy thing to get right, but is a massive help in providing cohesion between disparate marketing elements. But we're not done yet. The devil is in the detail, and strong brand cohesion also implies discipline on colours, typefaces, music, brand icons and the general feel and tone of the material. It would be nice to be able to write here that there is something magical about a Passionbrand identity that makes for perfect unity in these matters and guarantees that different creative disciplines will pull together and

Figure 12.3 'Your perfect hour of Sanctuary' advertisement

stick to the guidelines. But no such guarantee exists. In the end, brand cohesion at the detail level comes down to clear lines of communication and an iron will. Somewhere in the shadows, behind every truly cohesive brand, is a single, senior person with a very big stick.

Consistency over time

This can also be hard to get right. Everyone knows, of course, that it takes time to deepen the affections of consumers for the brand and its new identity. But that won't stop your own people getting itchy feet long before the consumer has even begun to connect. Even the most powerful, inspiring statements of identity induce a sense of over-familiarity in the only people who see them day in, day out. Vital, then, to remind everyone on the team how long truly consistent brands have been sticking to the same message: L'Oréal has said 'You're worth it' for over 15 years; Nike has said 'Just do it' for over 20; BMW has been 'the ultimate driving machine' for over 30; Sure deodorant has promised not to let you down since 1965; Lux has rooted its brand in stardom since 1928; and a diamond has been forever, since forever. Consumers are only ever half-concentrating, at best, on your brand message, which competes for finite brain space with thousands of other stimuli every day. So stand by what you stand for. Over the years you might vary the expression, manipulate the theme, ride the zeitgeist to keep the message fresh – as all these great brands do – but you should never be persuaded to waver at the core.

A big opportunity to anchor the brand identity over time comes from recruitment. When you first launch the identity internally, you must do so with the people you already have, some of whom might not be natural sympathizers. But over the years, as employees come to be replaced, you can recruit with brand belief as a guiding factor. This will require co-operation between all areas of the business, and real understanding of the brand in HR, but it can pay dividends, particularly in service industries, as Colin Mitchell (2002) shows:

> Hollywood Video, which regards its passion for movies as its differentiation from the mammoth Blockbuster chain, requires that employees show knowledge of and enthusiasm for movies. Southwest Airlines is known for rigorously assessing candidates' personalities during interviews, rating all potential hires – from pilots to mechanics – on a scale of one to five on seven traits corresponding to the brand's core values. While other companies might consider only more traditional values like honesty or responsibility, Southwest preserves its unique brand personality by hiring only people who are a perfect fit.

Ultimately, though, the rigours of ensuring consistency and cohesion bring us back to the need for genuine inspiration in the first place. If you want everyone to really stick to the identity – there's nothing quite like having an identity that people really want to stick to.

Principle no 6: Link measurement to action

Imagine you are sitting in the cockpit of a modern jet and your pilot is looking with concern at the altimeter. The pilot tells you the plane is too low – but does nothing about it. How do you feel about that?

Measurement is meaningless without action. We expect the pilot not simply to note the dangerously low altitude with interest, or casually to record it for posterity, but to do something to correct the position. This implies three units of knowledge: the altitude of the plane right now, the minimum altitude for safety and a knowledge of what to do if that minimum is not achieved. For any dimension on which your brand is to be measured, you will need three analogous pieces of knowledge. These can be captured in a simple grid, as shown in Figure 12.4.

If we take a basic measure like awareness, for example, a brand team might have hoped for 35 per cent, got 28 per cent and decided that the media mix could be improved. So our grid would be filled in like that shown in Figure 12.5.

	What did we hope for?	What did we get?	What will we change?
Measure			

Figure 12.4 Capturing the pieces of knowledge in a simple grid

	What did we hope for?	What did we get?	What will we change?
Awareness	**35%**	**28%**	**Media strategy**

Figure 12.5 Awareness example

The next step is to group linked measures together, to give a more rounded view of achievement and future strategy. Brand perception measures, for example, might be captured in an extended grid, like that shown in Figure 12.6.

In this way, future actions can be harmonized, so that they orchestrate better with one another. In certain circumstances, of course, taking no action at all is an option – when targets are met and current strategy is judged to be optimal for the time being. In this case, in the box entitled 'What will we change?', you would write 'Nothing'. But it should be noted like that, as a positive decision, not something that just comes about through aimlessness or inertia. The discipline of attaching a committed action to each measurement of progress is one of the simplest, most effective and most commonly ignored ways to ensure brand health and growth.

What should be measured?

Let's go back inside that cockpit. Suppose the plane has just two instruments, the altimeter and an airspeed indicator. It's easy to see that this

	What did we hope for?	What did we get?	What will we change?
Spontaneous Awareness			
Prompted Awareness			
Image Dimension 1			
Image Dimension 2			
Image Dimension 3			
Customer Satisfaction			

Brand Perception

Figure 12.6 Grouping linked measures in an extended grid

would offer only limited reassurance. What about a fuel gauge? Don't reserves of fuel matter too? And an 'artificial horizon'? Don't you need to know whether the plane is flying straight and level? In fact, don't you need a whole range of measurements to ensure that your destination will be reached both promptly and safely?

You do. And the same is true for brands. But most contemporary brand measurement practice is the equivalent of flying with just two instruments. Perception is almost always measured, performance sometimes and other factors rarely. But since Passionbrands strive for high integrity, since they reflect a balance of many internal and external ambitions, the measurements required for maintenance and growth will need to be more holistic.

Although precise details for each brand will vary, the aim for a Passionbrand should be a framework like the one shown in Figure 12.7. This is based on the Balanced Scorecard technique for assessing business performance, which was developed by Kaplan and Morton (1994) (to whom we are also indebted for the aircraft analogy).

At the centre is the Passionbrand implementation strategy, which influences, and is influenced by, measured actions in four spheres: brand perception, brand performance, the brand inside and brand currency.

Brand perception, as we have seen, would include dimensions like prompted and spontaneous awareness, relevant image measures and measures of customer satisfaction.

Brand performance implies harder-edged numbers that relate directly to profitability. They would typically include measures for loyalty, frequency of purchase, new customer generation, customer atrophy, customer churn and price premium.

The brand inside measures the knowledge and commitment of the people who work on the brand, which would ideally include both employees and important suppliers and partners. Dimensions might typically be employee turnover, job satisfaction, and employee and supplier brand knowledge.

Brand currency aims to quantify the social capital and goodwill of the brand. This will include measures of corporate reputation, brand trust, frequency of recommendation, and extent of brand community activity.

For each of the dimensions in the four spheres above your researchers will need to design appropriate quantitative metrics. These will vary by brand, and their detailed description is beyond the scope of this book. There are also methodologies for converting each

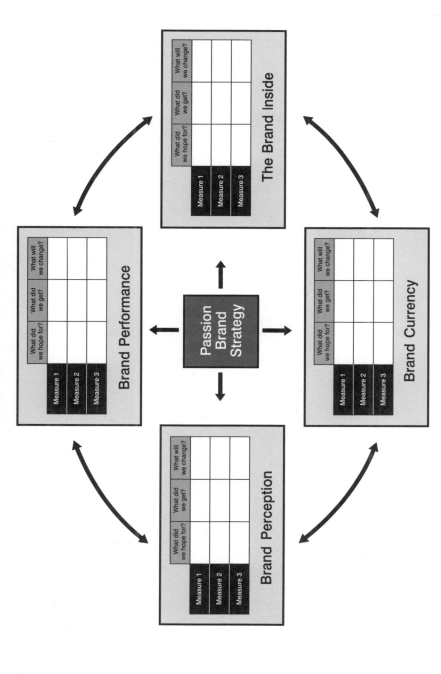

Figure 12.7 Passionbrand measurement framework

of the separate measures to scores out of 10, for ease of comparison. For more on both the metrics and methodologies involved in a Balanced Scorecard approach to measurement, see Kaplan and Morton's book, *The Balanced Scorecard: Translating strategy into action*, published in 1994 by Harvard Business School Press.

It has taken seven chapters to describe the journey from 'brand' to 'Passionbrand'. No stage of the journey has been easy, but hardest of all is the one described in this chapter – from identity to reality. This is where the grace and elegance of theory meet the seething chaos of markets, the cut and thrust of competition, and that most complex and unpredictable of phenomena: *people*. Perhaps, therefore, to our six guiding principles, we might have added a seventh: *never give up*. There is much to be said for a fighting spirit, with its concomitant traits of resourcefulness, grit and sheer determination to prevail in the face of adversity. If there is one common characteristic that unites the visionaries behind the world's great brands, it is probably that.

Note

The Ritz Carlton example is derived from Sucher and McManus (2002).

13 Leading from the heart

Leadership is a much discussed subject in business. *Harvard Business Review* alone dedicated 26 separate papers to this one topic between 2000 and 2005, with titles like 'Breakthrough leadership' and 'What leaders really do'. Ask what makes an effective business leader and you will hear about qualities like vision, drive, originality, courage and charisma. Especially charisma. In his massive textbook *Organizational Behaviour*, Stephen P Robbins (1998) breaks down the magic of charismatic leaders into seven 'key characteristics': self-confidence, a vision, ability to articulate the vision, strong convictions about the vision, behaviour that is out of the ordinary, change-agent mentality and environmental sensitivity. Robbins's list of leaders to display such qualities goes beyond the confines of business to include John F Kennedy, Martin Luther King, Jr, Walt Disney, Mary Kay Ash (founder of Mary Kay cosmetics), Ross Perot, Steve Jobs, Ted Turner, Lee Iacocca, Jan Carlzon (chairman of SAS Airlines) and General Norman Schwarzkopf. In business, as in politics and public affairs, the term 'leadership' carries with it a sense of greatness.

Except when it comes to brands. Ask what is meant by 'brand leadership' and you will hear nothing of charisma or vision or courage or conviction or change. What you will hear about is market share. Everyone reverts to the accepted definition, which comes down to no more than 'the biggest brand in the category by share'. Brand leadership is a measure not of greatness but of bigness – which means it is a snapshot of the current situation, on one dimension only, with no accounting for the forces of momentum or change.

To define leadership in this way is to encourage, among some 'leading brands', the smugness and paralysis that sheer dominance can foster. And it is to paint a queer picture, one that runs counter to observation. By the standard definition, some stick-in-the-mud brands are 'leaders' and some brands that display charismatic leadership are mere followers. Reuters, for example, is the brand leader in financial data systems but, for innovation, daring and speed to market, it is Bloomberg that displays charismatic leadership. In consumer electronics the brand leader is Sony but these days the charismatic leader, with its sharp eye for detail and its genius in convergence technology, is Samsung. In airlines the brand leader is Aeroflot; for the charismatic leader, it's a tussle between Virgin, Singapore and Emirates. But this isn't to fall into the trap of attributing charismatic leader status only to 'challenger brands'. In internet search the brand leader is Google and the charismatic leader is also Google. The point is that charismatic leadership is not dependent on size.

But it won't be long before size becomes dependent on charisma. Dominance today has already ceased to be predictive of dominance tomorrow. Gone are the days when unassailable positions could be maintained through the possession of finite assets: airport landing slots, broadcast licences, a prime-site retail portfolio, government patronage. The global economy is too fluid, distribution channels too varied, markets too open for this kind of privilege to confer lasting protection. And business is now too transparent, whether it wants to be or not. The internet, and especially the proliferation of weblogs, has given brands nowhere to hide. Ask Ingersoll-Rand, whose subsidiary Kryptonite lost over $10 million in 10 days, after bloggers exposed flaws in its patented bike locks. Or look at Mazda, which saw its reputation tarnished after it tried to infiltrate and influence widely read sites. Twenty-three thousand weblogs are created every day, many by company insiders, and every one is part of 'the inescapable trend', as *The Business* phrases it, 'towards the democratisation of power and opinion' (Kirkpatrick and Roth, 2005). This bottom-up swell of millions of consumers, connected but undirected, deciding as individuals yet acting in concert, is a power that renders leadership by mere size a fragile commodity. In recent years its force has assailed some of the mightiest bastions of capitalist enterprise. Marks & Spencer, Kodak, Polaroid, Sainsbury's, Toys R Us, WH Smith, GM and the Conservative Party have all been reduced from power-brand status to brands that journalists seldom refer to without the accompanying adjective 'belea-guered'. The truth is starting to dawn: to achieve and maintain brand leadership status, brands have got to get out there and do some leading.

And it is axiomatic that leading cannot be achieved by following. It's not enough simply to follow the consumer any more. Charismatic brands must understand consumers, just as charismatic business leaders must understand employees, but to this understanding must be fused something a little more uplifting than just eagerness to please. Those seven constituents of charisma, with their themes of confidence, vision, conviction, communication and change, owe more to the heart than to the head; they describe the *emotional* connection that we expect of great leaders. Through concepts like *brand belief, extraordinary core, forever values* and *zone one communication*, it is this kind of emotional connection, this charismatic leadership, that we have sought to define for Passionbrands. It is leading from the heart.

There is a second strand of meaning to that phrase: marketing lead-ership must come from the heart of the organization, from its centre, from its innermost, senior circle. Marketing is too important to be left just to a single department, often poorly understood and poorly supported, and rarely represented at the highest echelons of business. Brands belong in the boardroom, and CEOs need to stay as close to the discipline of marketing as they do to the discipline of finance. For every brand we have featured positively in this book, that kind of committed leadership, from the heart of the business, has been manifest.

Brands can survive without any of this of course, can survive without belief, can survive without emotional connection, can survive by leaving marketing to marketers, by trying to second-guess consumers, by resorting to me-too strategies, by sticking to the category assump-tions, by undercutting, by luck. 'But mere survival is a so-so aspi-ration.' The words are those of Theodore Levitt, from 'Marketing Myopia', written way back in 1960. This is what he went on to say: 'The trick is to survive gallantly, to feel the surging impulse of commercial mastery; not just to experience the sweet smell of success, but to have the visceral feel of entrepreneurial greatness.' Forty-five years on, who in their right mind would settle for anything less?

Postscript

Cast your mind back to the Preface, and put yourself back in that auditorium. The hush descends as before. Anticipation is as high as ever. The keynote speech is about to begin.

This time the speaker grabs you from the word go. This is someone who seems to have an instinctive feel for the audience, who talks your language and knows your hot buttons – but uses neither gratuitously. The talk moves at a pace, never fails to keep your interests to the forefront and yet has something strong of its own at the core: a heartbeat, a theme, a belief that infuses everything.

This time you get the sense of conviction passionately held, but sensitively communicated. The wit is spot on; the graphics are stunning; even the features of the hall are used cleverly, and with apparent spontaneity, to illustrate points.

Body language draws you in as much as the power of the argument itself. You find yourself feeling that the speaker is talking specifically to you. But there is no pandering, no ducking of contentious issues. The speaker wants to win friends, but not at the expense of deeply felt principles. This is confidence, and it's thrilling to watch. Here is someone who fuses an unshakeable belief with a clear, intuitive feel for what it might mean to the people at whom it is directed.

At the end the applause is thunderous, but the most noticeable effect comes immediately after that. Everyone is talking, heatedly, animatedly, about this speech. There is a real buzz of excitement around the hall, and you certainly would not want to be the speaker going on next. Not everyone agrees with the beliefs that the speaker made so vivid, and the antis stoically hold their ground – but the pros are passionate in their advocacy, quoting ideas from the talk verbatim. You find yourself thinking, and talking, about the experience hours, days, even weeks later.

This is the feeling that only a few, special brands manage to confer on modern consumers. They are brands that have belief at the core – but also an understanding that belief alone is not enough. They excite; they surprise; they capture imaginations by marrying their belief with an intuitive feel for people and a flawless grasp of contemporary life. They are savvy about changing conditions, and they work with zeal and imagination to maintain the capability to deliver everything they believe in. They get talked about, create strong communities around them, inspire loyalty, shrug off dissent.

They are Passionbrands, and the future belongs to them.

References

Aaker, DA and Joachimsthaler, E (2000) *Brand Leadership*, Simon & Schuster, New York

Aaker, JF, Fournier, S and Brasel, SA (2004) When good brands do bad, *Journal of Consumer Research*, **31**

Anthony, R (1992) *A Note on Service Mapping*, Harvard Business School Press, Boston, MA

Arnould, E and Wallendorf, M (1994) Market-oriented ethnography: interpretation building and marketing strategy formulation, *Journal of Marketing Research*, **XXXI**, November

Arnould, E, Price, L and Zinkhan, G (2004) *Consumers*, McGraw-Hill, New York

Baudrillard, J (2001) The system of objects; and The consumer society, *Jean Baudrillard: Selected writings*, ed Mark Poster, Stanford University Press, Stanford, CA

Bauman, Z (2000) *Liquid Modernity*, Polity Press, Cambridge

Benady, David (2004) The future's bright, but only if you care, *Marketing Week*, 4 March

Bergstrom, A, Blumenthal, D and Crothers, S (2002) Why internal branding matters: the case of Saab, *Corporate Reputation Review*, **5** (2)

Bocock, R (1993) *Consumption*, Routledge, London

Borkowski, Mark (2004) McDonald's braces for attack, *Marketing*, 25 August

Bower, JL and Christensen, CM (1995) Disruptive technologies: catching the wave, *Harvard Business Review*, January–February

Boyle, D (2003) Consumers and authenticity, *Financial Times*, London, 8 August

Bullmore, J (2003) *More Bullmore: Behind the scenes in advertising (Mark 3)*, 3rd edn, World Advertising Research Centre, Henley-on-Thames

Butterfield, L and Waters, K (2000, unpublished) Turning back the tide: a Co-operative success story

Carroll, J (1998) *Globalization: The human consequences*, Polity, London

Chartered Institute of Marketing (2003) *Eight Ways to Revive Your Brand for Better Business Performance*, Chartered Institute of Marketing, London

Collins, JC and Porras, JI (2000) *Built to Last*, Random House, London

Corstjens, J and Corstjens, M (1995) *Store Wars: The battle for mindspace and shelfspace*, John Wiley, Chichester

Crister, G (2003) *Fat Land: How Americans became the fattest people in the world*, Prentice Allen Lane, London

Davenport, TH, Prusak, L and Wilson, HJ (2003) Who's bringing you hot ideas (and how are you responding)?, *Harvard Business Review*, 1 February

Denzin, NK and Lincoln, YS (1998) *The Landscape of Qualitative Research: Theories and issues*, Sage, Thousand Oaks, CA

Doyle, P (1994) *Marketing Management and Strategy*, Prentice Hall, Englewood Cliffs, NJ

Doyle, P (2001) Building value-based branding strategies, *Journal of Strategic Marketing*, **9**

Drucker, P (2003) *On the Profession of Management*, Harvard Business Review Books, Boston, MA

Economist, The (2003) A survey of food, *The Economist*, 13 December

Elliott, R (1996) Discourse analysis: exploring action, function and conflict on social texts, *Market Intelligence and Planning*, **14** (6), pp 65–69

Elliott, R and Wattanasuwan, K (1998) Brands as symbolic resources for the construction of identity, *International Journal of Advertising*, **17**

Elliott, R *et al* (1995) Overt sexuality in advertising: a discourse analysis of gender responses, *Journal of Consumer Policy*, **18** (2), pp 71–92

ESOMAR (2003) *Industry Report*, ESOMAR, Netherlands

Featherstone, M (1992) *Cultural Theory and Cultural Change*, Sage, London

Feldwick, P (1991a) *Advertising Works 6: Papers from the IPA Advertising Awards, Institute of Practitioners in Advertising, 1990*, NTC Publications, London

Feldwick, P (1991b) *Understanding Brands: By 10 people who do*, Kogan Page, London

Finskud, L (2004) *Competing for Choice: Developing winning brand strategies*, Vola Press, London

FitzGerald, Niall (2003) Understanding people to build brands, Institute of Grocery Distribution, Annual Convention, 14 October

Fournier, Susan (1998) Consumers and their brands: developing relationship theory in consumer research, *Journal of Consumer Research*, **24**, March, pp 343–73

Freeman, R and Rogers, J (1999) *What Workers Want*, Cornell University Press, Ithaca, NY

Furedi, F (2003) Buy nothing anti-brand day in the US, *The Times*, London, 28 November

Gabriel, Y and Lang, T (1995) *The Unmanageable Consumer: Contemporary consumption and its fragmentations*, Sage, London

Garnett, R George (1968) *A Century of Co-operative Insurance*, Allen & Unwin, London

Giddens, A (1991) *Modernity and Self-Identity: Self and society in the late modern age*, Stanford University Press, Stanford, CA

Gladwell, M (2000) *The Tipping Point: How little things can make a big difference*, Little, Brown, New York

Goffee, R and Jones, G (1996) What holds the modern company together?, *Harvard Business Review*, November–December

Hammond, Keith H (2003) How Google grows... and grows... and grows, *Fast Company*, April

Heron, J (1996) *Co-operative Inquiry: Research into the human condition*, Sage, London

Kaplan, RS and Morton, P (1994) *The Balanced Scorecard: Translating strategy into action*, Harvard Business School Press, Boston, MA

Keller, KL, Sternthal, B and Tybout, A (1998) *Strategic Brand Management: Building, measuring and managing brand equity*, Prentice Hall, Englewood Cliffs, NJ

Keller, KL *et al* (2002) Three questions you need to ask about your brand, *Harvard Business Review*, 1 September

Kendall Tarrant (2003) *Review of 2003*, Kendall Tarrant, London

Kim, W Chan and Mauborgne, Renée (2004) Value innovation: the strategic logic of high growth, *Harvard Business Review*, 1 July (first published 1997)

Kirkpatrick, David and Roth, Daniel (2005) Email is for old people: blog is the new word, *The Business*, 16 January

Klein, N (2000) *No Logo*, Flamingo, London

Levitt, T (1960) Marketing myopia, *Harvard Business Review*, July–August

Levitt, T (1975) Marketing myopia, *Harvard Business Review*, September–October

Levitt, T (1983) *The Marketing Imagination*, Free Press, New York

Levitt, T (2001) Excerpts from 'Marketing myopia', *Harvard Business Review* classic

Marketing (2004) Has British Gas got it back to front?, *Marketing*, 28 July

Markides, C (2000) *All the Right Moves: A guide to crafting breakthrough strategy*, Harvard Business School Press, Boston, MA

Maslow, A (2002) *Maslow's Need Hierarchy: Consumers*, McGraw-Hill/Irwin, New York

McCracken, G (1988) *Culture and Consumption: New approaches to the symbolic character of consumer goods and activities*, Indiana University Press, Bloomington, IN

Mitchell, C (2002) Selling the brand inside, *Harvard Business Review*, 1 January

Mitroff, IIA and Murat, C (2003) Preparing for evil, *Harvard Business Review*, 1 April

Morgan, A (1999) *Eating the Big Fish: How challenger brands can compete against brand leaders*, John Wiley, Chichester

Morita, A (1987) *Made in Japan: Akio Morita and Sony*, Collins, London

Norris, Trevor [accessed October 2004] Hannah Arendt and Jean Baudrillard: pedagogy in the consumer society, *Infed* [Online] www.infed.org

O'Guinn, T and Muniz, A (2001) Review of 'Brand community', *Journal of Consumer Research*, **27**, March

Olins, W (2003) *On Brand*, Thames and Hudson, London

Parikh, J and Neubauer, F (1993) *Corporate Visioning. International review of strategic management*, John Wiley, Chichester

Pascale, R, Milleman, M and Gioja, L (1997) Changing the way we change, *Harvard Business Review*, 1 November

Pendlebury, M and Groves, R (1999) *Company Accounts: Analysis, interpretation and understanding*, International Thomson Business Press, London

Pendleton, Andrew *et al* (2004) *Behind the Mask: The real face of corporate social responsibility*, Christian Aid, London

Prahalad, C and Hamel, G (1990) The core competence of the corporation, *Harvard Business Review*, 1 May

Price, L and Feick, L (1987) The market maven: a diffuser of market-place information, *Journal of Marketing*, January

Reason, P (ed) (1988) *Human Inquiry in Action*, Sage, London

Reeve, Diane, Brooke, Carole and Williams, Simon (2003) *Biography of The Co-operative Bank*, Lincoln University, Lincoln

Ritson, M (2003) Ethnography: what's going on?, Ethnographic Research, Kansas City

Robbins, SP (1998) *Organizational Behaviour: Concepts, controversies, applications*, Prentice Hall, Englewood Cliffs, NJ

Ryder, Sarah (1994, unpublished) Profit with principles: Co-operative Bank case history 1992–1993

Schouten, JW and McAlexander, JH (1995) Subcultures of consumption: an ethnography of new bikers, *Journal of Consumer Research*, **22**

Seth, A and Randall, G (1999) (new edn 2001) *The Grocers: The rise and rise of the supermarket chains*, Kogan Page, London

Sucher, S and McManus, S (2002) *The Ritz-Carlton Hotel Company*, Harvard Business School, Boston, MA

Sutcliffe, T (2003) Interview with Wally Olins, *Independent on Sunday*, London, 12 October

Temple, K (2000) Naomi Klein: who's the rock star now?, ChartAttack.com, ChartAttack

Thompson, C, Locander, W and Pollio, HR (1989) Putting consumer experience back into consumer research: the philosophy and method of existential-phenomenology, *Journal of Consumer Research*, **16**

Thompson, JB (1990) *Ideology and Modern Culture*, Polity Press, Cambridge

Tran, Mark (2004) *Guardian Unlimited*, 22 January

Trevelyan, GM (1942) *English Social History: A survey of six centuries, Chaucer to Queen Victoria*, Penguin, London

Twitchell, JB (1999) *Lead Us into Temptation: The triumph of American materialism*, Columbia University Press, New York

Wilson, AN (2003) *The Victorians*, Arrow Books, London

Zangwill, WI (1998) *Lightning Strategies for Innovation*, Free Press, New York

Index